Social Justice in EAP and ELT Contexts

Also available from Bloomsbury

Locating Social Justice in Higher Education Research, edited by Jan McArthur and Paul Ashwin
Decolonizing University Teaching and Learning, D. Tran
Language and Decoloniality in Higher Education, edited by Zannie Bock and Christopher Stroud

Social Justice in EAP and ELT Contexts

Global Higher Education Perspectives

Edited by Paul Breen and Michèle le Roux

BLOOMSBURY ACADEMIC
LONDON • NEW YORK • OXFORD • NEW DELHI • SYDNEY

BLOOMSBURY ACADEMIC

Bloomsbury Publishing Plc, 50 Bedford Square, London, WC1B 3DP, UK
Bloomsbury Publishing Inc, 1385 Broadway, New York, NY 10018, USA
Bloomsbury Publishing Ireland, 29 Earlsfort Terrace, Dublin 2, D02 AY28, Ireland

BLOOMSBURY, BLOOMSBURY ACADEMIC and the Diana logo are trademarks of
Bloomsbury Publishing Plc

First published in Great Britain 2024
This paperback edition published in 2025

Copyright © Paul Breen, Michèle le Roux and Contributors, 2024

Paul Breen, Michèle le Roux and Contributors have asserted their right under
the Copyright, Designs and Patents Act, 1988, to be identified as Authors of this work.

For legal purposes the Acknowledgements on p. xxiii constitute an extension of
this copyright page.

Cover design: Grace Ridge
Cover image © Brain light/Alamy Stock Photo

All rights reserved. No part of this publication may be: i) reproduced or transmitted in
any form, electronic or mechanical, including photocopying, recording or by means of any
information storage or retrieval system without prior permission in writing from the publishers;
or ii) used or reproduced in any way for the training, development or operation of artificial
intelligence (AI) technologies, including generative AI technologies. The rights holders expressly
reserve this publication from the text and data mining exception as per Article 4(3) of the
Digital Single Market Directive (EU) 2019/790.

Bloomsbury Publishing Plc does not have any control over, or responsibility for,
any third-party websites referred to or in this book. All internet addresses given in
this book were correct at the time of going to press. The author and publisher regret
any inconvenience caused if addresses have changed or sites have ceased to exist,
but can accept no responsibility for any such changes.

A catalogue record for this book is available from the British Library.

A catalog record for this book is available from the Library of Congress.

ISBN: HB: 978-1-3503-5120-2
       PB: 978-1-3503-5124-0
       ePDF: 978-1-3503-5121-9
       eBook: 978-1-3503-5122-6

Typeset by RefineCatch Limited, Bungay, Suffolk

For product safety related questions contact productsafety@bloomsbury.com.

To find out more about our authors and books visit www.bloomsbury.com
and sign up for our newsletters.

Contents

List of Figures	vii
List of Tables	viii
List of Contributors	ix
Foreword *John Gray*	xviii
Acknowledgements	xxiii

Introduction: A Reflection Upon Social Justice in EAP and ELT Contexts *Paul Breen* — 1

1 The Evaluation and Evolution of a Framework that Integrates the Awareness of Social Justice into EAP Teaching and Learning Materials *Robert Farag, Katherine Mansfield, Hilary McDowell, Svetlana Page and Ignez Pereira* — 17

2 Curriculum for Change *Jo Kukuczka* — 39

3 Critical EAP: A Marginalised Friend? *Natalia Fedorova and Kashmir Kaur* — 57

4 Placing Assessment in the Vanguard of Social Justice in English for Academic Purposes *Jan McArthur* — 73

5 The White Gaze and Translanguaging: Getting Multilingual Students' Voices Heard *Nguyet Luu* — 91

6 Becoming Socially Just Educators: A Trioethnographic Study of Exploring Professional Identity Through Dialogue, Ethics of Care and Creativity *Lorraine Mighty, Tomasz John and Iwona Winiarska-Pringle* — 99

7 What Silence Tells Us *D. Tran* — 117

8 Adopting a Social Justice Lens in EAP: The Application of Cognitive Skills of Compassionate Communication (CSCC) in Online Task-focused Group Meetings *J.M.P.V.K. Jayasundara* — 121

9   English for Academic Purposes for Students in Fragile
    Environments   *Yvonne Fraser*   137

10 Contesting Narratives of the Deficit Writer: A Writing for
    Publication Workshop Programme for Displaced Syrian
    Academics   *Marion Heron and Tom Parkinson*   157

11 A Reflection on Social Justice in International EAP:
    Addressing (or Not ...) Gender Inequality Through English
    Instruction   *Magdalena Rostron*   177

12 The Journey of *Develop EAP*: From a Single Step to a More
    Sustainable and Shared Practice   *Averil Bolster*   189

13 English for Research Purposes and Linguistic Diversity:
    Researcher Reflexivity and Social Justice
    Magdalena De Stefani, Richard Fay and Zhuomin Huang   197

14 *Los de la UABJO*: Resisting Linguistic Imperialism in Southern
    Mexico Through the Indigenisation of Language Pedagogy
    *Alexander Black and Mónica Sánchez-Hernández with
    contributions from Mario E. López-Gopar and Katia González*   211

Conclusion: Concluding Reflections Upon Social Justice
    in EAP and ELT Contexts   *Paul Breen*   231
Index   237

Figures

1.1	Digital Teaching and Learning Ecosystem (DTLE)	21
1.2	Overview of the Community of Inquiry Model and the categories developed by Akyol et al. (2011)	22
1.3	Vygotsky's triangular model of action	24
1.4	Engeström's third-generation activity theory	24
1.5	A framework for integrating awareness of social justice into teaching and learning materials in an EAP curriculum	26
1.6	Results from Question 1 from the online survey	29
1.7	Results from Question 2 from the online survey	30
1.8	Results from Question 3 from the online survey	30
1.9	A teacher's path through the production of new or adapted materials	33
2.1	Curriculum for change	49
14.1	*Los de la UABJO* graphic depiction one	212
14.2	*Los de la UABJO* graphic depiction two	213
14.3	*Los de la UABJO* collage for stimulating conversation	220
15.1	The SJ-ELT or SJ-EAP model of activity	232

Tables

3.1	Study participants in a small-scale qualitative study to investigate EAP practitioners' attitudes to CEAP	60
10.1	Workshop for Cara Research Grant Winners	174
13.1	Insider and outsider perspectives in the research	203

Contributors

Alexander Black, EAP Lecturer and English Language teacher
Institute of Education, University College London, UK

Alexander Black has previously worked in France, Spain, Switzerland, Russia, and most recently, Mexico. Previous research projects have included a participatory action research project involving assessment practices in Mexico and ESOL materials development using practices from the Theatre of the Oppressed. X (Twitter) handle: @universe_circus.

Averil Bolster, Teacher of English
University of Turku, Finland

Averil Bolster's research interests focus on academic oral presentations, materials development, and collaborative learning. Her most recent book chapters (co-authored with Peter Levrai) include 'Are we Talking About the Same Thing? Researcher and Practitioner Perspectives of Student Collaboration' (2022a) in the *Proceedings of the 2019 BALEAP Conference* and 'Fast-Forwarding Toward the Future of EAP Teaching in "the Happiest Country in the World": Lessons Learned in Turbulent Times' (2022b) in *International Perspectives on Teaching and Learning in Academic English in Turbulent Times*.

Paul Breen, Senior Digital Learning Developer and Senior Lecturer in EAP
Academic Communication Centre, University College London, UK

Paul Breen gained his Masters and PhD qualifications at the University of Manchester in the field of education, with a particular focus on English Language Teaching, English for Academic Purposes and Educational Technology. He has worked in academic and media contexts in Britain, Ireland and overseas. His publications include both academic and non-academic output, ranging from textbooks to the 2018 book version of his PhD, entitled *Developing Educators for the Digital Age*. He is the co-editor of this publication.

Magdalena De Stefani, Head of the Research Department
Instituto Universitario de Artes Escénicas, Montevideo, Uruguay

Magdalena De Stefani (she/her) is a Lecturer in Research Methods and currently serves as Honorary Head of Research at Instituto Universitario de Artes Escénicas (IUDAE). She has been extensively involved in pre- and in-service teacher training for EFL teachers. Her research addresses issues of intercultural communication; action research; blended learning; and professional development.

Robert Farag, Lecturer in English for Academic Purposes and Director of Phoenix International Education and Teacher Training
University of Westminster, London

Robert Farag's research interests revolve around language teacher education, English for Specific Purposes, Content and Language Integrated Learning (CLIL) and English Medium Instruction (EMI).

Richard Fay, Senior Lecturer in Education
Manchester Institute of Education at the University of Manchester, UK

Richard Fay (he/him) is a Senior Lecturer in Education (TESOL / Intercultural Communication) at The University of Manchester. He teaches researcher education, intercultural communication through language education, and klezmer ensemble performance. His research addresses the languaging of research; epistemic injustice and a critical intercultural ethic in knowledge-work; and critical intentionality.

Natalia Fedorova, Lecturer in English
University of Coimbra, Portugal

Natalia Fedorova is responsible for designing and teaching an Academic English course to bachelor-level students. Previously, she worked at the Language Centre, University of Leeds, UK, teaching English for Academic Purposes on pre-sessional courses. Before she began teaching EAP, she taught General English and exam classes (IELTS and PET) to various students/young learners and adults in both the UK and Russia. Her research interests include EAP learner needs, critical EAP, neoliberalism, translanguaging, linguistic imperialism, native-speakerism, English as a Lingua Franca, and language and migration. Her latest publication is on EAP learners' attitudes towards grammar instruction (Autumn 2022) in the *International Journal of English for Academic Purposes: Research and Practice*.

Yvonne Fraser - ELT Consultant and Teacher Trainer.

Yvonne Fraser comes from a background of English language teaching, teacher training, academic and project management. She worked overseas for over twenty years, predominantly with the British Council, in Turkey, Egypt, Malaysia, Jordan, Tunisia and Libya, where she specialised in working with learners and educators living in challenging contexts. She returned to the UK four years ago and has consulted on remote English for Academic Purposes and teacher training projects in Tajikistan, Afghanistan, Myanmar and China. She is currently coordinating pre-Master's programmes at a Higher Education Institute in the UK. Yvonne has a bachelor's degree in Politics and International Relations, the Cambridge DELTA and qualifications in project management. She has recently completed a Master's degree in TESOL and Applied Linguistics at Manchester Metropolitan University, UK.

Mario E. López-Gopar, Professor of Applied Linguistics
Universidad Autónoma Benito Juárez de Oaxaca (UABJO), Mexico

Mario's main research interest is intercultural and multilingual education of indigenous peoples in Mexico. He has received over fifteen academic awards. His PhD thesis was awarded both the 2009 AERA Second Language Research Dissertation Award and the 2009 OISE Outstanding Thesis of the Year Award. He has published numerous articles and book chapters in Mexico, USA, Canada, Argentina, Brazil and Europe. Some of his most notable works include *Decolonizing Primary English Language Teaching* (2016) and *International Perspectives on Critical Pedagogies in ELT* (2019).

John Gray, Professor of Applied Linguistics and Education
University College London Centre for Applied Linguistics, UK

John Gray has a first degree in English from Trinity College, Dublin and a Master's degree and a PhD from the University of London (IOE). His background is in English language teaching and English language teacher education. He is the author of 'The Construction of English: Culture, Consumerism and Promotion' in *The ELT Global Coursebook* (2010) and *Critical Perspectives on Language Teaching Materials* (2013). He is also the author, along with David Block and Marnie Holborow, of *Neoliberalism and Applied Linguistics* (2012) and *Social Interaction and English Language Teacher Identity* (2018), written with Tom Morton.

Marion Heron, Associate Professor in Educational Linguistics
University of Surrey, UK

Marion Heron is responsible for overseeing and supporting the Surrey Excellence in Teaching (SET) Framework, as well as contributing to the MA in Higher Education and Continuing Professional Development (CPD) workshops and sessions. Her doctoral research focused on the construction of teaching knowledge in pre-service trainees, and this interest in the application of sociocultural theory to different learning contexts remains her main area of scholarly work.

Michèle le Roux, Lecturer in EAP
University of Ulster

Michèle le Roux has over thirty years' experience of teaching EFL and EAP both in the UK and abroad. She has also worked as a course/materials designer, a teacher trainer and in management roles in HE, most recently as Course Leader in the Academic Skills Centre at the University of Bath. Michèle supervises MATESOL students at Durham University and the Departments of Education at the Universities of Glasgow and Bath. She is a founder member of two BALEAP SIGs (Social Justice and Academic Listening), is a member of the Steering Group of the EAP strand of the Cara Syria Project, and teaches for the Institute of Ismaili Studies. Michèle has also trained in Catechesis and Spiritual Accompaniment and is developing her practice in the facilitation of non-violent communication and circles of trust. She seeks to position herself with integrity at the interface of several of these professional identities and to build bridges, trust and community. She is co-editor of this publication.

Zhuo Min Huang, Lecturer in Education
Manchester Institute of Education, University of Manchester, UK

Zhuomin Huang (she/her) is a Lecturer in the Manchester Institute of Education at The University of Manchester. She has interests in teaching and research regarding intercultural/international education. Her recent work examines: epistemic injustice and a critical intercultural ethic in knowledge-work; intercultural experience; intercultural personhood; mindfulness; and creative-arts methods.

J.M.P.V.K. (Viji) Jayasundara, PhD student and Senior Lecturer
University of Hertfordshire, UK and Uva Wellassa University of Sri Lanka

Viji Jayasundara is currently reading for her PhD in Developing Cognitive Skills of Compassionate Communication for Online Group Management. Her research interests are in the areas of Applied Linguistics, Psycholinguistics, Teacher Education, Testing and Evaluation and Compassionate Communication. She has published more than thirty research papers in her academic career.

Tomasz John, Teaching Fellow in TESOL and Intercultural Communication
University of Strathclyde, Glasgow, UK

Tomasz John worked as an ESOL lecturer for three years, then as an EAP practitioner and Head of EAP for over ten years. He is a Co-convener and Comms Officer of the BALEAP EAP4SJ SIG. Tomasz cares about ethical and comprehensive internationalisation of HE, the decolonization of the curriculum and representation in ELT. X (Twitter) handle: @ tomaszjohn84.

Kashmir Kaur (SFHEA), Lecturer in English for Academic Purposes
University of Leeds, UK

Kashmir Kaur for the last three years was responsible for designing and teaching on the pre-sessional English for Academic Purposes for Postgraduate Researchers. In the academic year 2022/3, Kashmir commenced teaching EAP to in-sessional postgraduate students in the School of the Earth and Environment and the Institute of Transport. She is also the Module Lead for the pre-sessional Language for Engineering. Her research interests intersect student identity and internationalization including critical EAP, 'decolonizing' the curriculum, linguistic imperialism, native-speakerism, translanguaging, digital literacies and 'criticality' in higher education. Her latest publication is 'Embed Sustainability in the Curriculum: Transform the World' (December 2022) in the *Language Learning in Higher Education: Journal of European Confederation of Language Centres in Higher Education (CercleS)*.

Nguyet Luu, PhD student
University of Roehampton, UK

Nguyet Luu is pursuing research in Applied Linguistics. Prior to her doctoral studies, she worked as an ESL (English as a Second Language) and EAP (English for Academic Purposes) teacher at Thang Long University in Vietnam. Before that, she earned her Master's degree in TESOL from the University of Westminster, where she gained a deep understanding of academic writing and experienced it first-hand as a multilingual writer.

Hilary Key McDowell, Lecturer in Academic Skills, Critical Thinking and EAP
University of Westminster, UK

Hilary Key McDowell has recently become involved in the Prison Project, through which the university delivers preparatory courses to students at nineteen UK prisons.

Jo Kukuczka, educational development and English for Academic Purposes (EAP) professional, PhD student and Assistant Professor (Educational Development)
University of Warwick, Academic Development Centre, UK

Jo Kukuczka is a Senior Fellow of Advance HE, Fellow of BALEAP, Member of BERA, Associate Member of LCT Centre for Knowledge-Building, an academic journal peer reviewer, assessor, mentor and external examiner. Her expertise includes HE curriculum development, teacher education, teaching EAP, and, recently, practitioner research. She is passionate about learning, teaching, research and sharing knowledge on curriculum, education for social change, and the union of theory and practice. She is currently undertaking a PhD on the social impact of an EAP curriculum for change.

Katherine Mansfield, Senior Lecturer and researcher in Academic English
University of Westminster, UK

Katherine Mansfield is a module leader for undergraduate and postgraduate Academic English courses. Her research interests include academic writing, online pedagogy, the acculturation of international students, and bi/multilingualism. She has recently published on how to re-engage Higher Education students and demonstrate compassion to first year undergraduates. Her most recent book is *International Perspectives on Teaching and Learning Academic English in Turbulent Times* (2022).

Jan McArthur, Senior Lecturer in the Department of Educational Research
Lancaster University, UK

Jan McArthur has previously worked in Monash University in Melbourne, Australia and the University of Edinburgh UK. Her research interests mainly span two themes: education and social justice, and the nature of higher education. Her most recent work has looked at the nature of assessment and feedback as well as the role of failure in learning including the relationship between conceptions of failure and social justice. Amongst the lengthy list of publications she has produced in this field, one of her best known is *Assessment for Social*

Justice: Perspectives and Practices within Higher Education published by Bloomsbury Academic (2018).

Lorraine Mighty, People and Organisational Development Consultant
University of Birmingham, UK

Lorraine Mighty previously worked as an English for Academic Purposes Practitioner and Programme Manager for over ten years. She is the Treasurer of the BALEAP EAP for Social Justice SIG. Her research interests include the internationalization of higher education, staff and students' experiences of higher education, critical and inclusive pedagogy and academic identity. X (Twitter) handle: @mighty_write.

Svetlana Page, Lecturer in Academic English
University of Westminster, UK

Svetlana Page's research interests cover cultural studies and international student teaching, action research, world literature and postcolonial theories, minority cultures and Eastern European translation studies. Her latest publications include *Self-Translation and Power: Negotiating Identities in European Multilingual Contexts* (co-edited with Olga Castro and Sergi Mainer, 2017) and 'Maxim Gorky and World Literature: Challenging the Maxims' in *Translation and World Literature* (edited by S. Bassnett, 2019).

Tom Parkinson, Reader and Programme Director
Centre for the Study of Higher Education in the University of Kent, UK

Tom Parkinson chairs the Academic Development steering group for the 'Council for At-Risk Academics' (Cara) Syria Programme, which supports Syrian academics in continuing their academic work in exile. His research interests are higher education in conflict, post-conflict and refugee contexts, internationalization of higher education and music education. He is currently nearing completion of a historical study of Turkish music education funded by the British Academy.

Ignez Pereira-Norris, EAP Lecturer
University of Westminster, UK

Ignez Pereira-Norris' research interests focus on material development, language teacher education and inclusive practices in the teaching of English as a second language.

Magdalena Rostron, Teaching Faculty
Georgetown University, Qatar

Magdalena Rostron has an educational background that includes an MA in English Literature and TEFL from Warsaw University and a PhD in Education from the University of Manchester. She works in the Academic Bridge Program (teaching Academic Composition and co-ordinating Literature courses), and as adjunct faculty at Georgetown University in Qatar. She has published articles in Polish and English, in academic journals and other publications.

Mónica Sánchez Hernández, PhD student of Social Policy
Bristol University, UK

Mónica Sánchez Hernández is an indigenous-rooted, working-class woman from the Global South/Global Majority. She previously studied at universities in Brazil, Belgium, Mexico and France. Her work experience has centred on education programmes for incarcerated men in Mexico City, and her current research examines understandings of manhood within and without prison using art-based methods and decolonising methodologies. X (Twitter) handle: @monicabrsh.

D. Tran, Director of Education and Reader in Developmentally Disruptive Practices and Pedagogies
University of the Arts London (UAL), UK

D. Tran manages the Teaching, Learning and Employability Exchange and leads on the delivery of the UAL Learning and Teaching Enhancement Strategy. She previously held the role of Interim Dean of Learning, Teaching, Enhancement, and Associate Dean of Academic Enhancement at UAL. Prior to this, D. Tran was Associate Professor of Higher Education Learning and Teaching at the University of Greenwich, UK. She is a Principal Fellow (AdvanceHE) and has worked at various UK HE institutions across different roles and areas. Her research interests include decolonizing teaching and learning, belonging, and reflective practice. Her most notable recent publications include *Decolonizing University Teaching and Learning* published by Bloomsbury Academic in May 2021.

Iwona Winiarska-Pringle, Lecturer in English for Academic Purposes
University of Glasgow, UK

Having taught English for General and Specific Purposes for seven years, Iwona Winiarska-Pringle moved to teaching academic English and literacies in 2013, developing an interest in oracy and educational dialogue, ethical internationalization, and relational pedagogies. Her additional role at Glasgow involves overseeing support for refugee-background students and she is the Events Officer of the BALEAP EAP4SJ SIG. X (Twitter) handle: @IwonaPringle.

Foreword
Foreword and Forward: A Personal Reflection

John Gray
Centre for Applied Linguistics, University College London

Although the concept has a long history, social justice has become something of a key term across a range of domains and disciplines in recent years. For those of us who work in language education, it has provided a useful conceptual tool for thinking about the structures within which we are imbricated, the roles we are ascribed and the identities to which we are able to lay claim, as well as to matters of pedagogical practice and student flourishing. From my own perspective as a queer educator whose thinking about the social is indebted to Marx, I am also aware that the concept is understood very differently depending on attitudes to capitalism, and in particular to capitalism in its increasingly fractured neoliberal guise. Thus, despite Friedrich Hayek's (1982: 82) repudiation of social justice as belonging 'not [...] to the category of error but to that of nonsense', many of the inheritors of his creed of market fundamentalism have more recently engaged with the idea as potentially useful, as the negative social consequences of neoliberalism have become ever more evident.

A cursory look at the website of the centre-right British Centre for Social Justice is instructive in this regard. Its mission statement declares that the organisation's vision is for 'those living in the poorest and most disadvantaged communities across Britain to be given every opportunity to flourish and reach their full potential' (Centre for Social Justice 2023). It aims to do so by addressing what it sees as the root causes of poverty, which are listed as: family breakdown, educational failure, worklessness, addiction and crime and problem debt and housing. Unsurprisingly, educational failure (as the factor most directly relevant to readers of this volume) is discussed in terms of the 'upskilling' and 'reskilling' needed 'as our jobs market is rapidly being remoulded by technology and the world economy' (ibid.). No mention here (or anywhere on the website) of the depredations of neoliberal capitalism or the need for structural change – rather a predictable focus on the need to meet the challenges demanded by 'the economy' and the role of education in facilitating this. My point in raising this in the foreword to this volume is that what social justice means is intimately bound up with our political understanding of the purpose of education. As Kevin Harris (1982) put it some years ago, what capitalism requires for its reproduction is *schooling* rather than *education* – a distinction in which the former is understood as the inculcation of the values of the system and the production of school leavers and graduates with the appropriate dispositions needed to service the economy, while the latter is construed in terms of the development of human potential and the critical consciousness necessary to effect change. 'Educated people' he writes, 'are a threat to an oppressive or repressive social system' and, under capitalism, education 'is kept from rather than provided for the vast proportion of the population' (Harris 1982: 23). We do not have to accept Harris' assessment completely though, as he tends to neglect the role of teachers' agency (despite the many constraints on it) in striving to educate their students. But it is certainly the case that the political right seeks to commandeer the concept of social justice with a view to rendering it subservient to the needs of capital. Thus, teachers and scholars whose view of education resonates more with that of Harris than that of the Centre for Social Justice have an important role to play in articulating and implementing a view of social justice in which social critique is central.

In thinking about such a view of social justice, the work of a number of scholars has been important for me – in particular that of Nancy Fraser (1995) on redistribution and recognition and, more recently, that of Donaldo Macedo (2019) on decolonising the curriculum. Fraser argues that social justice in the world today requires redress on two fronts. On the one hand, she identifies the *socioeconomic injustice* which requires a politics of redistribution. On the other hand, there is the *cultural injustice* suffered by minority groups (e.g. racial, linguistic, religious, etc.) whose marginalisation calls out for a politics of recognition. Of course, there is overlap between the two and, as Fraser points out, the distinction between them is analytical. With regard to the cultural injustice experienced by non-normative sexuality and gender-identifying minorities there has been a plethora of protective and recognition-granting legislation introduced by governments globally in recent years (e.g. decriminalisation of homosexuality, introduction of equal marriage and the rights of transgender people to change their birth certificate, passport, etc. in line with their chosen gender identification, etc.). However, very little of this social change is reflected in the pedagogical materials for use in classrooms. These remain in large part relentlessly heteronormative and cisnormative in terms of content (Gray 2023), thereby perpetuating the symbolic violence of erasure that LGBTQ+ students endure in educational settings. Calls for recognition are therefore important, but to forget about the ways in which cultural injustice and socioeconomic injustice articulate with one another runs the risk of our redress being co-opted by a neoliberal homo- and cisnormativity which is celebratory of diversity, individualism and choice, but which remains blind to structural inequalities of class society. The challenge, Fraser (1995: 69) suggests, is to: 'see ourselves as presented with a new intellectual and practical task: that of developing a *critical* theory of recognition, one which identifies and defends only those versions of the cultural politics of difference that can be coherently combined with the politics of social equality.'

Hence the argument for an approach to recognition that is both intersectional and attentive to the realities and lived experience of students from the Global South. And here the spectre of colonialism rears its head. In a recent edited volume, *Decolonizing Foreign Language Education: The Misteaching of English and Other Colonial Languages*, Donaldo Macedo (2019) and colleagues argue that the teaching of colonial languages needs to change if colonial legacies and linguistic hierarchies are to be challenged. As well as making the case for alternative forms of carrier content in language teaching materials to those currently on offer, in which all mention of colonialism is erased and language spread is seen as a natural and apolitical phenomenon, many of the contributors make the case for a translanguaging approach to pedagogy. It is one in which the monolingualism associated with communicative language teaching is viewed as politically retrograde, educationally shallow and ethically unsustainable. These contributors do so in line with the manifesto recently issued by a group of translanguaging scholars (García et al. 2021: 211) who contend that:

> academic language is not a set of empirically derived linguistic features, but rather a category that emerges as part of broader raciolinguistic ideologies that overdetermine racialised communities as linguistically deficient and unacademic, even as the concept of academic language itself remains impossible to define objectively. That is, racialised populations are often perceived by the white listening subject as using non-academic language that needs to be corrected even when engaging in ostensibly the same linguistic practices that are unmarked for white subjects.

The manifesto is a powerful argument in favour of a very different kind of second language classroom, and one in which a concern with social justice moves centre stage. That said, as Jürgen Jaspers (2018) points out, we need to be realistic about what we as educators can achieve. There is no doubt that we are well positioned to address cultural injustice by actively taking steps to accord recognition to marginalised groups in the materials we use to teach, and we can allow our students to draw on the full range of their linguistic and semiotic repertoires in the classroom as they engage in meaning making in ways which undermine the privileging of English monolingualism. When it comes to socioeconomic injustice things are a little different. Structural change also requires political activity *outside* the classroom – but the case for such activity can certainly be made *within* the classroom. Here the tradition of critical reading is helpful in encouraging students to begin to imagine alternatives to the versions of the world currently on offer in so many second language classrooms. Thinking about ways of exploring heteronormativity (but clearly relevant to so many other issues), Joshua Paiz (2022: 98) recommends posing post-comprehension questions of the following kind:

> What relationships do we see represented in the text?
> What do we notice about the structure of these relationships as it is related to gender, age, race, etc?
> What does this suggest to us about what the text values?
> How are these views supported by the graphic elements of the text?
> Do the pictures that go with the text reinforce these ideas or others?
> Who is ignored by this view? Who is given preference?
> What would alternatives look like?

Such an approach – and it is only one of many – is representative of a pedagogy of social justice in which education (as understood by Harris) is the driving force. It is one that encourages students to think critically about the materials and ideas they are asked to engage with, and that seeks to elicit their own responses in imagining alternative ways of construing and creating the world. In the pages that follow, a group of international scholars offer a global perspective on social justice in a range of EAP and ELT contexts in which issues of theory and practice are insightfully explored. It is a much needed and welcome addition to the literature.

References

Centre for Social Justice (2023). Available at: https://www.centreforsocialjustice.org.uk/ (accessed 08/01/2023).

Fraser, N. (1995) 'From Redistribution to Recognition? Dilemmas of Justice in a "Post-Socialist" Age', *New Left Review*, 212: 68–149.

García, O., Flores, N., Seltzer, K, Li, W., Otheguy, R. and Rosa J. (2021) 'Rejecting abyssal Thinking in the Language and Education of Racialised Bilinguals: a Manifesto', *Critical Inquiry in Language Studies*, 18 (3): 203–28.

Gray, J. (2023) 'Between Recognition and Redistribution – the Political Economy of Taboos in Foreign Language Education', in C. Ludwig and T. Summer (eds), *Taboos and Controversial Issues in Foreign Language Education*, pp. 23–30. Abingdon: Routledge.

Harris, K. (1982) *Teachers and Classes: a Marxist Analysis*, London: Routledge and Kegan Paul.

Hayek, F. A. (1982) *Law, Legislation and Liberty*, London: Routledge.

Jaspers, J. (2018) 'Language Education Policy and Sociolinguistics: Toward a New Critical Engagement', in J. W. Tollefson and M. Pérez-Milans (eds), *The Oxford Handbook of Language Policy and Planning*, pp.704–724, Oxford: Oxford University Press.

Macedo, D., ed. (2019) *Decolonizing Foreign Language Teaching: the Misteaching of English and Other Colonial Languages*. Abingdon: Routledge.

Paiz, J. M. (2020) *Queering the English Language Classroom: a Practical Guide for Teachers*. Bristol: Equinox.

Acknowledgements

Thanks to all who have contributed to this publication, in ways that might have been big or small but are all equally valuable. This has been a journey in which we have worked closely with all of our authors and we, as editors, thank you for your participation in this project. We also thank all those authors who have given us their permission to replicate or reference their frameworks as a stimulus for those we have developed ourselves. It has been an honour to collaborate with some very prestigious names not just in EAP and ELT but the wider higher educational domain.

Equally, we thank our team of editors at Bloomsbury for their assistance, patience and dedication along the way. We also extend that thanks to everyone who has played any part in the publication process, from proofreading through to marketing. Within that, we would also include the external reviewers who gave us plenty of food for thought along the way. That has helped cultivate the seed of an idea into a final output. Significantly, we have never seen our work as the finished or definitive word on the topics we are writing about. We thank all those who are contributing to the conversation in so many different ways in the wider world, including the EAP for Social Justice Group that is part of BALEAP. UCL also deserves thanks for contributing to an environment highly conducive to the demands of taking an edited book through to completion. Lastly, special thanks to the team in the university's Academic Communication Centre for their continuous encouragement and camaraderie.

Every effort has been made to trace copyright holders and to obtain their permission for the use of copyright material. However, if any have been inadvertently overlooked, the publishers will be pleased, if notified of any omissions, to make the necessary arrangement at the first opportunity.

INTRODUCTION

A Reflection Upon Social Justice in EAP and ELT Contexts

Paul Breen

John Gray's foreword addresses some of the philosophical and political challenges faced by those of us who work in language education, before concluding where this chapter begins. That is situated at a juncture of belief in finding 'a pedagogy of social justice in which education', as distinct from mere schooling (Harris, 1982) is 'the driving force.' My belief is that education lies at the heart of the activity system that we inhabit and it co-habits this terrain, equally and inseparably, with language. Throughout my life, both personally and professionally, I have been committed to the cause of social justice, believing strongly in Jan McArthur's argument that education and society are 'intrinsically interrelated' and a fundamental purpose of education is the attainment of social justice (McArthur 2010: 493).

Such values have always been at the heart of English Language Teaching (ELT), in spite of this often being a highly commercialised and precarious industry. Similarly, there is a strong sense of social justice embedded in the more scholastic area of English for Academic Purposes (EAP). Increasingly, this is evident in all areas of EAP practitioners' work, particularly at curricular, material and epistemological levels. Values of care, compassion, inclusivity and fairness are being put into practice on an everyday basis. A shift is happening too in terms of lessening our Western-centrism. Having worked most of our lives with international students, language teaching professionals understand what a multipolar world might mean in practice. Through the type of work we do, we understand the power of such things as patience, shared understanding, intercultural communication, consensus and negotiation. Sometimes these might seem like the sort of essential values that have been lost or forgotten. Perhaps then part of our role as language educators is to create a pathway of access for marginalised voices within an increasingly polarised and xenophobic world.

Though our own voice in the various domains of education is not always a mainstream one, it is unique. Language teachers are often situated at intersections of activity. As such, we are well-placed to address another of the challenges of our times. Currently we live in an age of fragmented and even competing causes. Often, we see valuable tenets of social justice activity taking place on a disparate rather than cohesive basis. At times there can even be contradictions in what we are trying to do. Perceptions of social justice vary across contexts as seen in this publication. Similarly too, there are challenges around what is meant by the term 'social justice' itself. Throughout this work you will hear a range of voices stretching from global East to West and North to South. Each context is unique, with very different forms of activity being enacted. Though good work is being done in so many places, these are not always knitted together in a clear pattern. As such, there is a recognisable need to draw together these tenets and also to define a common set of principles through which they operate. That is one core objective of this publication alongside a desire to thread together these stories of different contexts into one tapestry.

In order to give this work a strong theoretical foundation, it has drawn upon an application and adaptation of Engeström's (1993, 1999, 2001) conceptualisation of Activity Theory. Once regarded as 'the best kept secret in academia' (Engeström 1993: 64), this theory rose to higher prominence at the start of the millennium (Roth 2004). Increasingly, it has come to play a significant role across disciplines providing a bridge between theory and practice that is ultimately focused upon the production of outcomes. This makes it political in its ideology but practical in its enactments. Previously, I have used this as part of the conceptual framework in a PhD study of EAP teacher development (Breen 2018). Since it focuses on intersections of activity, it is most useful for holding together aspects of theory and practice in situations where there are challenges, contradictions and changes. As such, Activity Theory serves as a scaffold for facilitating intersectional connections, allowing for the types of development suggested in Vygotsky (1934/1978) who Roth (2004: 8) labels as one of 'the fathers of activity theory', alongside Marx, Engels and Leont'ev.

More information on this is provided in Chapter 1 which introduces third-generation Activity Theory in greater detail. For now, in this introduction, the goal is not to delve too deeply into theoretical aspects but to situate the work. An important first step in this is probably to clearly define the parameters of what the book is about. In the words of my co-editor Michèle le Roux, this work is intended 'to inform, to provoke thought and to allow light, air and variety into our thinking about EAP/ELT in terms of boundaries and territories.' At times, it is hard to define such boundaries. Are we all part of the same family in English Language Teaching? Or are we as broken up as the organisations and bodies we often see in the world of professional sports? Personally, I think we are fighting many of the same battles. As such, I share the stance of Jennifer MacDonald who lumps together the entire ELT sector in her 2016 paper drawing on the work of Goodson and Hargreaves (1996) in discussing postmodern professionalism. Therein, she alludes to a shared knowledge base in EAP and ELT whilst acknowledging that there is no one agreed epistemology of professional knowledge for the English teacher (Liyanage, Walker and Singh 2015; MacDonald 2016: 108). Although we may occupy different habitats in the world of English Language Education, we are all part of the same interrelated ecosystem.

The notion of an educational ecosystem is one that fits well with Activity Theory in that our relations within an ecosystem as within a system of activity are socially mediated. They are also historically situated and interdependent, with the educational workplace needing a synergy of different components in order to thrive, just as a plant requires a combination of light, water and air so as to photosynthesise. Increasingly too, the term ecosystem is one that has become synonymous with a vocabulary of risk, challenge and endangerment. As we face the existential threat of climate change, we are becoming ever more aware of the ways in which the local feeds into the global. That is often termed as 'glocal' in Roland Robertson's (1992: 8) classic definition, first espoused in the 1980s as an advancement upon the idea of globalisation, which is a term that lacks a sense of mutual dependency and interconnectedness.

ELT and EAP have always had a strong consciousness of glocalisation in my opinion, and that for me is most strongly evident in our field's historical work with technology. Right from the early period of Computer Assisted Language Learning (Warschauer 2002, 2003) up to the present, we have been at the forefront of technology being used to open doors of opportunity 'rather than creating digital divides' (Motteram 2016). That was seen in how language educators generally reacted to the demands of the Covid-19 pandemic as in Blaj-Ward et al. (2021) and Prevatt-Goldstein et al. (2021). Perhaps through our precarious position and our work in what might be seen as a chameleon discipline responding to demands of the moment, we have become equipped with a pedagogic knowledge heavily imbued with adaptability. I have consistently believed that although we are language educators, pedagogy plays just as crucial a role in who we are, particularly in a time of great contemporary disruption with the new wave of 'AIEd technologies' such as Open AI's ChatGPT (Zhang and Aslan 2021; Mhlanga 2023). Perhaps as the nature of language itself begins to change as a result of the tools through which we mediate our shared practices, the focus of our activity needs to broaden in order to make our future more sustainable.

Already though, there appears to be a growing desire within our field to have a greater impact on the world, whether in the islands of academia or the shores of wider society. Around us, projects small and large are taking shape in the scattered archipelago of English Language Teaching. These can be found in such initiatives as the Cara Syria Programme which features later in this book; the work of BALEAP's EAP for Social Justice Special Interest Group; the efforts of RefugEAP (Palanac 2022a) to facilitate educational efforts for refugee students; and a growing engagement with Education for Sustainable Development in all domains of language teaching. This is also evidenced in *Develop EAP: A Sustainable Academic English Skills Course* by Averil Bolster and Peter Levrai (2017), The British Council's *Climate Connection* podcast series, and *FutureLearn* Black Lives Matter resources.

In recent times, an increasing number of English language educators are also bringing issues of social justice into their classrooms in the form of teaching materials. This includes Leah Mortenson's (2022) work on highlighting racial inequalities. Further to this, both John Gray (2021) and Tyson Seburn (2021) have provided robust examples of incorporating LGBT awareness into materials design, in very different contexts. By making such issues a part of our activity, we are showing a broader awareness of what Mason et al. (2019) describe as the wider 'campus climate'. Today's campuses are becoming sites of political action in which students themselves aspire to a protest against and a deconstructing of past prejudices and injustices. A further way of developing this could come with the creation of what are known as 'brave' spaces (Arao and Clemens 2013) in our classrooms, work environments and wider societies. Such spaces allow for the courage to feel empowered so that we can engage in the 'challenging dialogues' that are necessary to impact meaningful change (ibid.: 149). Further to that, it moves the emphasis off 'therapeutic education' as discussed in Ding and Bruce (2017: 35–9), drawing on the work of Kathryn Ecclestone (2009, 2014). Brave spaces put an emphasis upon action, which fits in well with Activity Theory's focus on transformative impact and socially-mediated outcomes.

Through having the bravery of desiring change, we can draw on the compassionate, empathetic and transformative pedagogic approaches of ELT/EAP to advocate for the design of assessments, curriculum and materials shaped by principles of social justice. Ultimately though, social justice is always more of a fossil-free fuel that runs through the engine of activity rather than being the vehicle itself. It is important to guard against being seen as advocating a pedagogic approach that does not have tangible outcomes. Ken Hyland rolls some very strong stones of criticism in this direction with his seminal paper 'in defence of EAP' (2018). Jan McArthur also acknowledges that critical pedagogic approaches are sometimes seen as 'more successful in critiquing educational and social practices than in achieving actual change' (2010: 493). As part of her argument she warns against 'romantic possibilitarian' rhetoric (ibid.), drawing on earlier arguments made by Geoff Whitty (1974) and Michael Apple (2000). This means that more than aspiration is required. In order to be taken seriously as a conceptually-sound force for change, our work in these areas has to have real impact. Everything that we do has to have twin aims: to enhance teaching and learning at the same time as trying to improve the world around us.

One instance of this comes in the way in which my workplace, UCL, has integrated so much of a focus on climate change into its educational systems. This ranges from the creation of a Climate Hub through to exhibitions involving interdisciplinary work. That includes a speculative account of the future worlds we may well face if we don't look after our planet, in an exhibition labelled as *Objects of the Misanthropocene*. There, the university is interacting with the outside world in a collaboration between *The Illegal Museum of Beyond* and UCL's Museums and Cultural Programmes, at the same time as drawing together different disciplines into a shared space of activity. Other such initiatives include our Centre for Languages and International Education having its own Climate Action Team, putting principles of sustainability into practice rather than purely for strapline purposes. They participate in such localised ventures as advocating on behalf of charities like *Trees for Life*, whilst at the same time promoting awareness of the need for coordinated global action to safeguard the preservation of the planet for future generations. In doing so, they are using the platform of higher education to leave a sustainable legacy that might outlive the present 'unsustainable marked propensity towards the marketisation of education' (Molesworth, Nixon and Scullion 2009: 278, cited in Palanac 2022b).

'Marketisation' is a recurring term in twenty-first century educational literature (Apple 2000; Bunzel 2007; Sauntson and Morrish 2011; Ding and Bruce 2017; Bond 2020; Palanac 2022b). Alex Ding and Ian Bruce (2017) refer to this as a state of 'financialisation' (pp. 13–45) that reflects 'the vagaries of the current political, economic and social forces' (p. 10), probably now worsened in Britain by the deregulation playground of Brexit. A further problem is the 'increasing casualisation of academic labour' throughout 'the global North' in which a culture of 'short-term temporal logics' has taken hold (Leathwood and Read 2022: 756). This creates precarity for staff (Le Roux 2022a) and has left many teachers trapped for a lifetime in the vagaries of the gig economy. The prioritisation of numbers without deep consideration of implications has also caused 'technicisation' of language (Turner 2004: 95), reducing it to proficiency test scores to satisfy an entry requirement, as cited in MacDonald (2016: 108). As a consequence of this, English language educators are often forced into a role of gatekeeper (Smithwick 2014; MacDonald 2016; Palanac 2022b) with EAP courses labelled as 'sheltered and adjunct' to mainstream activity (Gilbert 2013: 119). There is a short-termism here, a fossil fuel mentality of sucking up the oil of international student recruitment before the well runs dry. And yet paradoxically, many in our field depend on such a state for their very employment.

Social justice then must also entail an economic element in order to be meaningful and impactful. That is recognised right from the outset of this book with John Gray's foreword and is a theme that recurs through many of the chapters. Within these chapters too there are some great instances of philosophies being put into practice. There are suggestions not just for what can be done at curricular, material and epistemological levels, but also ideas that can be used in everyday teaching. These range from the creation of elective classes based around issues in contemporary social justice to the use of blackout poetry as one means of developing voice. Another powerful impact of this book is the way in which authors do not just give us a lens into new situations but also make us see the world through the eyes of others.

Many of the pedagogies and ideas that are shared put forward radical views of what needs to be done. The experience of those in other contexts, particularly the more challenging environments we encounter, adds another dimension to the work and further strengthens a move away from seeing hierarchies within EAP and ELT. Rather than viewing everything in a singularly Western gaze, we have tried to bring in voices that don't just tell but show how others see the world. Indeed at times, whether considering the socio-political climate of Mexico, or marrying together the mindsets of East and West in academic writing, there is a powerful call to action happening. Amidst these voices, there are advocates of such changes that would make many of today's language learning environments unrecognisable. Whether it is a call to arms for turning away from *Turnitin* or a greater acceptance of translanguaging, projects small and large are given voice the length and breadth of a very diverse world.

Right from the outset of putting this publication into motion, the goal was to bring more marginalised voices centre stage. Indeed, throughout this book, there is a very strong and consistent female presence with every subsequent chapter featuring a woman's voice. Those chapters also span as many contexts as possible, creating a sense of equal ownership. It is important that social justice's role in English education is not seen as 'some new Trafalgar' as David Graddol once warned against in recommendations for the future of English Language Teaching (1998: 9). The aforementioned translanguaging is one way of enhancing that sense of equal ownership. Equally importantly, the empowerment of students is another and that is something which comes across strongly throughout. At this stage then, I will briefly introduce the chapters themselves which have been sequenced around common themes, whilst at the same time allowing a natural rather than forced rhythm.

In a practice-rich opening **Chapter 1**, four of the five authors are female, alongside mixed race, multilingual and international aspects. Together, that group of authors take on the baton of Activity Theory from this opening reflection, by trying to fine-tune a theoretical understanding of social justice. That group of EAP practitioners from London's University of Westminster discuss the evaluation and evolution of a framework that integrates the awareness of social justice into teaching and learning materials. This chapter has its roots in a BALEAP-funded project to explore and develop a framework for embedding principles of social justice into the design of such materials. Therein, Engeström's (1999, 2001) Activity Theory plays a critical role and offers scope for the development of a new model of design practices in which pedagogy and language can sit more comfortably together.

This particular chapter has also got a unique significance for me because I formerly worked in the same environment as these practitioners, developing the course that they used as the focus of their research. In that environment, we always tried to educate students not just about the linguistic diversity of today's world but also the cultural diversity that will help them become better citizens of a more glocal future. In one instance of cultivating such a climate, on the pre-sessional course, I brought in guest lecturers from subject-specific disciplines to provide a weekly optional lesson for a predominantly Chinese cohort. These included Professor Pippa Catterall, a historian at Westminster who spoke on the topic of 'LGBT and transgender history'.

Through this, students were exposed to new ideas and perspectives which could then be related to the types of criticality that would be useful in challenging established canons and assumptions in their own disciplines. Therefore, in such an enactment, Pippa's lecture was the tool used to mediate an eventual outcome of students becoming more critical, rather than the content or its core message as an outcome in itself. These lectures were never intended as one-shot workshops. Instead of that, they served as a deep intramuscular approach to learning (Breen 2014) in which students are prompted to make that intellectual and psychological shift towards a zone of development. Such environments strengthen participation in academic life, in ways espoused in the Academic Literacies' literature (Lea and Street 1998). In this sense, social justice acts as a vehicle for student empowerment. Added to this, within the opening chapter, issues of practitioner justice are also touched upon.

Following on from this, Jo Kukuczka introduces the concept of a Curriculum for Change in **Chapter 2**, with the recommendation of a tailored framework for specific EAP contexts. This is a chapter that is again advocating the infusion of social justice into academic English courses, in a way that translates theory into practice. A lot of what Jo discusses has really strong echoes with what has gone before and introduces ideas to be explored further in subsequent chapters. One such area is assessment, particularly the contradictions that come from high-stakes, decontextualised language assessments. That is something further discussed by Jan McArthur in Chapter 4. It has also been discussed externally in the work of Jayne Pearson (2017, 2021). Above all though, this is a passionate call for social change, for a move beyond a focus on simply concentrating on the here and now of getting through language courses. Instead, there is a need for what might be defined as legacy – empowering our students in such a way that they go out into the world equipped as better citizens.

Chapter 3 continues in such a vein, with Natalia Fedorova and Kashmir Kaur's timely and necessary defence of Critical EAP. This chapter draws on the work of Sarah Benesch (1996, 2001) and others to show what critical pedagogies can offer in terms of actual practice. Within that, there is a sense of an approach that has much to offer not just to the Social Sciences but even those subjects considered as the hard sciences, wherein critical thought and critical engagement is so crucial at this moment in time. Moreover, although EAP's significant contribution to the more textual aspects of what we do (Hyland 2018: 389) should be cherished, there is genuine value to those other parts of our activity which prioritise pedagogy. With an increasing emphasis upon the types of transformation that John Gray and Jo Kukuczka have already spoken of, this could be an age when Critical EAP is very much back in vogue. It is important then to understand what such approaches mean in practice and what they can contribute. Together, these authors provide such a statement of purpose.

Chapter 4 then brings us to the work of Jan McArthur who advocates a radical change to the way students are assessed, not just in our local EAP/ELT contexts but also more globally in higher education. Just like Jo in Chapter 2, Jan is a powerful advocate of the cooperative nature of social life and of learning. Throughout her work and her practice, she emphasises the importance of the human dimension to education. Although not an English Language practitioner, the values that she espouses are very much in tune with those of ELT's compassionate pedagogy. She emphasises empathy over examination and champions care for teaching, transformation and trust over testing, particularly over-reliance on technological tools such as *Turnitin*. Added to that, this chapter is of particular importance because it reminds us that practitioners do not necessarily have to be directly from the EAP/ELT domain to make important contributions to its discussions and debates.

In **Chapter 5**, a new international voice comes to the fore, continuing where Jan left off in many ways. This work also speaks out against the sense of policing language that criss-crosses so much of our epistemological habitat, in an 'eats shoots and leaves' (Truss 2005) approach to judging the worthiness of international students. Here, Nguyet Luu challenges the sense of correction that constricts the entire academic journey for such students in offering an outsider's perspective of academia's 'white gaze'. Her call for change and a greater incorporation of such approaches as translanguaging serves as a rallying cry for 'decolonisation' of educational habitats (Tran 2019; Jivraj 2020; Tran 2021; McArthur 2022). Indeed, reading such work might even evoke a sense of historical guilt and a questioning of our practices. Arguably, so many parts of our professional ecosystem are dependent upon the need for remedial work, whether we ourselves see it through such a lens or not. If we began to unpick the threads of such systems of activity, perhaps the whole tapestry of what we do might unravel. However, by thinking outside the box, as in this chapter, we can perhaps move to a point of using a different kind of expertise to interact with the international students who are such a part of the fabric of today's Western universities. This chapter then is a call for co-creation and not correction, adding further support to the voices and the arguments that have preceded it.

Chapter 6 shifts the themes from those that are overarching to something that is more individual, relating to the shaping of the self rather than the wider context. Within this chapter, there is a stance on social justice that may seem different to what has gone before, but is actually rooted in the very same set of values, such as those human elements stressed in Jan McArthur's work. In this chapter, Lorraine Mighty, Tomasz John and Iwona Winiarska-Pringle bare their inner selves. They discuss and situate their personal existence within what they describe as 'an ecosystem of knowledge of our lived and professional experiences as English language teachers.' They do this through a trioethnographic study which explores professional identity through dialogue, ethics of care and creativity, as a group of individuals get to learn how the personal shapes the professional. As such, it is a deeply personal story; one that will leave readers with a sense of coming to know the authors as people – perhaps something not so common in the world of academic writing.

D. Tran's **Chapter 7** continues with themes relating to voice and identity. Within this short reflection, the emphasis is on the skill of listening. Perhaps that is a skill neglected or forgotten in today's polarised socio-political world. That is why, in this chapter, the author presents an argument for the power of silence. Within this, critical listening is a key element because it facilitates critical thinking. The idea is not to remain quiet but to use silent reflection as a means of identifying and addressing gaps in our knowledge. Again, that ties in with recurring themes in the book. The enactment of social justice is not simply achieved by talking about it. Sometimes we have to sit back and think about what all of these aspirations mean in practice. Through doing so we might also be better able to see and navigate the tensions, contradictions and challenges within our systems of activity.

In a further call for change to our communicative practices, Vijitha Jayasundara integrates Compassionate Communication into her pedagogy in **Chapter 8**. This work strongly resonates with the Arao and Clemens' (2013) call for a 'brave' space in which to scaffold our students towards development. The inclusion of a research journey and story linking Britain with Sri Lanka in Vijitha's case further illustrates how glocal our work really is. The chapter also has a resonance with wider external work, like that of my co-editor Michèle le Roux and others in exploring the application of compassionate pedagogy in a Circles of Trust approach (Le Roux 2022a, b).

The next group of chapters are so interlinked that they are best discussed together. Each of these touch upon places and practices that bring an even more international flavour to the book as a whole. The work of Yvonne Fraser in **Chapter 9** further shows the importance of what we do in our teaching and how that can have significant impact in real-world situations. Her work in physical, political and philosophical terms is the very enactment of that aforementioned 'brave space' (Arao and Clemens 2013). Similarly, Marion Heron and Tom Parkinson in **Chapter 10** take us into the heart of positive action – highlighting the work of the Council for At-Risk Academics (Cara) Syria Programme. Therein we see pedagogy and language working in synch. And, most strikingly, each of these chapters reminds us that the work of English language educators and EAP educators is indeed glocal.

This broad geographic canvas then extends to the context of Qatar in the case of Magdalena Rostron's **Chapter 11**, where she explores attempts to apply social justice-aligned pedagogy in a non-Western EAP classroom. There, the challenges are cultural and at times uncomfortable, highlighting new tensions and contradictions. Perhaps the most powerful message to come out of these chapters is that social justice is not something that is enacted only in woolly, safe spaces. The places and the people that these authors are writing about face a very different set of challenges from those that we encounter on a daily basis in the classrooms of the Western world.

Averil Bolster's **Chapter 12** explores her experience of designing materials around a platform of the United Nations' Sustainable Development Goals – turning a personal passion into an act of professional practice. This chapter ties in particularly well with the work of the Westminster practitioners because they actually investigate the usage of these materials in their context. As such too, this is one of those chapters that is designed to give readers not just food for thought but something they can actually use. As authors it has been important for us not just to make this a work of theory, but also one that contributes to everyday practice. This chapter by Averil Bolster, linked into highly versatile and usable materials for the classroom, really achieves that.

Chapter 13 again shifts the focus back towards the non-EAP end of our family spectrum. The central discussion on English for Research Purposes and Linguistic Diversity brings together voices from three distinct linguistic and cultural backgrounds. Magdalena De Stefani, Richard Fay and Zhuo Min Huan share ideas that resonate with those expressed throughout the book, right from John Gray's foreword. The discussion around English as a global lingua franca for both academic purposes (EAP) and research purposes (ERP) also adds to issues that Nguyet Luu highlighted. This chapter, composed of three voices, is one that provides not just food for thought but sustenance and substance to issues that are sometimes discussed on a superficial level but not considered at the depth this chapter attains. Most importantly, at a scholarly level, it looks at things from a methodological perspective too, explaining, exemplifying and enacting the role of reflexivity in practice.

Penultimately, Alexander Black, Mónica Sánchez-Hernández and Mario E. López-Gopar take us on something of a revolutionary road trip in **Chapter 14**, alongside artistic contributions from Katia González. This chapter takes a radical approach to narrative, influenced heavily by the context that is being written about, in Oaxaca. Through a dialogue of duoethnography, the authors report on what is essentially a sociocultural case study of resistance to linguistic imperialism in southern Mexico through the indigenisation of language pedagogy. Although quite different terrain in cultural terms, this chapter strongly resonates with the work of other authors writing about what Yvonne Fraser describes as 'fragile environments'. At the same time, the Oaxaca context is a unique one that to my mind has a *Motorcycle Diaries* (1995) ambience to the way in which the narrative is shaped, storied and shared.

To complete the work there is then a concluding reflection. However, the goal is not to end the conversation at that point. This work is primarily intended as a discussion starter, a trigger, a stimulus, fresh fuel for the growing fires of social justice. If you imagine this book as a journey, there is a huge geographic spread with stopovers in places that go from south to north, east to west – Uruguay to Qatar, Finland to Sri Lanka – and then to such fragile environments as Syria, Afghanistan and more. Throughout the work there is a sense of educators wanting to make a difference to their own EAP and ELT contexts, but at the same time to connect with others. And perhaps presently that connection is the missing ingredient, which is where Activity Theory can make a significant contribution, pulling disparate elements together.

Within all of these chapters, there are challenges and contestations which further support the theoretical approach that I and the authors in Chapter 1 have taken. Activity Theory is highly pertinent to environments where there are elements of contradiction, contestation and conflict. Such disputed territory is not found within the parameters of EAP and ELT alone, though. Within wider society, so much of the language of social justice has been colonised and commodified to a sales pitch. Causes are often readily embraced at a superficial level with detachment from social or political context. The greatest beneficiary of such division is capitalism because when the various elements are divided, they are less of a force for change, just as those who are schooled are less of a threat than the educated (Harris 1982).

When we are divided, as the history of colonialism has taught us, we are less capable of situating ourselves as an independent force. Together, as English Language Educators we have to create an ecosystem in which our habitats pull together in the interests of social and educational betterment. Rather than unquestioningly servicing structures of power, we can seek to reshape them and by doing so enrich them with a broader tapestry of cultural equilibrium. To achieve this, we must move away from policing weaknesses in the manner of a constabulary in one of the last colonial outposts of education. Throughout this work there is a demand for change to so many areas of our practice and these are changes that we can and should enact where possible, whether in assessment or the way we work with international students.

We as English Language educators should be drivers towards a place of change rather than passengers. We have time to make this happen because a growing consciousness of social justice is here to stay. As a consequence it will continue to play a part in all levels of our classroom activity. That though needs to be on more than a topical basis. Social justice has to take its place at the heart of all we do because it is not in competition with the main focus of our work, which is language teaching. Rather, it sits perfectly naturally alongside what we do, whether working with refugees, teaching Business English to improve our students' work prospects or empowering them academically by developing their writing practices. All these elements are a part of facilitating the improved forms of communication this divided world needs right now. Social justice can help provide the mood music for the lyric of change that is needed.

References

Apple, M. W. (2000), 'Can Critical Pedagogies Interrupt Rightist Policies?', *Educational Theory*, 50(2): 229–54.

Arao, B., & Clemens, K. (2013). 'From Safe Spaces to Brave Spaces: a new way to frame dialogue around diversity and social justice'. In Landreman, L. (ed.), *The Art of Effective Facilitation: Reflections from Social Justice Educators* (pp. 135–150). Sterling, VA: Stylus Publishing.

Benesch, S. (1996), 'Needs Analysis and Curriculum Development in EAP: An Example of a Critical Approach', *Tesol Quarterly*, 30(4): 723–38.

Benesch, S. (2001), *Critical English for Academic Purposes: Theory, Politics, and Practice*. New York: Routledge.

Blaj-Ward, L., Hultgren, A.K., Arnold, R. and Reichard, B. (2021), *Narratives of Innovation and Resilience: Supporting Student Learning Experiences in Challenging Times*, Renfrew: BALEAP.

Bolster A. and Levrai, P. (2020), 'A Sustainable Academic English Skills Course', *Develop EAP*. Online: https://developeap.weebly.com/ (accessed 12 November 2020).

Bond, B. (2020). *Making Language Visible in the University: English for Academic Purposes and Internationalisation*, New Perspectives on Language and Education 82, United Kingdom: Multilingual Matters.

Breen, P. (2014), 'An Intramuscular Approach to Teacher Development in International Collaborative Higher Education', in Mukerji, S. and Tripathi, P. (eds), *Handbook of Research on Transnational Higher Education*, Hershey, PA: IGI Global. pp. 368–390.

Breen, P. (2018), *Developing Educators for the Digital Age: A Framework for Capturing Teacher Knowledge in Action*, London: Westminster University Press.

Bunzel, D. (2007), 'Universities Sell their Brands', *Journal of Product and Brand Management*, 16(2): 152–3.

Ding, A. and Bruce, I. (2017), *The English for Academic Purposes Practitioner: Operating on the Edge of Academia*, Switzerland: Springer International.

Ecclestone, K., and Hayes, D. (2009), *The Dangerous Rise of Therapeutic Education*, Abingdon: Routledge.

Ecclestone, K. (2014), 'Turning Students into Nervous Wrecks', *Spiked*, 6 March 2014. Online: https://www.spiked-online.com/2014/03/06/turning-students-into-nervous-wrecks/ (accessed 1 March 2023).

Engeström, Y. (1987), *Learning by Expanding*, Helsinki: Prienta-Konsultit Oy.

Engeström, Y. (1993), 'Developmental Studies of Work as a Testbench of Activity Theory: the Case of Primary Care Medical Practice', in S. Chaiklin and J. Lave (eds), *Understanding Practice: Perspectives on Activity and Context*, 64–103, Cambridge: Cambridge University Press.

Engeström, Y. (1999), 'Activity Theory and Individual and Social Transformation', in Y. Engeström, R. Miettinen and R-L. Punamäki-Gitai (eds), *Perspectives on Activity Theory*, 19–38, Cambridge: Cambridge University Press.

Engeström, Y. (2001), 'Expansive Learning at Work: Toward an Activity Theoretical Reconceptualization', *Journal of Education and Work*, 14(1): 133–56.

Gilbert, J. (2013), 'English for Academic Purposes', in G. Motteram (ed.), *Innovations in Learning Technologies for English Language Teaching*, London: British Council.

Goodson, I. and Hargreaves, A. (1996), *Teachers' Professional Lives*, London: Falmer Press.

Graddol, D. (1998), *The Future of English*, London: The British Council.

Gray, J. (2021), 'Addressing LGBTQ Erasure Through Literature in the ELT Classroom', *ELT Journal*, 75(2): 142–51.

Guevara, C. (1995). *The Motorcycle Diaries: a Journey around South America*, New York: Verso.

Harris, K. (1982), *Teachers and Classes: a Marxist Analysis*, London: Routledge and Kegan Paul.

Hyland, K. (2018), 'Sympathy for the Devil? A Defence of EAP', *Language Teaching*, 51(3): 383–99.

Jivraj, S. (2020), 'Decolonizing the Academy–Between a Rock and a Hard Place', *Interventions*, 22(4): 552–73.

Lea, M. R. and Street, B. V. (1998), 'Student Writing in Higher Education: an Academic Literacies Approach', *Studies in Higher Education*, 23(2): 157–72.

Leathwood, C. and Read, B. (2022), 'Short-Term, Short-Changed? A Temporal Perspective on the Implications of Academic Casualisation for Teaching in Higher Education', *Teaching in Higher Education*, 27(6): 756–71.

Le Roux, M. (2022a), 'The Predicament of PEAPPs: Practitioners of EAP in Precarity' in Bruce, I. & Bond, B. (eds), *Contextualizing English for Academic Purposes in Higher Education: Politics, Policies and Practices*, London: Bloomsbury Academic, 165–80.

Le Roux, M. (2022b), 'Pedagogies in English for Academic Purposes: Teaching and Learning in International Contexts', *ELT Journal*, 76(3): 418–420.

Liyanage, I., Walker, T. and Singh, P. (2015), 'TESOL professional standards in the "Asian Century": Dilemmas facing Australian TESOL Teacher Education', *Asia Pacific Journal of Education*, 35(4): 485–97.

MacDonald, J. (2016), 'The Margins as Third Space: EAP Teacher Professionalism in Canadian Universities', *TESL Canada Journal*, 34(1): 106–16.

Mason, D. P., McDougle, L. and Jones, J. A. (2019), 'Teaching Social Justice in Nonprofit Management Education: a Critical Pedagogy and Practical Strategies', *Administrative Theory and Praxis*, 41(4): 405–23.

McArthur, J. (2010), 'Achieving Social Justice within and through Higher Education: the Challenge for Critical Pedagogy', *Teaching in Higher Education*, 15(5): 493–504.

McArthur, J. (2022), 'Critical Theory in a Decolonial Age', *Educational Philosophy and Theory*, 54(10): 1681–92.

Mhlanga, D. (2023), 'Open AI in Education, the Responsible and Ethical Use of ChatGPT Towards Lifelong Learning', *SSRN*, 11 February 2023. Online: https://ssrn.com/abstract=4354422 or http://dx.doi.org/10.2139/ssrn.4354422 (accessed 1 March 2023).

Molesworth, M., Nixon, E. and Scullion, R., eds (2011), *The Marketisation of Higher Education and the Student as Consumer*, London: Routledge.

Mortenson, L. (2022), 'Integrating Social Justice-Oriented Content into English for Academic Purposes (EAP) Instruction: A Case Study', *English for Specific Purposes*, 65: 1–14.

Motteram, G. (2016), 'Socially Just Practice in the Use of Learning Technologies in Language Learning and Teacher Education', in Gómez Chova, L.; López Martínez, A.; Candel Torres, I. , *INTED2016 Proceedings*, 3349–55, Valencia, Spain: IATED.

Palanac, A. (2022a), 'Towards a Trauma-Informed ELT Pedagogy for Refugees', *Language Issues: The ESOL Journal*, 33(1): 34–45.

Palanac, A. (2022b), 'A Shift from Handmaidens to Enlightened Waiters: EAP Practitioners for a Grassroots Sanctuary Movement', in M. Evans, B. Bond and A. Ding (eds), *Proceedings of the 2019 BALEAP Conference: Innovation, Exploration and Transformation*, 207–14, UK: Garnet Education.

Pearson, J. (2017), 'Processfolio: Uniting Academic Literacies and Critical Emancipatory Action Research for Practitioner-Led Inquiry into EAP Writing Assessment', *Critical Inquiry in Language Studies*, 14(2–3): 158–81.

Pearson, J. (2021), 'Assessment of Agency or Assessment for Agency?: a Critical Realist Action Research Study into the Impact of a Processfolio Assessment within UK HE Preparatory Courses for International Students', *Educational Action Research*, 29(2): 259–75.

Prevatt-Goldstein, A., Thomas, D. and Smart, A. (2021), 'Learning How to Build a Learning Community Online', in L. Blaj-Ward, K. Hultgren, R. Arnold, and B. Reichard (eds), *Narratives of Innovation and Resilience: Supporting Student Learning Experiences in Challenging Times*, 6–12, Renfrew: BALEAP.

Robertson, R. (1992), *Globalization: Social Theory and Global Culture*. London: Sage.

Roth, W.M. (2004), 'Activity Theory and Education: an Introduction', *Mind, Culture, and Activity*, 11(1): 1–8. Available online: DOI: 10.1207/s15327884mca1101_1 (accessed 1 March 2023).

Sauntson, H. and Morrish, L. (2010), 'Vision, Values and International Excellence: the 'Products' that University Mission Statements Sell to Students', in Molesworth, M.; Scullion, R.; and Nixon, E., *The Marketisation of Higher Education and the Student as Consumer*, 87–99, London: Routledge.

Seburn, T. (2021), 'How to Write Inclusive Materials.' ELT Teacher 2 Writer.

Smithwick, N. A. (2014), ' "It's Like all of Campus Life Inside a Little Classroom": How an English for Academic Purposes (EAP) Program Operates within a University Setting', PhD diss., University of Waterloo, Canada.

Tran, D. (2019), Why we Shouldn't Shy Away from Discussions around Decolonising Curricula', *Compass: Journal of Learning and Teaching*, 12(1).

Tran, D. (2021), *Decolonizing University Teaching and Learning: an Entry Model for Grappling with Complexities*, UK: Bloomsbury Publishing.

Truss, L. (2005), *Eats Shoots and Leaves*, London: Profile Books.

Turner, J. (2004), 'Language as Academic Purpose', *Journal of English for Academic Purposes*, 3(2): 95–109.

Vygotsky, L. S. ([c.1934] 1978), *Mind in Society: The Development of Higher Psychological Processes*, trans. A. R. Luria, M. Lopez-Morillas and M. Cole, with J. V. Wertsch, Cambridge, Mass: Harvard University Press.

Warschauer, M. (2002), 'A Developmental Perspective on Technology in Language Education', *TESOL Quarterly*, 36(3): 453–75.

Warschauer, M. (2003), 'Demystifying the Digital Divide', *Scientific American*, 289: 42.

Wenger, E. (1998), *Communities of Practice: Learning, Meaning, and Identity*, Cambridge: Cambridge University Press.

Whitty, G. (1974), 'Sociology and the Problem of Radical Educational Change', in M. Flude and J. Ahier (eds), *Educability, Schools and Ideology*, 112–137, London: Routledge.

Zhang, K. and Aslan, A. B. (2021), 'AI Technologies for Education: Recent Research and Future Directions', *Computers and Education: Artificial Intelligence*, 2: 100025.

The Evaluation and Evolution of a Framework that Integrates the Awareness of Social Justice into EAP Teaching and Learning Materials

Robert Farag, Katherine Mansfield, Hilary McDowell, Svetlana Page and Ignez Pereira

Introduction

EAP is a research-informed discipline which considers the complex and diverse communicative demands of the modern university, the students' needs and the interconnectedness of their contexts (Hyland and Shaw 2016). Critical approaches in EAP teaching and materials design have been well-documented in recent decades, although the inclusion of contemporary, ideological content on socially relevant issues in EAP courses tends to be avoided (Mortenson 2021). Scholars such as Kumaravadivelu (2003) or Hyland and Hamp-Lyons (2002: 3) have suggested that 'EAP has a vulnerability to claims that it ignores students' cultures', and it has been established that there is a gap in synthesising together the disparate aspects of social justice that are relevant to the EAP world today (Breen and Le-Roux 2023). Since EAP should have an aspiration to be interdisciplinary, inclusive and above all intercultural (Bond 2020), the field is ideally placed to meet the challenge of bringing together different aspects of social justice under one umbrella, considering both student-facing and practitioner-facing perspectives.

EAP and the University of Westminster

The University of Westminster (UoW), a multicultural and multilingual university based in central London, offers both in-sessional and pre-sessional Academic English (AE) courses which attract domestic and international students. Both courses aim to develop students' written and spoken academic language skills and provide a solid foundation for university studies and university life (Mansfield and Spinillo, 2022). In 2022, in response to climatic, economic and demographic challenges, UoW committed to the UN Sustainable Development Goals (SDG's) and listed 'Global engagement' as one of its key aims, focusing on global alumni benefiting from an authentic learning experience (UoW 2022). That same year, a number of EAP tutors employed on the summer pre-sessional course, together with the in-sessional module leader, set out to develop a framework for integrating awareness of social justice into EAP teaching and learning materials.

Social justice in the EAP environment

It soon became apparent that there were several competing tensions. These tensions included: (1) the issue of how far the EAP classroom, be it in person or virtual, is part of, or separate from, the various crises and inequities that beset the globe and possibly today's higher educational institutions; (2) to what extent the unresolved legacy of geographic and linguistic colonialism still distorts activity within an EAP class; (3) whether it is possible to attempt to address SJ issues therein without falling into the 'British values' soft power trap; (4) whether it is socially just to raise issues that might resonate with students from, or still in, countries where their discussion is potentially dangerous; and (5) how EAP tutors can honestly orientate themselves to the themes of SJ when they are subject to moral torsion; empowered by their ability to impart a dominant language and mark assessments, yet simultaneously disempowered by the creeping casualisation of their work and incomplete recognition of the field as an academic discipline in its own right.

Several guiding principles were useful as a steadying influence. First, the recognition that this project should involve practitioner reflection, alongside scrutiny of existing and newly designed materials plus students' own reactions to the SJ topics covered, and perceptions of their value. Second, the project incorporates a 'leaning in' approach wherein student confidence in participation was the priority, especially when discussion might be challenging or uncomfortable. As noted by Mortenson (2021: 118) 'there is a gap not only in being informed on the issues, but also being equipped to address moments of discomfort, disagreement, ambiguity, and conflict so that the teachable moments that could come out of such tensions are not sacrificed'. The third principle, perhaps most importantly, was the application of the Activity Theory model

(Engeström 2001), which fosters recognition that tutors are an intrinsic, internalised part of such discussion despite their simultaneous positions of guidance in the overall activity.

All principles outlined above were shaped by an acceptance of EAP tutors' responsibility to ensure students learn to recognise conventions of academic English language usage. These include the 'cultural competencies' of Zamel and Spack (2006), featuring persuasive powers of argument, demonstration of objectivity within conveyance of personal opinion, the need to martial and acknowledge sources, and student capabilities of thinking critically, participating in discussion, questioning the stances of experts including their lecturers, and participating in the political life of their cohort and the wider world (Benesch 2001).

However, there was a range of views as to the role of SJ related materials within EAP as relating to the exercise of these freedoms, indicating no resolution to the debate over whether English can be taught hermetically sealed off from its histories and cultural accretions. This is despite Mortenson's compelling argument that 'Uncritical and/or pragmatist approaches leave EB [emergent bilingual] students unprepared to engage successfully in university-level content-area work, which necessitates understanding ideological issues' (2021: 108).

Quite early on, the authors identified the need for a framework to guide EAP tutors wishing to incorporate SJ materials meaningfully into their classes, or for materials' designers avoiding common pitfalls. These might include alienating binarisms of 'developed/developing world' and the cultural appropriation of suffering without associated empowerment. Given priorities and tensions identified, it was clear that such a framework would need to place the student learning experience front and centre, in the recognition that learning is an activity inseparable from the wider world and that teachers, while aiming to equip students with criticality, are learning too.

Finding a framework

Guided by these principles, with the student learning experience at the centre, the authors began exploring existing sets of EAP materials for theoretical expression of these guiding SJ principles and their practical application in existent or hypothetical courses and materials. Of the existing teaching materials and courses which incorporated SJ discourse, the authors unearthed the following:

1. Bolster and Levrai's (2020) course materials from 'Develop EAP: A Sustainable Academic English Skills Course.'

2. The British Council's 'The Climate Connection Course', a ten-part podcast series from the British Council which explores the relationship between the climate crisis and language education (British Council n.d.).

3. The curriculum and a set of materials used on the University of Westminster's pre-sessional courses.

The first two sets of materials highlighted the importance of sustainability and the application of the UN's SDGs within EAP courses, especially taught either exclusively online or using blended methodologies (Bonk and Graham 2012; Dalziel 2015). Contemporarily, a growing chorus of researchers and practitioners have advocated inclusion of sustainability and environmental issues into EFL and EAP curriculums (e.g. Nkwetisama 2011; Nanni and Serrani 2015; Putri 2018). Thus, it was deemed necessary to seek a framework which would incorporate those and, potentially, other SJ themes, within e-learning in EAP classroom contexts.

Digital Teaching and Learning Ecosystem model

Jorge Reyna's work on digital teaching and learning – while written for a different discipline – has nevertheless offered potential answers to the sustainability and sustainable development of teaching EAP, regaining attention with COVID-19's triggering of a worldwide switch to online learning (Reyna 2020). Reyna's original Digital Teaching and Learning Ecosystem (DTLE) provided a framework 'to assess and rank the quality of online learning environments, taking into account elements such as design layout and navigability, accessibility, content and interactivity, assessment and student engagement' (2011: 1084). Presented in a graphic form (see Figure 1.1), the virtual classroom, all participants, teaching and learning platform and contents exist either in biotic-biotic or biotic-abiotic interactions.

While providing some helpful guidance on digital classroom contents and its participants' interactions, when applying the framework to SJ in EAP contexts, it is clear that a number of tensions arise. These may firstly include differing roles of Tutors, Lecturers and E-Learning Officers who rarely form a working trio within EAP. Added to this, there are such complexities as teaching with cameras on/off and managing various forms of interaction as well as issues of access with digital resources and a shift in expectations around lesson roles and responsibilities. Moreover, considering the complex systems and both human as well as digital and energy resources necessary for sustaining the e-learning in this model, it remains unclear whether digital resources offer the best option of

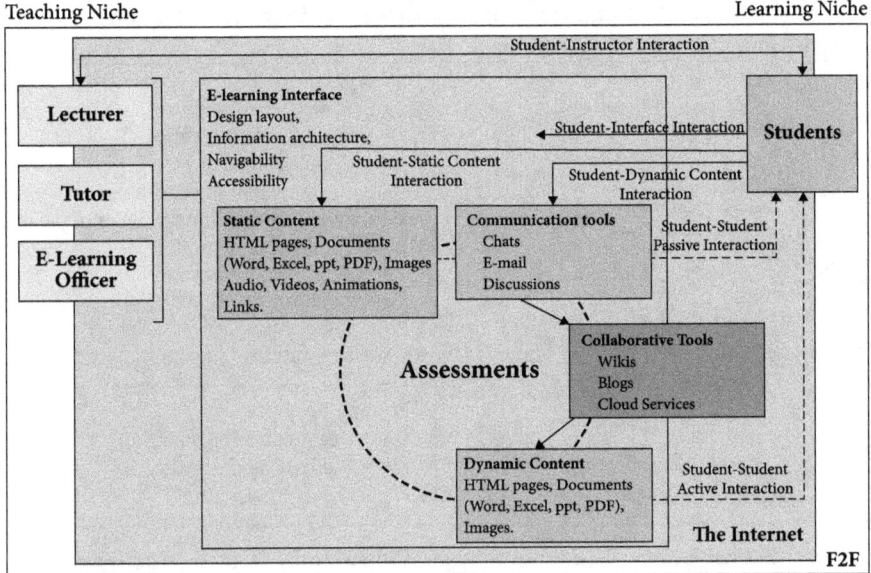

Figure 1.1 Digital Teaching and Learning Ecosystem (DTLE) (Reyna 2011: 1085).

eco-sustainability. Finally, content appears to lie at the heart of the model, rather than the learner, which contradicts the values inherent to the current research. Thus, it appeared more apt to consider a framework which would put the learner – and learning – at its core.

Community of Enquiry model

The Community of Inquiry (COI) model was developed between 1996–2001 by a research group in Alberta, Canada, who were principally involved in distance learning (Garrison et al. 2010; Anderson 2005). The COI model, and the categories subsequently developed by Akyol et al. (2011) (see Figure 1.2), places the learning experience in its centre.

The association of critical thinking inherent in the authors' understanding of the Cognitive Presence, and the elevated status of the latter within the model, made it attractive to the current research goals and themes, as SJ issues often go hand-in-hand with critical thinking development discussions in class. The teaching presence and the social element of the triad were also important for the research as they are all vital in EAP courses, with the learning experience being the cornerstone of the EAP process. Its focus on independent learning, problem solving, critical engagement, teamwork and knowledge retention also make it a

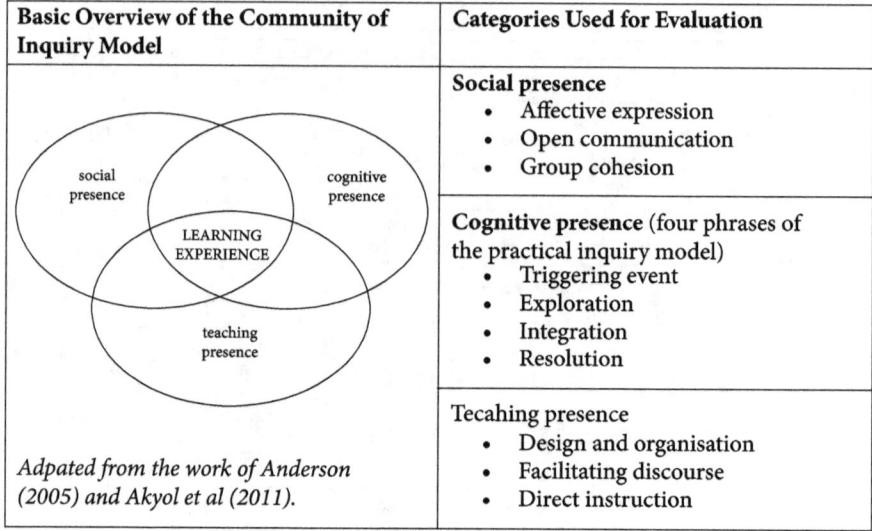

Figure 1.2 Overview of the Community of Inquiry model (Anderson 2005) and the categories developed by Akyol et al. (2011).

useful tool for the purposes of this research. Although the model and subsequent categories developed by Akyol (2011) were valuable when analysing qualitative data within the specific context, the authors found this model incompatible as a framework for designing EAP materials.

The main reasons why it was not deemed appropriate stem from multiple arising tensions. For instance, as the COI authors later admit, the framework 'emerged in the specific context of computer conferencing in higher education – i.e., asynchronous, text-based group discussions – rather than from a traditional distance education theoretical perspective assumed that students worked independently from each other' (Garrison et al. 2010: 5). The authors 'believed at the time that the effect of lack of nonverbal cues in online communication was exaggerated' (Garrison et al. 2010: 6) and thus placed emphasis on the written text, rather than immediate communication. This comes into conflict with the nature of EAP courses and types of social presence and communication happening therein. Hence, whilst providing useful guidance on e-learning and teaching context, during the investigation it became clear that it was not fully covering the 'divisions of labour' happening during the teaching/learning process. This was partly due to some complexities in terms of the stakeholders and their roles, including the students' reluctance to actively participate, which is often the case with many students of EAP courses, especially when online. Additionally, there are other problems. These might include the teacher's reluctance to raise certain topics and their potential discomfort with either the issues themselves or with the audience they are facing. Additionally, the nature of SJ content is 'messy' and constantly changing, which influences the materials, teaching methods and teaching/learning interactions and other issues. Given these tensions with the application of the model, the need to find and subsequently adapt a theoretical framework, which would both cover the complexities of our guiding principles as well as seek to alleviate the tensions arising at their practical application, have been highlighted. The answer to these, it is argued, has been found in re-evaluating Activity Theory.

Activity Theory

Activity Theory (AT) is described as 'a cross-disciplinary framework for studying how humans purposefully transform natural and social reality, including themselves, as an ongoing culturally and historically situated, materially and socially mediated process' (Roth et al. 2012: 1). It can be used as a lens through which human activity can be analysed (Jonassen and Rohrer-Murphy 1999), and as a framework employed to confront deep social transformations, as it acknowledges human activity as being multifaceted. AT is especially applicable in circumstances with a strong historical and cultural background, within which the participants, their tools and the goals are undergoing fast and ongoing change (Engeström 1999; Hashim and Jones 2014).

The first generation of AT was established by Vygotsky (1934) when he created the triangular model of action (see Figure 1.3). In his framework, the *subject* is the participant(s) executing the activity, the *tool/mediating artifact* is the prior knowledge the participant(s) uses to influence the activity and the *object* is the purpose of the activity/mediated action. The mediated action aims to demonstrate the process by which humans develop their consciousness with the conviction that 'individuals make meaning of the world through interactions with artefacts and other individuals in a particular environment' (Gedera 2016: 53). Vygotsky believed that humans do not simply behave differently because of stimuli; rather it is the creation of certain artifacts/tools that prompts a person to modify their actions (Engeström 1987).

The second generation founded by Alexei Leontiev (1978, 1981), focused mainly on 'activity' and not action as in Vygotsky's framework. Leontiev believed that actions are performed by individuals or groups to achieve a concrete goal,

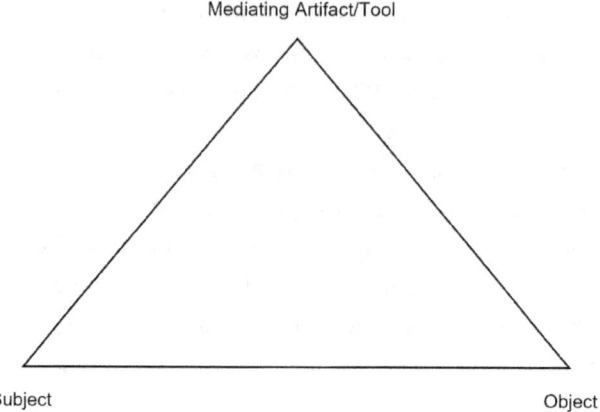

Figure 1.3 Vygotsky's (1934) triangular model of action.

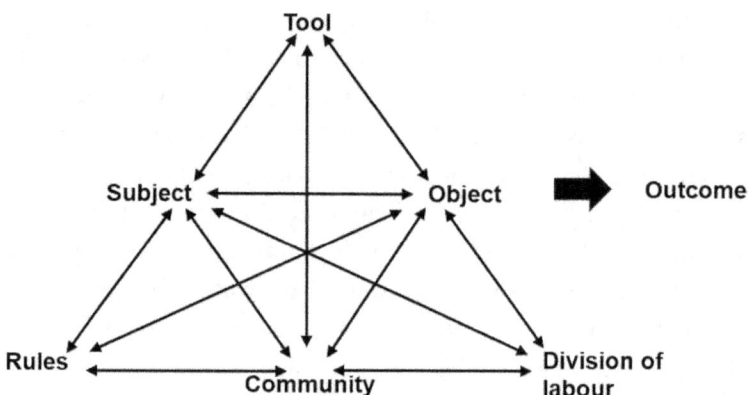

Figure 1.4 Engeström's third-generation activity theory (2001).

whilst an activity is conducted by a community with a specific object and motive in mind. In the 1980s and 1990s, Engeström further developed AT, and a third generation framework became prevalent (1987, 1999) (see Figure 1.4). Engeström breaks down activity into numerous components: *subject*, *object* and *tools*. In this framework, the *subject* is analysed, the *object* is the intended activity, and the *tools* are the mediating instruments used to perform the activity (Hasan 1998).

This third-generation adaptation proposes two units of analysis: (1) *rules* and (2) *division of labour* which implicitly affect the activity in question. *Rules* are seen as certain circumstances which guide how and why people act the way they do. The *division of labour* highlights the community of workers responsible as the vehicle for distributing the actions. Both *rules* and *division of labour* contribute to what is known as a *community* and can equally be analysed within the wider spectrum of activity. According to Kuutii (1996), activities are not static and are affected by constant changes in the environment. These external influences are capable of manipulating the activities by causing an imbalance. Such imbalances can be referred to as 'contradictions' and demonstrate the presence of problems, tensions, and so on. In AT, these contradictions are not viewed as issues, but as areas in need of development (Uden 2007).

Why Activity Theory?

There are several reasons why AT is appropriate for the design and development of EAP materials and/or curricula that incorporate themes of social justice. From an epistemological perspective, AT acknowledges that social interaction facilitates learning, and that learning is situated within a specific context (Engeström 1987). Lave and Wenger (2002) portray learning as a 'legitimate peripheral participation' which takes place within a community of practice (CoP). In our case, CoP refers to EAP practitioners and EAP learners. Herein, learners start with little knowledge on themes related to social justice, but this changes with increased participation (engaging with the materials/curricula), and progression from the periphery towards mastering participation; as characteristic of COP formation.

With the intention of our framework for the teachers (the more capable peers) to guide their students through the Zone of Proximal Development (ZPD) (Vygotsky 1978), and assist performance (awareness of social justice), the EAP practitioners are bridging the gap between what the students consciously know and what they do not know (specific topics/details/facts related to social justice). It is therefore through the interaction with other learners and the practitioners mediated by the materials/curricula that the ZPD emerges. The aim of AT is to deal with real-world issues, which are messy, constantly changing and in need of development (Mwalongo 2016), and as demonstrated in the first part of this chapter, SJ is one of those landscapes. With its emphasis on human activity, Engeström's (2001) AT framework can be reworked in a bid to include themes of social justice into the future design and development of materials and/or curricula.

Framework for incorporating social justice

Activity theory and social justice

In our framework (see Figure 1.5), elements of AT are represented as follows:

1. *Subject* refers to EAP practitioners teaching on an EAP course
2. *Object* is the use of EAP materials which include and promote topics related to social justice
3. *Tools* refer to the overarching EAP curriculum and the materials themselves which are used as a vehicle to input the topics
4. *Community* is the EAP practitioners and their students
5. *Rules* are what need to be considered when including topics of social justice into the curriculum and/or materials. In this case: (1) the appropriacy of language covered, (2) the relevance of that language and subject matter content, having considered the intended audience, and (3) the purpose of the material and accompanying task

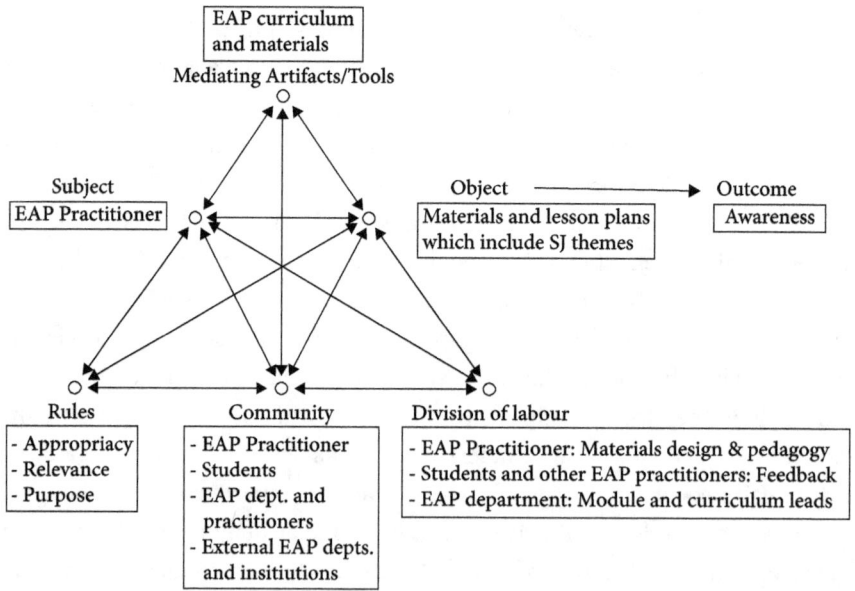

Adapted from Engeström (2001)

Figure 1.5 A framework for integrating awareness of social justice into teaching and learning materials in an EAP curriculum, adapted from Engeström (2001).

6. *Division of labour* refers to the curriculum leads tasked with writing the main curriculum, the materials writers, and the EAP practitioners
7. *Outcome* refers to the awareness of topics which discuss and promote social justice.

Further explanation of the key areas

Two areas, *rules* and *outcome* need some further clarification. Regarding *rules*, we identified three main areas for consideration when writing or adapting materials which incorporate SJ themes, for an EAP curriculum:

1. Appropriacy was considered linguistically:
   a. Is the word, phrase or structure on this material suitable for the context of the lesson, and the specific task I want the students to do?
   b. What additional support might need to be prepared, so that students can ask questions about the content, express different viewpoints, negotiate, etc.?
2. Relevance of the material and accompanying task, needs to be considered in light of students' language level, language needs, and age; also, in light of the overall aims of the EAP course, with the particular objective of raising awareness of a social justice topic:
   a. Why might students require practice of this particular language, or language skill?
   b. Is the material of a suitably academic standard for the level of the students e.g., pre-university, UG or PG?
   c. Does the material address a SJ topic? In sufficient detail? From what perspective, or with what bias, if any? Are there issues I should avoid, and why?
3. Purpose considers the points above, as well as other practical considerations for the material's use in the classroom:
   a. Can this material and task actually give practice of a relevant language aim, or other convention of academic English, which students require at this level?
   b. Does the material enable students to think critically and ask questions about the stated SJ topic?
   c. Is the task supported by this material student-centred? What type of classroom interactions (e.g., T-Ss, S-S, S-Ss etc.) are supported? Are the instructions clear on the face of the material?

These *rules* were particularly important for assessing authentic materials (or materials from non-EAP sources) on SJ, before adapting them for use on the UoW pre-sessional course. Regarding *outcome*, we have stated 'awareness', as it is our goal to make students consciously aware of contemporary global affairs and where tensions may lie. By indicating and discussing these areas of SJ, and equipping students with the language they need to exchange views in an academic context, our hope is that they will be able to think critically about societal issues, asking questions or taking more active roles, should they choose.

Practical application of framework

Seeking to address real-world issues and subsequently increase students' awareness of social justice, a set of materials was designed for deployment with undergraduate and postgraduate international students holding a B2 level of English and considered as our proposed framework (see Figure 1.5). Each lesson addressed one topic of social justice and was divided into two parts: one hour for input and another for conversation, involving speaking activities about the addressed theme. A range of themes were covered, such as the Black Lives Matter movement, the United Nations sustainable goals, climate change, race and gender, and other relevant topics. The materials were written with the *'rule'* component in mind, paying particular attention to their *appropriacy, relevance and purpose*. Although many of the source materials were informed by principles of academic language acquisition, teachers needed to draw from different sources, including the British Council's podcasts on climate change and climate action, and numerous YouTube videos. Explorations revealed that many existing mainstream EAP materials do not explore themes of social justice, and therefore adaptations of non-EAP sources were also deemed necessary. The resulting materials therefore anticipated and addressed the needs of EAP learners in general and were relevant not only to the wider EAP curriculum, but also to the specific cohort being taught. The desired *outcome* of raising students' awareness of social justice was flexible enough and included informing and/or discussing the topics depending on students' previous knowledge.

Assessing the impact of the materials

To assess the impact of the materials used in the classes, and consequently verify if the desired outcome (awareness) had been achieved, a questionnaire consisting of six questions was given out at the end of each session (see **Appendix 1**). Students were sent a link and invited to respond to questions that aimed to find out: (1) whether the lectures made them more aware of topics of social justice; (2) whether they are now able to discuss these topics in English; (3) if their views on society and on the world have been impacted by those lectures; (4) if they are likely to become agents of social justice in the future; and (5) which skills they developed the most during those sessions. On average, the number of students per session was between ten and fifteen. Teachers were also asked to give written feedback on how they felt materials were received, their perceived strengths and possible tensions.

Findings

1. Students

The results of the survey show that most students agree that they now know more about social justice themes and are better equipped to discuss these topics in English (see Figures 1.6 and 1.7).

Although many of the respondents were uncertain as to whether they would campaign against areas of social justice in the future or not, a great number do see the likelihood of becoming agents of social justice in the future (see Figure 1.8).

Considering the desired outcome of the materials was raising *awareness*, it appears that the developed materials achieved this goal.

2. Teachers

The teachers who designed and delivered the materials found that they were generally well-received. Amongst the strengths of the materials was that many students had never heard about some topics, nor had the opportunity to discuss them in English. Students also indicated that such an opportunity was welcome

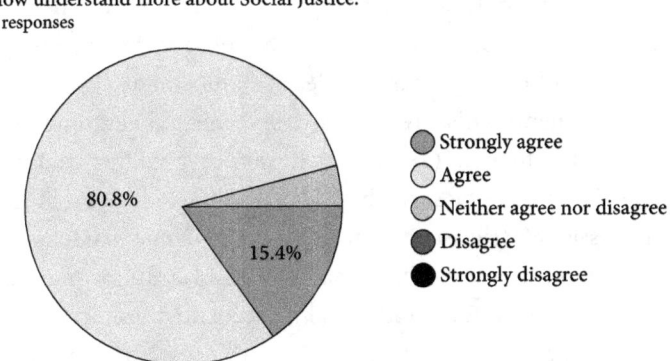

Figure 1.6 Results from Question 1 from the online survey.

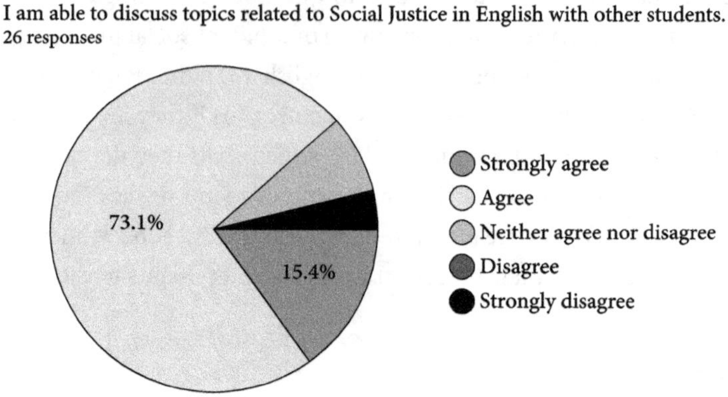

I am able to discuss topics related to Social Justice in English with other students.
26 responses

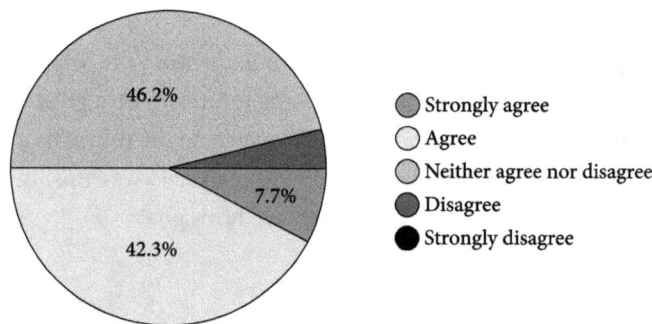

- Strongly agree
- Agree
- Neither agree nor disagree
- Disagree
- Strongly disagree

73.1%
15.4%

Figure 1.7 Results from Question 2 from the online survey.

In the future, I am more likely to campaign against this area of social justice.
26 responses

46.2%
7.7%
42.3%

- Strongly agree
- Agree
- Neither agree nor disagree
- Disagree
- Strongly disagree

Figure 1.8 Results from Question 3 from the online survey.

since the materials were authentic, the topics are current, and may prepare them to take part in academic discussions in the UK. One of the teachers mentioned that her students felt that 'the materials were up-to-date and that the lessons were preparing them to discuss these topics in the future' (Teacher 1).

Regarding the possible tensions, one teacher observed that although students were appreciative of the opportunity to learn about and discuss those matters, 'it was difficult for them to disagree or provide compelling arguments at times as the topics were new to them' (Teacher 2). It was observed that students 'felt more comfortable discussing topics which had been addressed within the main course of the pre-sessional (e.g., feminism). However, some students still lacked language of a level that could have made the conversations more meaningful' (Teacher 2). It was also noted that to some students those lessons might have been perceived purely 'as more content to absorb' (Teacher 3) and thus 'not meet their immediate need to be approved in the pre-sessional' (Teacher 1).

Lessons learnt

To ease possible future tensions and improve students' feelings towards the designed materials, the teachers suggest the following:

1. Beginning with topics which have either been highlighted in the course previously or which are usually discussed in students' home countries. 'More challenging topics would then be introduced later, after teachers have paved the way to such discussions through feelers or homework in previous lectures' (Teacher 2).
2. Creating a strong classroom community where the students feel safe, comfortable and not judged when they share their views.
3. Considering the mode of delivery of the materials i.e., online or face-to-face as this can impact the depth of discussion of the particular SJ topics. Students wishing to discuss culturally sensitive topics can feel inhibited talking online, for fear of being overheard.
4. Really contemplating the *rules* (see Figure 1.5), as these are essential to the achievement of desired outcomes, and considering students' cultural values and beliefs in the choice and presentation of the SJ topic.
5. Using authentic 'objects', for example, TedTalks, newspaper articles, journal articles which address world issues, as they tend to be more efficient and often differ from more mainstream materials used in the UK.

How our framework addresses the different tensions

A theoretical understanding of internal relationships

This chapter raises several competing tensions for the EAP practitioner to be aware of before designing materials which incorporate SJ themes. Many of these can perhaps be attributed to the very nature of ideological content; that through the analysis of different ideas, beliefs and attitudes related to social order, we create the opportunity for discussion, but also disagreement and possibly discomfort. Other tensions might arise because of the language of the discussion, the 'dominance' of the EAP practitioner over their students, the hegemony of English and its legacy of linguistic colonialism; and quite possibly for the practitioner, the risk of being seen by their students as a promoter of an Anglo-centric, or Western-centric bias to an SJ issue. Tensions can also exist because the setting for these discussions is the EAP classroom, where some students (or practitioners) may not feel SJ topics, or authentic and non-standardised teaching materials, typically belong. Finally, there will be tensions related to SJ that are exclusive to the EAP practitioner in their workplace, particularly in situations of precarity, when their institution's commitment to supporting additional developmental work could be a key factor in determining the amount of time they commit to creating resources which accurately reflect contemporary societal issues.

With all this potential for tension, the EAP practitioner may choose to abandon addressing SJ themes altogether. However, with the foresight that comes from understanding their students, due preparation, and open exchange with colleagues, even these difficult issues can be navigated. Understanding the different relationships involved in the creation of such materials will go some way to providing answers for most situations – managing them, avoiding them, or perhaps exploiting them as a (language) teaching point. This is the utility of the activity theory framework, in that it allows us to recognise the *subject*, in this case the EAP practitioner, as just one of the contributing elements in the process of *object* creation. The source materials which the practitioner uses, adapts, or just learns from, are clearly vital to this process, but so too is the *community*, with whom the practitioner shares the work required. Some examples of the framework 'in use' are listed below:

1. Tension because the SJ EAP material/*object* presents issues which students are normally discouraged from discussing in their country. This is anticipated through interactions with the students/*community* before materials creation begins in earnest. Knowledge of students' background will influence the practitioner/*subject's* choice of source material/*mediating artifact*, perhaps to find a range of examples of the SJ topic from different countries.
2. Tension because students do not see the connection between SJ, critical thinking skills, and the EAP classroom can be approached by the practitioner through explaining the relevant *rules (appropriacy, relevance and purpose)* for the process to students beforehand – i.e. saying that the material/lesson aim is rooted in academic English language use, and is relevant for the course.
3. If the practitioner thinks there is bias in an authentic source material/*mediating artifact* but is uncertain, they can ask colleagues/*community* for their interpretation before deciding whether to find an alternative, or to just exploit the material as is, discussing the topic of bias in a broader sense.

A practical guide for materials design

The considerations above suggest that the practical steps required for SJ EAP materials design are more extensive, or more carefully considered, than for standard EAP lessons. Our adapted activity theory framework shows practitioners that they do not, or should not, act alone in the design process, even if they are working independently. When designing SJ EAP materials, therefore, we propose a tailored interpretation to Jolly and Bolitho's framework for materials writing (2011) (see Figure 1.9) where we suggest an optional additional stage zero to the process (consultation), and provide alternative definitions for subsequent stages, to better fit our interests in this context, provide some linkage with our proposed activity theory framework (Figure 1.3), and acknowledge the tensions previously discussed.

The various steps in the materials writing process are:

0. **Consultation** – with the module or curriculum lead, considering whether there are any policies, conventions, or cultural values that might be relevant at that institution when choosing a SJ topic for EAP materials. Clarifying expectations for the *object* that is to be the end product, and collaboration over when SJ is going to be introduced in the curriculum, and how it will be raised with students initially (all these could be viewed as additional practitioner-facing *'rules'* on the proposed activity theory framework).

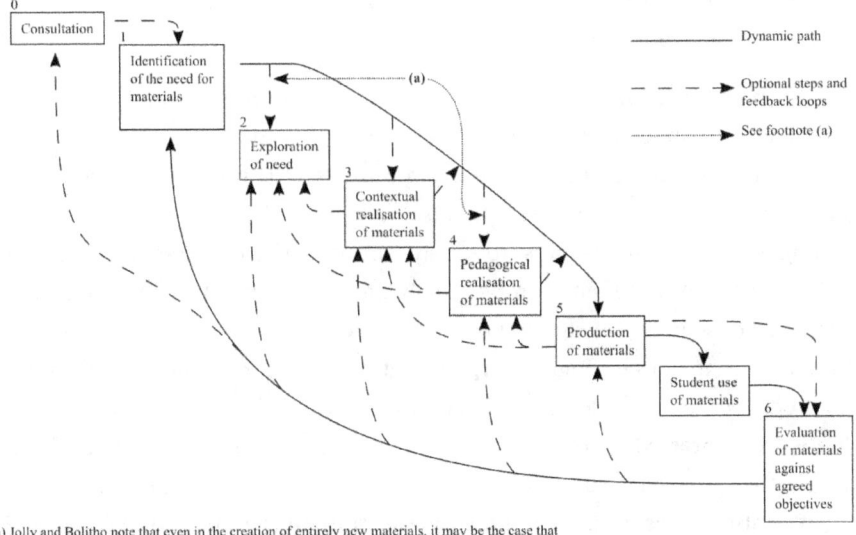

(a) Jolly and Bolitho note that even in the creation of entirely new materials, it may be the case that some of the steps envisaged here will have already been done for the materials designer.

Figure 1.9 A teacher's path through the production of new or adapted materials, adapted from Jolly and Bolitho (2011).

1. **Identification** – by teacher or learner(s) of a SJ topic and EAP skills area to give practice of, requiring the creation of materials.
2. **Exploration** – of the area of SJ topic in terms of content understanding, and any anticipated tensions that may arise; analysis of linguistic need, what language, what meanings, what functions, what skills, etc. to carry out the task, negotiate, and respond to (potentially differing) viewpoints.
3. **Contextual Realisation** – of the proposed new materials by the finding of suitable ideas, contexts, or texts with which to work. Consideration of *'rules'* – *appropriacy* and *relevance* as outlined in our adapted activity theory framework.
4. **Pedagogical Realisation** – of materials by the finding of appropriate exercises and activities AND the writing of appropriate instructions for use. Again, consideration of *'rules'* – *appropriacy* and *relevance* as outlined in our adapted activity theory framework
5. **Physical Production** – of materials, involving consideration of layout, type size, visuals, reproduction, audio length, etc. Materials for online teaching may require the practitioner/writer to consider accessibility in other ways.
6. **Evaluation** – of materials, forcing the practitioner/writer to examine whether they have met objectives. A failure to meet objectives may be related to any or all the intervening steps between initial identification of need and eventual use.

As can be seen from Figure 1.9, the process of writing materials consists of a sequence of distinct activities, not necessarily followed in a precise order. It can be seen as a dynamic and self-adjusting process; firstly, because 'excellence in materials lies less in the products themselves than in the appropriate and unique tuning for use that teachers routinely engage in' (Jolly and Bolitho 2011: 113), and secondly, because problem-solving is not a linear thought process. In materials design, a re-evaluation of one stage of the process, e.g. the production of materials, may well trigger the re-evaluation of an earlier stage, e.g. the text or audio proposed for the lesson – the contextual realisation. This self-regulation is therefore expressed through optional pathways and feedback loops. On the whole then, materials' design is a reflective process and the hope is that this chapter also serves to increase greater reflection on the incorporation of social justice into EAP's ecosystem.

References

Akyol, Z., Vaughan, N., and Garrison, N. D. (2011), 'The Impact of Course Duration on the Development of a Community of Inquiry', *Interactive Learning Environments*, 19(3): 231–46. Available online: https://doi-org.uow.idm.oclc.org/10.1080/10494820902809147 (accessed 23 August 2022) [this link is not open access].

Anderson, T. (2005), 'Distance Learning – Social Software's Killer App? 17th Biennial Conference of the Open and Distance Learning Association of Australia, 9–11 November 2005. Available online: http://hdl.handle.net/2149/2328 (accessed 7 September 2022).

Benesch, S. (2001), *Critical English for Academic Purposes*. New York: Routledge.

Bolster A. and Levrai, P. (2020), *Develop EAP: A Sustainable Academic English Skills Course*. [Online Course with materials]. Available online: https://developeap.weebly.com/ (accessed 29 July 2022).

Bond, B. (2020). *Making Language Visible in the University: English for Academic Purposes and Internationalisation*. Bristol, Blue Ridge Summit: Multilingual Matters. https://doi.org/10.21832/9781788929301 (accessed 7 September 2022).

Bonk, C. J. and Graham, C. R. (2012), *The Handbook of Blended Learning: Global Perspectives, Local Designs*, Hoboken, New Jersey: John Wiley and Sons. Available online: https://tinyurl.com/bonk-graham-2012 (accessed 21 September 2022).

Breen, P. and Le-Roux, M. (2023), *Social Justice in EAP and ELT Contexts*, London: Bloomsbury.

British Council (n.d.), *The Climate Connection*. Online: https://www.britishcouncil.org/climate-connection (accessed 24 May 2022).

Dalziel, J. (2015), *Learning Design: Conceptualizing a Framework for Teaching and Learning Online*, New York: Routledge. Available online: https://doi.org/10.4324/9781315693101 (accessed 26 August 2022).

Engeström, Y. (1987), *Learning by Expanding : An Activity Theoretical Approach to Developmental Research*. Helsinki, Finland: Orienta-Konsultit.

Engeström, Y. (1999), 'Activity Theory and Individual and Social Transformation', in Y. Engeström, R. Miettinen and R.-L. Punamäki (eds), *Perspectives on Activity Theory*, 19–38, Cambridge: Cambridge University Press.

Engeström, Y. (2001), 'Expansive Learning at Work: Toward an Activity Theoretical Reconceptualization', *Journal of Education and Work*, 14(1): 133–56.

Garrison D. R., Anderson T. and Archer W. (2010), 'The First Decade of the Community of Inquiry Framework: a Retrospective', *Internet and Higher Education*, 13: 5–9. Available online: doi:10.1016/j.iheduc.2009.10.003 (accessed 30 August 2022).

Gedera, D. (2016), 'The Application of Activity Theory in Identifying Contradictions in a University Blended Learning Course', in D. Gedera and J. Williams (eds), *Activity Theory in Education*, 51–69, Rotterdam: Sense. https://doi.org/10.1007/978-94-6300-387-2_4 (accessed 5 September 2022).

Hasan, H. (1998), 'Activity Theory: a Basis for the Contextual Study of Information Systems in Organisations', in H. Hasan, E. Gould and P. N. Hyland (eds), *Information Systems and Activity Theory: Tools in Context*, 19–38, Sydney: University of Wollongong Press.

Hashim, N. H. and Jones, M. L. (2007), *Activity Theory: A Framework for Qualitative Analysis*, 2007: University of Wollongong. Available at: http://ro.uow.edu.au/commpapers/408 (accessed 7 August 2022).

Hyland, K. and Hamp-Lyons, L. (2002), 'EAP: Issues and Directions', *Journal of English for Academic Purposes* 1(1): 1–12. Available online: https://doi.org/10.1016/S1475-1585(02)00002-4 (accessed 30 August 2022).

Hyland, K. and Shaw, P. (2016), *The Routledge Handbook of English for Academic Purposes*, Oxford: Routledge.

Jolly, D. and Bolitho, R. (2011), 'A Framework for Materials Writing', in B. Tomlinson (ed.) *Materials Development in Language Teaching*, 107–34. 2nd edn, Cambridge: Cambridge University Press.

Jonassen, D. H. and Rohrer-Murphy, L. (1999), 'Activity Theory as a Framework for Designing Constructivist Learning Environments', *Educational Technology Research and Development*, 47(1): 61–79. Available online: https://doi.org/10.1007/BF02299477 (accessed 6 September 2022).

Kumaravadivelu, B. (2003), 'Problematizing Cultural Stereotypes in TESOL', *Tesol Quarterly*, 37(4): 709–19. Available online: https://doi.org/10.2307/3588219 (accessed 8 September 2022).

Kuutti, K. (1996), 'Activity Theory as a Potential Framework for Human–Computer Interaction Research', in B. A. Nardi (ed.), *Context and Consciousness: Activity Theory and Human–Computer Interaction*, 17–44, Cambridge: MIT Press.

Lave, J. and Wenger, E. (2002), 'Legitimate Peripheral Participation in Communities of Practice', in M. R. Lea and K. Nicholl (eds), *Distributed Learning, Social and Cultural Approaches to Practice*, 111–26, London: Routledge Falmer.

Leontiev, A. N. (1978), *Activity, Consciousness, and Personality*, Englewood Cliffs, NJ: Prentice-Hall.

Leontiev, A. N. (1981), 'The Problem of Activity in Psychology', in J. V. Wertsch (ed.), *The Concept of Activity in Soviet Psychology*, 4–33, New York: Sharpe.

Mansfield, K. and Spinillo, M. (2022), 'Pre-Sessional and In-Sessional Academic English Courses', *CETI on the Scene* (University of Westminster Newsletter), July: 2–4.

Mortenson, L. (2021) 'White TESOL Instructors' Engagement with Social Justice Content in an EAP Program: Teacher Neutrality as a Tool of White Supremacy', *BC TEAL Journal* 6(1): 106–31. Available online: https://doi.org/10.14288/bctj.v6i1.422 (accessed 29 July 2022).

Mwalongo, A. (2016), 'Using Activity Theory to Understand Student Teacher Perceptions of Effective Ways for Promoting Critical Thinking through Asynchronous Discussion Forums', in D. Gedera and J. Williams (eds), *Activity Theory in Education*, 17–34, Rotterdam: Sense.

Nanni, A. and Serrani, J. (2015), Teaching Sustainability in the English for Academic Purposes Classroom. The Second Asian Conference on Education for Sustainability, 1–5. Available online: https://www.academia.edu/12314655/Teaching_Sustainability_in_the_English_for_Academic_Purposes_Classroom (accessed 29 September 2022).

Nkwetisama, C. (2011), 'EFL/ESL and Environmental Education: Towards an Eco-Applied Linguistic Awareness in Cameroon', *World Journal of Education*, 1(1), 110–118. https://eric.ed.gov/?id=EJ1159052

Putri, I. G. A. P. E. (2018), 'Critical Environmental Education in Tertiary English Language Teaching (ELT): a Collaborative Digital Storytelling Project', *Indonesian Journal of Applied Linguistics*, 8: 336–44.

Reyna, J. (2011), 'Digital Teaching and Learning Ecosystem (DTLE): a Theoretical Approach for Online Learning Environments', in *Ascilite 2011: Changing Demands, Changing Directions : Wrest Point, Hobart, Tasmania, Australia, 4-7 December 2011 : Proceedings*, 1083-88. University of Tasmania. Available online: https://www.ascilite.org/conferences/hobart11/downloads/papers/Reyna-concise.pdf (accessed 27 September 2022).

Reyna, J. (2020), 'Twelve Tips for COVID-19 Friendly Learning Design in Medical Education' *MedEdPublish*, 9:103. Available online: https://doi.org/10.15694/mep.2020.000103.1 (accessed 24 October 2022).

Roth, W.M., Radford, L. and LaCroix, L. (2012), 'Working with Cultural-Historical Activity Theory', *Forum Qualitative Sozialforschung / Forum: Qualitative Social Research*, 13(2): article 2, 1–21. Available online: https://doi.org/10.17169/fqs-13.2.1814 (accessed 26 October 2022).

Uden, L. (2007), 'Activity Theory for Designing Mobile Learning', *International Journal of Mobile Learning and Organisation*, 1(1): 81–102.

UoW (=University of Westminster) (2022), *Being Westminster: 2022-2029.* (Prospectus), Available online: https://www.westminster.ac.uk/sites/default/public-files/prospectuses/Being-Westminster-2022-29.pdf (accessed 22 June 2022).

Vygotsky, L. S. ([1934] 1978), *Mind in Society: the Development of Higher Psychological Processes*, Cambridge, Mass: Harvard University Press.

2

Curriculum for Change

Jo Kukuczka

Introduction

This chapter reports on preliminary findings from a larger study, and relates to the nature of a social change-oriented EAP curriculum where advancement of social justice is one of the key outcomes. As such, the chapter aims to introduce the concept of *curriculum for change* and how it relates to social justice, to justify the need for such a curriculum in EAP, and to suggest a curriculum for change framework as a first step to turning theory into practice.

To set the scene, the troubled relationship between higher education (HE) and social justice is outlined and followed by a discussion of the literature on social change, social impact, and social value, as they relate to education. Those broad discussions then pave the way for more specific considerations relating to sustainable development and, within it, social justice. Drawing on those key terms, the chapter then discusses HE curricula as one means of supporting social change and advancing social justice, introduces the concept of curriculum for change, and explores constituents of such a curriculum, culminating in a proposal of a curriculum for change framework. The chapter concludes by summarising the key constituents of curriculum for change, exploring limitations and implications of the proposed approach to curriculum development, and inviting the reader to critique and test curriculums for change in their EAP context(s).

Setting the scene

The problem

Society and education are interrelated. As such, the purpose of education is not only to educate, but to do so in such a way that contributes to the sustainable development of society (QAA and Advance HE 2021; Ashwin 2020). Since the transformation of the ways of being, knowing and doing is essential to achieving this purpose, the role of education is to instigate change, and measuring the impact of this change becomes the gateway to success.

In the context of UK HE, universities appear to recognise the social purpose of education, and increasingly prescribe to notions of sustainable development such as widening participation, inclusion, decolonisation, internationalisation, global citizenship, climate justice, diversity, inclusion, and gender, racial, cultural, and economic equality (McArthur 2018). Consequently, graduates becoming global citizens engaged in civic life (Barker, Hibbins and Woods 2012) is one of the expected outcomes of such social change agendas. However, while widening participation, for example, results in growing numbers of students (ONS 2017; UKCISA 2019), there is little or no evidence suggesting that university education results in graduates indeed becoming agents of change. Additionally, it appears that widening participation does not, in fact, support access and success in equal measure, meaning that although a greater number of students from a variety of socio-political backgrounds access HE, a lower proportion of those students succeed (Bottrell and Manathunga 2018; Clarence 2021). Similarly, literature on decolonisation and internationalisation in HE rarely focuses on the impact of educational practices on society. This suggests that policies and intentions alone do not carry sufficient force to develop global citizens actively reinforcing change. In fact, without normalised rigorous measurements of the intended impact, those policies pose a risk of achieving the opposite effect, such as internationalisation actively recolonising, rather than decolonising, global HE by, for example, increasing pressure to publish in academic English worldwide.

Turning to the connected concept of sustainable development, and specifically the United Nations Sustainable Development Goals (SDGs) (United Nations 2021), here too literature suggests that the notion of setting goals alone is insufficient in achieving desired outcomes (Clifford and Barnes 2022). This is partly due to the current *top-down* approach enacted by those in power, which disempower intended beneficiaries. Moreover, historically, innovation has succeeded when approached *bottom-up*, involving active local and regional initiatives supported by governing bodies. Such empowerment of beneficiaries appears essential in achieving sustainable change (Hazenberg and Paterson-Young 2022b).

EAP curriculum for change as a potential solution

Since the role of HE curricula (including EAP) in addressing social change is under researched (Abbas, Ashwin and McLean 2016; Shay and Peseta, 2018), investigating the nature of a curriculum for change, followed by the development of a bespoke EAP framework, could substantially contribute to closing this knowledge gap.

EAP, as a field enculturating students into HE (Cowley-Haselden 2020b), is an ideal site for a curriculum for change, bridging the gap between universities' visions and actual practices leading to producing global citizens advancing social justice. In theory, the social aspects of EAP curricula and their potential to contribute to transformation of HE should be widely researched and disseminated. In practice, however, literature from the seminal Hyland and Hamp-Lyons (2002) up to the more contemporary Riazi, Ghanbar and Fazel (2020) paints a very different picture of EAP as a field largely reluctant to critically engage with institutional values (such as social justice) for example, and fairly comfortable with its traditional accommodationist orientation.

Simultaneously, a growing body of EAP, socio-linguistic, and socio-educational research argues that, in order to be effective, academic communication and therefore, EAP, must be underpinned by understanding that language is a social practice (Halliday 1978), and academic language, behaviour, and knowledge develop in unison and should not be segmented (Coffin and Donohue 2014; Maton, Hood and Shay 2016; Monbec 2018; Cowley-Haselden 2020b). Linguistic and sociological theories employed by some EAP practitioners echo the above, alongside a view of academic discourse providing a gateway to educational success and 'worlds of imagination and discovery' (Martin, Maton and Doran 2020: 1). Consequently, understanding academic discourse (which is, arguably, the flesh of EAP) and helping everyone access, shape and change this knowledge, is critical to achieving social, epistemological, or axiological power, and therefore, enabling change through, for example, advancing social justice (ibid.).

This dichotomous image of EAP calls for attention and provides sound reasoning for an EAP curriculum for change; enabling EAP students to not only succeed as effective academic and professional communicators in their disciplinary communities of practice, but also advance social justice by becoming active global citizens.

The study

The larger study that shaped this chapter had two aims; first, to investigate the nature of a curriculum for change, and second, to measure social impact of that curriculum on students' views and practices related to sustainable development (including social justice). A thematic approach to background literature has been taken, employing the use of academic databases and Google search engines of such key terms as those that recur throughout this chapter.

The selection criteria included relevance, credibility, and currency, with active emphasis on sources published after 2000, except for key texts (e.g. conceptual underpinnings). Furthermore, to support inclusion and ethical selection, works of diverse authors were sought out, including publications by female and non-Western academics or peer-reviewed literature published outside of Western academia. This gave rise to much of the knowledge that follows.

Social change

Social change and education

Understanding social impact, and social justice as its outcome, might be limited without exploring the meaning of social change first. After all, it is social change within which social impact occurs. Moreover, since the idea of addressing and instigating social change underpins the very purpose of HE, it must be given prominence in any review on the social impact of a curriculum (Ashwin 2020; Clarence 2021; McArthur 2018).

According to Rucker (1955), social change is a change in people's relationships with each other and their environment. However, it also encompasses the change *within* individuals, in their beliefs and evaluations, which often triggers or results in the above-mentioned changes. For example, Wilterdink and Form (2022) state that social change is 'the alteration of mechanisms within the social structure, characterised by changes in cultural symbols, rules of behaviour, social organizations, or value systems', as an ever-present phenomenon in any society.

To deepen the understanding of change, it is important to consider its various aspects, as emphasised by different theoretical schools. Marxist theory suggests that changes in modes of production can lead to changes in class systems, which, in turn, can incite class conflict. Conflict theory, on the other hand, argues that conflict may not be purely divisive and may, in fact, bring about changes that promote social integration (Wilterdink and Form 2022). This leads to further considerations about the origins of social change, with literature evidencing that it can evolve from a variety of different sources such as contact with other societies, changes in the ecosystem, technological change, demographic variables, and socio-political movements (Fairclough 1993). All appear to have played a part in the current resurrection of interest in social change, with globalisation being the contact with other societies, climate change being the changes in the ecosystem, rapid developments in technology, and movements such as Me Too and Black Lives Matter being the socio-political notions for change (Lin and Yang 2019).

Education with its sustainable development agenda aims to address the above challenges by inspiring a positive transformation of society. Whether or not, and to what extent this educational endeavour succeeds, remains a question, and to support attempts at answering it, it is important to conceptualise social impact and its underpinning idea of social value.

Social impact and social value

Beginning with impact, it is crucial to differentiate between the broad concept of *impact*, and a more specialised term of *social impact*. Whilst impact means an effect on something in general, social impact refers to an influence on a social challenge. The review of literature on *social impact* and *social value* reveals that the concepts are intrinsically intertwined and ambiguous due to their fluid, socially constructed nature. Furthermore, despite the rise of the social impact and social value agenda in the early 2000s globally (Public Services (Social Value) Act 2012), and the widespread recognition of the need for mutual understanding as to what those terms mean (Burdge and Vanclay 1996; Hazenberg and Clifford 2016), it remains a challenging area.

In their edited book on social impact measurement for a sustainable future, Hazenberg and Paterson-Young (2022a), conclude that although the definitions continue to vary, those differences are subtle in nature, and allow for pinpointing fundamental principles that those understandings share. The definition proposed by the *Group d'experts de la commission sur l'entrepreneuriat sociale* (GECES) synthesises those shared principles and describes social impact as: 'the reflection of social outcomes as measurements, both long-term and short-term, adjusted for the effects achieved by others (alternative attribution), for the effects that would have happened anyway (deadweight), for negative consequences (displacement), and for effects declining over time (drop-off)'. (Clifford et al. 2014: 12). In other words, social impact can be understood as the effect on people as a result of an action or inaction, a project, or policy (Clifford and Barnes

2022). In terms of social value, Jain et al. (2019) have defined it as: 'a value that demonstrates change(s) in the live(s) of an individual or groups of individuals when tangible and intangible resources are employed at grassroots level by social actors, ultimately creating social change within the society.' (Jain et al. 2019: 10, as cited in Hazenberg and Paterson-Young 2022b).

Similarities are evident in both definitions focusing on how changes occur in the lives of individuals, communities and society, with social impact focused specifically on quantification of change, and social value focused on processes of driving that change. The recognition of this dual focus has implications for measurement practices with Hazenberg and Paterson-Young (2022b, 15) defining social impact measurement as a 'process of assessing changes rather than structures'.

Sustainable development and social justice

Following the conceptualisation of social change, social impact, and social value, the next key consideration is the notion of *sustainable development;* as the ultimate goal of a curriculum for change aiming at students becoming global citizens actively advancing social justice (Barker, Hibbins and Woods 2012; QAA and Advance HE 2021).

According to United Nations (2021), sustainable development 'meets the needs of the present society, without compromising the ability of future generations to meet their own needs'. Despite first coming to attention in 1972 at the United Nations Conference on the Human Environment, followed by its development as a solution to the problems of environmental degradation discussed in Brundtland's (1987) Common Future Report, sustainable development was first acknowledged as a major challenge at the United Nations Conference on Environment and Development in Rio de Janeiro in 1992. That summit marked the first global attempt to develop tangible strategies for moving towards a more sustainable future (Sustainable Development Commission 2011), and ultimately led to the development of the seventeen SDGs in 2015 (United Nations 2015).

Sustainable development can be interpreted in different ways, but has a core approach of aiming to balance a variety of competing needs against awareness of the environmental, social and economic challenges faced by societies internationally. SDGs are a useful framework through which to view those global needs as related to sustainable development. Clifford and Barnes (2022: 49) cite UN literature to show how the goals aspire to 'tell a story of a world beset by inequalities and entrenched in social and environmental challenges but do so in the context of a vision that by 2030 the world will be different.'

To avoid *unsustainable* development, it is critical to view those challenges as interrelated issues rather than occurring in isolation or seemingly irrelevant to one another. For example, Massey (2022) argues that none of the SDGs can be achieved without delivery of Goal 16 (peace, justice, and strong institutions) or Goal 17 (partnership for the goals). This interconnectedness means that everyone is part of the problem, and everyone's values, choices and practices have effects far greater than often anticipated. Because of that, everyone must be part of the solution.

Furthermore, since the SDGs are a compelling re-evaluation of what is important globally, and act to legitimise and shape a dialogue on what matters locally, their targets should be flexible and require local interpretation (Heleta and Bagus 2020; Clifford and Barnes 2022.). When viewed in this way, similarities to HE policies on sustainable development become apparent. There, too, it is critical to recognise that top-down approaches are ineffective, and inclusion of bottom-up innovation must be a more significant part of the solution (Hazenberg and Paterson-Young 2022b). Because the world is hierarchical, relational, and intricately interconnected, effective responses are constrained by structures that better serve centralised monitoring and system-wide learning (Capra and Luisi 2014: 297–321, 362–93). Such structures are not appropriate for governing programmes of complex social change (Clifford and Barnes 2022). Success, therefore, relies instead on collective action which aligns and amplifies the impact delivered through societies, communities and individuals. This collective action requires 'a shared focus, a sense of urgency, and engagement' (UN Sustainable Development Group 2021). Furthermore, the impact of this action must be rigorously measured, to demonstrate what works and to what extent, and what does not and why, enabling evaluation and further action leading to a more sustainable future as set out by the original goals.

Through the investigation of social impact of a curriculum, curriculum for change potentially becomes such a collective action, and, therefore, part of the solution to the *wicked problems* addressed by the SDGs (Dentoni, Bitzer and Pastucci 2016; Manning and Reinecke 2016). Before moving onto what the curriculum for change is, and how, from the literature point of view, such curriculums can impact on sustainable development and lead to the advancement of social justice, it is critical to consider the meaning of social justice itself.

A sense of social justice is central to sustainable development. It has also been equally important to education for the several past decades (Bernstein 2000; Nussbaum 2006). At the same time, the concept itself is complex and contested (McArthur 2020; Smith 2018). Depending on who talks about social justice, to whom, and how, may or may not define its specific purpose. Simple definitions sometimes hide a 'malign content' and can be used to 'subvert the concept' itself making it 'devoid of critical meaning' (McArthur 2020: 35). Ruitenberg and Vokey (2010) attach three principles of fairness to social justice: harmony, equity and equality. United Nations (2006) mentions fair and equitable division of resources, opportunities and privileges in society, while Honneth (2010) employs critical theory in his understanding of social justice as equal rights and opportunities. Nancy Fraser's theory of social justice (also underpinned by critical theory), on the other hand, recognises its three dimensions, redistribution (economic justice), recognition (cultural justice), and participation/representation (political justice) (Fraser 1998). Finally, the current universities' social justice agenda, with its initiatives on equality, diversity and inclusion, for example, utilizes all the above to a greater or lesser extent.

Similarly, the *advancement* of social justice in the educational context can mean different things, from *socially just* practices, as in assessment (McArthur 2020; Shay and Peseta 2018), to social justice as an *outcome* of practices, such as developing critical citizens through curricula (Abbas, Ashwin and McLean 2016; Benesch 2009; Masehela 2020). Herein, social justice is broadly understood as fair and equitable redistribution, representation, and participation, which can be specifically achieved through a curriculum committed to transforming students' views and practices related to sustainable development in a way that advances social justice further.

Curriculum for change

The nature of an EAP curriculum for change

What is the nature of an EAP curriculum for change? What might such a social change-oriented curriculum, intended to not only build knowledge of academic communication in English, but also to advance social justice through the change of students' views and practices related to sustainable development, look like? Knowledge acquisition is key to transformation of ways of being, knowing, and doing (for example, see Wang and Burris 1997), but is it sufficient? Is social justice-oriented content enough to support sustainable development and advance social justice (Abbas, Ashwin and Mclean 2016)?

While literature agrees that the notion of *social change* is central to higher education (Benesch 2009; Bernstein 2000; Freire 2005; Nussbaum 2006), there is little evidence of this centrality in practice, particularly in the context of HE practices which are persistently battling with seemingly unsolvable issues such as inequality or exclusion (McArthur 2018). Instead, a wealth of literature calls for HE to actively contribute to positive transformation of students and societies, and critiques the economic rationale underpinning current HE policies and decision-making processes (Ashwin 2020). Those voices suggest that the purpose of modern HE, particularly in the UK context but also beyond, is merely reproductive, and not transformative (Luckett and Shay 2017). Further literature views this deficient neoliberal approach as a problem disabling most attempts to address the world's current issues, and actively disempowering students as agents of change (Cho and Mosselson 2018).

This observation is particularly interesting when considered in the context of institutional attempts to alleviate *wicked problems* through introduction of policies on decolonisation, internationalisation, widening participation, sustainable development, and so on. However, due to limited success of those attempts, what is true in terms of ineffectiveness of top-down approaches to sustainable development, appears to apply to top-down approaches in the UK HE sector as well. Often, such top-down approaches disempower, rather than empower, the beneficiary groups, such as students, that it aims at supporting (Hazenberg and Paterson-Young 2022b, McArthur 2020). Yet, it is precisely student empowerment, achievable through knowledge acquisition, change of perspective, and reaching policy makers, that enables change (Wang and Burris 1997).

As suggested by the Education for Sustainable Development Guidance (QAA and Advance HE 2021) and research related to South Africa's Fees Must Fall movement (Luckett and Shay 2017), curricula might be one way of empowering students through a combination of top-down and bottom-up approaches; enabling them to become agents of change. However, knowledge on the extent to which a curriculum is successful in achieving such change, and what the nature of such a curriculum is, is limited, since the social role of the HE curricula is under researched (Abbas, Ashwin and McLean 2016; Luckett and Shay 2017).

However, the research that exists points to a *connected* curriculum (Fung 2017), assessment-driven curricula (Bond 2020; Kirk 2018), and specifically, theory informed assessment and feedback *for* learning (McArthur 2020; Shrestha 2020), as the most relevant types of curricula supporting education for sustainable development. Therefore, in this proposed approach, the HE curriculum is understood to include the broader values and goals of the programme such as assessment and feedback practices (Kirk 2018), where both assessment and feedback are part of pedagogy (Gillway 2020; Winstone and Carless 2020).

If the purpose of HE curricula is to teach, transform, and produce disciplinary and inter-disciplinary experts, as well as active change-makers (Ashwin 2020), the core *intention* must be to change students' ways of being, knowing and doing. Without this explicit pedagogical intention (Freire 2005) guiding the curriculum design and delivery processes, change may be impossible. Therefore, to enact such change, curriculum practices should be driven by this overarching transformative goal. Knowledge and knowledge building practices grounded in theory are key drivers of change and enlightenment (Coffin and Donohue, 2014; Maton, Hood and Shay 2016; Cowley-Haselden 2020b; Martin, Maton and Doran 2020; Shrestha 2020). McArthur (2020: 9) argues that social practice theories 'cast light on what is flawed in current arrangements and illuminate the way ahead towards a more just society'. Similarly, others claim that theory provides access to critical knowledge that enables change and empowers people (Maton, Hood and Shay 2016), and that the curriculum of the future should be the *curriculum of knowledge* (Brooke, Monbec and Tilakaratna 2019) enabling both, knowledge acquisition (content), and a critical change of perspective (criticality) on that knowledge.

Furthermore, students' engagement with community is also a major driver of change in ways of being, knowing and doing (Garibay 2015; Ginwright and Cammarota 2015; Gallor 2017). Interestingly, this *community* factor is largely absent in the literature on the HE curricula which, as discussed above, mainly focuses on the sustainable development content and theory-fronted critical approaches to knowledge acquisition.

What connects the community engagement and theory-informed criticality, is what they both *do*, and specifically, how they *empower* people to enact change. This explains the reported successes in the bottom-up approaches to sustainable development (Hazenberg and Paterson-Young 2022b), and strengthens the idea of a curriculum for change.

The proposed curriculum for change framework

Four principal considerations characterise a curriculum of change:

1. Explicit *intention* to transform and empower.
2. Theory-driven *criticality* aimed at the change of perspective.
3. *Content* related to sustainable development and social change.
4. Interaction with *community*.

Although current UK HE curriculum initiatives on decolonisation, inclusion or internationalisation may include some of those considerations, I have, so far, found no systemic evidence of any of them applying all four together (intention, content, criticality, community), nor reporting the extent of the social impact of those initiatives. Based on these findings, I propose an EAP curriculum for change framework (below) consisting of one core constituent, an explicit intention to change, underpinning three sub-constituents: sustainable development related content, theory-fronted criticality, and engagement with community.

In practice, the enactment of these principles could manifest themselves in a variety of ways. For example, a social change-oriented learning outcome, a debate or a text evaluation on a social justice related issue as assessment and/or coursework, or a transformative theory-driven curriculum design (e.g. based on Benesch's Critical EAP (2009)), would embody the explicit intention to transform and empower. The use of vocabulary, texts, and images focused on social justice issues such as gender, cultural and racial equality or poverty, would serve as curriculum for change content, while theory-fronted approaches to teaching of critical thinking would enable criticality. For example, the systemic functional linguistics concept of 'transitivity' has been proven to support multimodal critical discourse analyses (Machin and Mayr 2012), Seburn's (2016) academic reading circles have been used to support critical analysis and knowledge transfer (Cowley-Haselden 2020a; Kukuczka 2021), and the Legitimation Code Theory notion of 'axiological constellations' has been found helpful in evaluating

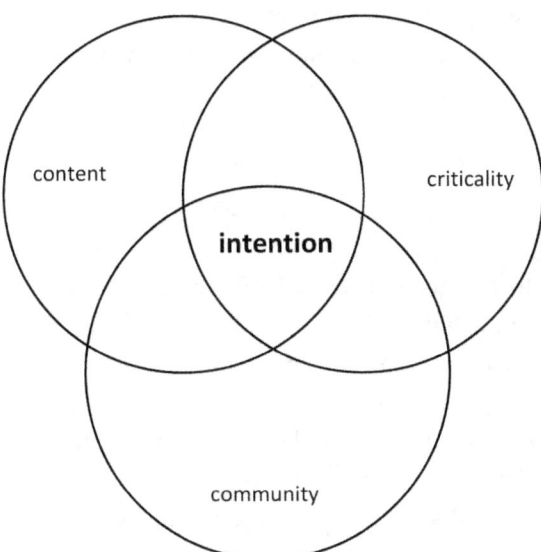

Figure 2.1 Curriculum for change.

values hidden in texts (Martin, Maton and Doran 2020). Finally, the interaction with community could take the form of a research project investigating local beliefs/practices in relation to social inclusion of ethnic minorities, or could involve taking students outside the classroom to reflect on physical spaces they and others occupy, and evaluate why those spaces exist, in what ways they include and exclude, and what impact might they have on community (Watson 2022). Another option could be a reflective photo diary where, in response to a social justice-related prompt (e.g. photograph anything related to poverty), students would take photos around their community and then discuss them with peers (Wang and Burris 1997).

According to the existing literature, it can be argued that in some EAP contexts, where the themes of sustainable development and global citizenship have been gaining momentum in recent years, an implicit or explicit intention to transform and empower has been present for a while, as has sustainable development-oriented content. Adding increasingly theory-driven approaches to critical thinking instruction in EAP (for example, Academic Literacies (Lea and Street 2006), Critical EAP (Benesch 2009), Critical Discourse Analysis (Machin and Mayr, 2012), Systemic Functional Linguistics (Halliday, 1978), Legitimation Code Theory (Maton, Hood and Shay 2016)) further increases the chances that some existing EAP curricula already *are* instigating social change to some extent. As to the interaction with community, I have, so far, found no published evidence suggesting this constituent as part of current EAP curricula, which, by no means proves that it does not exist. Rather, this might suggest a lack of prominence, especially in comparison with the sustainable development related content and criticality in EAP.

Conclusion

It is important to recognise that the EAP curriculum for change framework proposed here is in its infancy, and therefore not without limitations. To claim that it is (or might be) working effectively in EAP contexts, this theory must be rigorously tested and evaluated.

There are two main limitations to the approach presented here. The first is the fact that the curriculum for change framework is yet to be tested and evaluated in an EAP context, and second, that its inception has been based on a limited literature review. However, preliminary findings have been shared in the hope that the reader finds them inspiring enough to pursue their own search for an

EAP curriculum for change, be it through a critique of the ideas presented in this chapter, discussions with fellow EAP practitioners, or empirical study.

Although knowledge in EAP appears to be gaining momentum, explicit studies on the role of an EAP curriculum in supporting social justice are critical but scarce. To bridge this gap, this chapter proposes a literature informed *curriculum for change* framework and invites the reader to critique and test it in their own EAP context(s), alongside sharing their findings and comments with the author and wider EAP community. The implications of such collaborative quests for social justice-oriented curricular approaches in EAP could be far reaching, and not only supporting EAP students in becoming global citizens actively advancing social justice, but also advancing the field of EAP within and beyond wider academia.

Be part of this conversation.

References

Abbas, A., Ashwin, P. and McLean, M. (2016), 'The Influence of Curricula Content on English Sociology Students' Transformations: The Case of Feminist Knowledge', *Teaching in Higher Education,* 21(4): 442–56.

Ashwin, P. (2020), *Transforming University Education: A Manifesto*, London: Bloomsbury Academic.

Barker, M. C., Hibbins, R. T., Woods, P. (2012), 'Bringing Forth the Graduate as a Global Citizen: An Exploratory Study of Masters-Level Business Students in Australia', in S. Sovic and M. Blythman (eds), *International Students Negotiating Higher Education*, 132–45. London: Routledge.

Benesch, S. (2009), 'Theorising and Practicing Critical English for Academic Purposes', *Journal of English for Academic Purposes*, 8: 41–5.

Bernstein, B. (2000), *Pedagogy, Symbolic Control and Identity: Theory, Research and Critique,* Maryland: Rowman and Littlefield.

Bond, B. (2020), *Making Language Visible in the University: English for Academic Purposes and Internationalisation*, Bristol: Multilingual Matters.

Bottrell, D. and Manathunga, C., eds (2018), *Resisting Neoliberalism in Higher Education*, vol. 1: *Seeing Through the Cracks*, New York: Springer.

Brooke, M., Monbec, L. and Tilakaratna, N. (2019), 'The Analytical Lens: Developing Undergraduate Students' Critical Dispositions in Undergraduate EAP Writing Courses', *Teaching in Higher Education,* 24(3): 428–43.

Brundtland, G. H. (1987), *Our Common Future. Report of the World Commission on Environment and Development,* Oxford University Press: Oxford: United Nations.

Burdge, R. and Vanclay, F. (1996), 'Social Impact Assessment: a Contribution to the State of the Art Series, *Impact Assessment,* 14(1): 59–86.

Capra, F. and Luisi, P. (2014), *The Systems View of Life: a Unifying Vision*, Cambridge: Cambridge University Press.

Cho, H. S. and Mosselson, J. (2018), 'Neoliberal Practices Amidst Social Justice Orientations: Global Citizenship Education in South Korea', *Compare: A Journal of Comparative and International Education*, 48(6): 861–78.

Clarence, S. (2021), *Turning Access into Success: Improving University Education with Legitimation Code Theory*, London: Routledge.

Clifford, J. and Barnes, K. (2022), 'Why and What to Measure? The Justification for Social Impact Measurement', in R. Hazenberg and C. Paterson-Young (eds), *Social Impact Measurement for a Sustainable Future: the Power of Aesthetics and Practical Implications*, 49–74, Cham: Palgrave Macmillan.

Clifford, J., Hehenberger, L. and Fantini, M. (2014), *Proposed Approaches to Social Impact Measurement in European Commission Legislation and in Practice Relating to: EuSEFs and the EaSI*, European Commission Report 140605, June 2014. Available online: https://op.europa.eu/en/publication-detail/-/publication/0c0b5d38-4ac8-43d1-a7af-32f7b6fcf1cc (accessed 7 August 2023).

Coffin, C. and Donohue., J. (2014), *A Language as Social Semiotic-Based Approach to Teaching and Learning in Higher Education*, Malden, Mass.: Wiley.

Cowley-Haselden, S. (2020a), 'Building Knowledge to Ease Troublesomeness: Affording Theory Knowledgeability through Academic Reading Circles', *Journal of University Teaching and Learning Practice*, 17(2): - no page numbers available as electronic publication

Cowley-Haselden, S. (2020b), 'Using Learner Diaries to Explore Learner Relations to Knowledge on an English for General Purposes Pre-Sessional', *Journal of Academic Language and Learning*, 14(1): 15–29.

Dentoni, D., Bitzer, V. and Pascucci, S. (2016), 'Cross-Sector Partnerships and Co-Creation of Dynamic Capabilities for Stakeholder Orientation', *Journal of Business Ethics*, 135(1): 35–53.

Fairclough, N. (1993), *Discourse and Social Change*, Cambridge: Polity.

Fraser, N. (1998), *Social Justice in the Age of Identity Politics: Redistribution, Recognition, Participation*, Discussion Papers. SSOAR. Available online: https://www.ssoar.info/ssoar/bitstream/handle/document/12624/ssoar-1998-fraser-social_justice_in_the_age.pdf?sequence=1 (accessed 7 August 2023).

Freire, P. (2005), *Pedagogy of the Oppressed*, New York: Continuum.

Fung, D. (2017), *A Connected Curriculum for Higher Education*. London: UCL Press.

Gallor, S. (2017), 'A Social Justice Approach to Undergraduate Psychology Education: Building Cultural Diversity, Inclusion, and Sensitivity into Teaching, Research and Service', *Psi Chi Journal of Psychological Research*, 22(4): 254–7.

Garibay, J.C. (2015), 'STEM Students' Social Agency and Views on Working for Social Change: Are STEM Disciplines Developing Socially and Civically Responsible Students?', *Journal of Research in Science Teaching*, 52(5): 610–32.

Gillway, M. (2020), 'An Exploration of the Depths of Feedback in Higher Education: Bringing the Beliefs of Academic Teachers to the Surface', EdD thesis, University of Bath.

Ginwright, S. A. and Cammarota, J. (2015), 'Teaching Social Justice Research to Undergraduate Students in Puerto Rico: Using Personal Experiences to Inform Research', *Equity and Excellence in Education*, 48(2): 162–77.

Halliday, M. A. K. (1978), *Language as Social Semiotic: the Social Interpretation of Language and Meaning,* Baltimore: University Park Press.

Hazenberg, R. and Clifford, J. (2016), 'Developing Social Impact Measurement for Social Enterprise', in C. Durkin and R. Gunn (eds), *Social Entrepreneurship: A Skills Approach,* pp. 125–32, Bristol: Policy Press.

Hazenberg, R. and Paterson-Young, C., eds (2022a), *Social Impact Measurement for a Sustainable Future: the Power of Aesthetics and Practical Implications,* Cham: Palgrave Macmillan.

Hazenberg, R. and Paterson-Young, C. (2022b), 'The Development of Social Impact Measurement', in R. Hazenberg and C. Paterson-Young (eds), *Social Impact Measurement for a Sustainable Future: The Power of Aesthetics and Practical Implications*, 13–25. Cham: Palgrave Macmillan.

Heleta, S. and Bagus, T. (2020), 'Sustainable Development Goals and Higher Education: Leaving Many Behind', *Higher Education,* 81: 163–77.

Honneth, A. (2010), 'The Political Identity of the Green Movement in Germany: Social-Philosophical Reflections', *Critical Horizons,* 11(1): 5–18.

Hyland, K. and Hamp-Lyons, L. (2002), 'EAP: Issues and Directions', *Journal of English for Academic Purposes*, 1(1): 1–12.

Jain, P., Hazenberg, R., Seddon, F. and Denny. S. (2019), 'Social Value as a Mechanism for Linking Public Administrators with Society: Identifying the Meaning, Forms and Process of Social Value Creation', *Journal of Public Administration*, 43(10), 876–89

Kirk, S. (2018), 'Enacting the Curriculum in English for Academic Purposes: A Legitimation Code Theory Analysis', EdD thesis, Durham University.

Kukuczka, J. (2021), 'The Impact of Academic Reading Circles on Students' Academic Development', BALEAP Biennial Conference Talk: Glasgow 2021. Available online: https://www.youtube.com/watch?v=q9NMe8gXBlk (accessed 7 August 2023).

Lea, M. R. and Street, B. V. (2006). 'The "Academic Literacies" Model: Theory and Applications', *Theory into Practice,* 45: 368–77.

Lin, Z. and Yang, L. (2019), '"Me too!': Individual Empowerment of Disabled Women in the #metoo Movement in China', *Disability and Society,* 34(5): 842–7.

Luckett, K. and Shay, S. (2017), 'Reframing the Curriculum: a Transformative Approach', *Critical Studies in Education*, 61(1), 50–65.

Machin, D. and Mayr, A. (2012), *How to do Critical Discourse Analysis*, Los Angeles-London-New Delhi-Singapore-Washington DC: SAGE.

Manning, S. and Reinecke, J. (2016), 'We're Failing to Solve the World's "Wicked Problems": Here's a Better Approach', *The Conversation*, 3: 1–5.

Maton, K., Hood, S. and Shay, S. eds (2016), *Knowledge-Building: Educational Studies in Legitimation Code Theory*. Abingdon: Routledge.

Martin, J. R., Maton, K. and Doran, Y. J. eds (2020), *Accessing Academic Discourse: Systemic Functional Linguistics and Legitimation Code Theory*. London and New York: Routledge.

Masehela, L. M. (2020). 'Developing Critical Citizens by Changing the Higher Education Curriculum', in J. McArthur and P. Ashwin (eds), *Locating Social Justice in Higher Education Research*, 169–81, London: Bloomsbury.

Massey, A. (2022), 'Sustainable Development Goals and their Fit with Good Governance. Policy Insights', *Global Policy*, 13: 79–85.

McArthur, J. (2018), *Assessment for Social Justice: Perspectives and Practices within Higher Education*, London: Bloomsbury.

Monbec, L. (2018), 'Designing an EAP Curriculum for Transfer: A Focus on Knowledge', *Journal of Academic Language and Learning*, 12(2): 88–101.

Nussbaum, M.C. (2006). *Frontiers of Justice*, London, UK-Cambridge, US: Belknap Press of Harvard University Press.

ONS (= Office for National Statistics) (2017), 'Graduates in the UK Labour Market', *Office for National Statistics*, 24 November 2017, https://www.ons.gov.uk/employmentandlabourmarket/peopleinwork/employmentandemployeetypes/articles/graduatesintheuklabourmarket/2017 (accessed 15 January 2021).

Public Services (Social Value) Act (2012). Available online: https://www.legislation.gov.uk/ukpga/2012/3/contents (accessed 7 August 2023).

QAA (=Quality Assurance Agency for Higher Education) and Advance HE (2021), 'Education for Sustainable Development Guidance', *AdvanceHE*, 29 March 2021, https://www.advance-he.ac.uk/knowledge-hub/education-sustainable-development-guidance (accessed 7 August 2023).

Riazi, A. M., Ghanbar, H. and Fazel, I. (2020), 'The Contexts, Theoretical and Methodological Orientation of EAP Research: Evidence from Empirical Articles Published in the Journal of English for Academic Purposes', *Journal of English for Academic Purposes*, 48(2).- no page numbers as electronic only

Rucker, W. R. (1955), 'Social Change and Education', *The Phi Delta Kappan*, 36(8): 305–8.

Ruitenberg, C. and Vokey, D. (2010). Equality and Justice', in R. Bailey, R. Barrow and D. Carr (eds), *The SAGE Handbook of Philosophy of Education*, 401–14, Los Angeles-London-New Delhi-Singapore-Washington DC: SAGE.

Seburn, T. (2016), *Academic Reading Circles*, Toronto: The Round.

Shay, S. and Peseta, T. L., eds (2018), *Curriculum as Contestation*. Abingdon: Routledge.

Shrestha, P. N. (2020), *Dynamic Assessment of Students' Academic Writing: Vygotskian and Systemic Functional Linguistic Perspectives*, Cham: Springer.

Smith, E. (2018), *Key Issues in Education and Social Justice*, 2nd edn, Los Angeles-London-New Delhi-Singapore-Washington DC: SAGE.

Sustainable Development Commission (2011), 'What is Sustainable Development?', *Sustainable Development Commission*, http://www.sd-commission.org.uk/pages/what-is-sustainable-development.html (accessed 7 August 2023).

UKCISA (2019), 'International Student Statistics: UK Higher Education', *UK Council for International Student Affairs (UKCISA)*, https://www.ukcisa.org.uk/Research--Policy/Statistics/International-student-statistics-UK-higher-education (accessed 1 May 2022).

UN Sustainable Development Group (2021), *Leave No-One Behind*. Available online: https://unsdg.un.org/2030-agenda/universal-values/leave-no-one-behind (accessed 7 August 2023).

United Nations (2006), *Social Justice in an Open World: The Role of the United Nations*. Available online: https://www.un.org/esa/socdev/documents/ifsd/SocialJustice.pdf (accessed 7 August 2023).

United Nations (2015), *Transforming our World: The 2030 Agenda for Sustainable Development*. Available online: https://sdgs.un.org/2030agenda (accessed 7 August 2023).

United Nations (2021), *Sustainable Development Goals*. Available online: https://sdgs.un.org/goals (accessed 7 August 2023).

Wang C. and Burris M. A. (1997), 'Photovoice: Concept, Methodology, and Use for Participatory Needs Assessment', *Health, Education and Behavior*, 24(3): 369–87.

Watson, L. (2022), 'Developing Global Citizenship through Place-Based Learning', Unpublished Classroom Materials. International Foundation Year Programme, Southampton: University of Southampton.

Wilterdink, N. and Form, W. (2022), 'Social Change', *Encyclopaedia Britannica*. Available online: https://www.britannica.com/topic/social-change (accessed 7 August 2023).

Winstone, N. and Carless, D. (2020), *Designing Effective Feedback Processes in Higher Education: a Learner-Centred Approach*, London: Routledge.

3

Critical EAP: A Marginalised Friend?

Natalia Fedorova and Kashmir Kaur

Introduction

What is the purpose of higher education? Is it to mould students into a convenient shape suitable for a particular cultural and political environment? Or is it to foster agency, individuality, criticality and awareness of their socio-political contexts? While many would agree that the latter is the more worthy aspiration, this ideal is not always embodied in English for Academic Purposes (EAP) courses, which typically take place within HE institutions (MacDonald 2022). Writing as EAP practitioners, we might be charged with 'biting the hand that feeds you' by embarking on a critique of the premises upon which EAP stands. However, it would probably be more hypocritical (and harmful) to stay neutral, for neutrality in education is an illusion. 'Washing one's hands of the conflict between the powerful and the powerless means to side with the powerful, not to be neutral' (Freire 1985: 122). All aspects, from curriculum development and content selection to the choice of teaching methods in a single class, are shaped by certain beliefs and ideologies.

The aim of this chapter is to shine a light on the myth of the neutrality of EAP. We are not the first scholars to bring awareness to the political and ideological issues surrounding the teaching of EAP: prominent among our predecessors is Sarah Benesch and it is her construction of Critical EAP (CEAP) which is the focus of this chapter.

Benesch's *Critical English for Academic Purposes* (CEAP) was published in 2001. The CEAP framework stands in opposition to neoliberalism and the traditional skills-based teaching of EAP in that it aims to promote students' agency in shaping their own education. It is a democratic approach to teaching which entails stimulating students' active questioning of the existing socio-political processes and hierarchical structures, with the aim of raising their understanding of the context in which they are operating and of encouraging negotiation for more favourable learning conditions. As do approaches such as Academic Literacies (Lea and Street 1998) and Dialogic Interrogations (Chun 2009), CEAP aims to challenge the status quo of the traditional classroom. Yet CEAP has never been at the forefront of EAP research or teaching. In a corpus survey of papers from BALEAP proceedings and accounts from Professional Issue Meetings in the years 1975–2019, the term 'critical' was found to have a 'sustained, though low level of interest evident since 2010' (Charles 2022: 8). This low level of interest in CEAP and Benesch's seminal work is also reflected in the findings of the bibliometric analysis by Hyland and Jiang (2021) of a corpus of EAP-related articles in forty social science journals. With regards to its application in curriculum design or classroom practice, according to Mortenson (2022: 2), 'there has been minimal research into the adoption of critical, social justice-oriented content in such (EAP) programs to teach EB ('Emergent Bilingual') students about the historical legacy that informs the current socio-political context in which they are completing their studies.'

Even though there are 'pockets of resistance' across the world – that is, institutions and practitioners who resist the neoliberal turn (Harland and Pickering 2011; MacDonald 2022) – these are under-represented in the literature. Among the few studies of specific teaching contexts there is little evidence of overt use of CEAP (see, for example Fenton-Smith 2014). Except for the 2009 Special Issue of the *Journal of English for Academic Purposes* (JEAP), which showcased the theory and praxis of CEAP (Benesch 2009), there have been few articles dedicated to the practice of CEAP in real classroom settings. The latest issue of JEAP (at the time of writing) features an article (Pu and Xu 2022) which criticises EAP students' resistance to institutional requirements and socialization into discourse norms, branding such views as deviant. In the same special issue of JEAP, Bell (2022) highlights that methodological and pedagogical issues in an EAP classroom have received very little interest from researchers throughout the years. While Bell acknowledges the importance of equal partnership between EAP students and teachers and of having a process (i.e., co-constructed) rather than a product (i.e., pre-planned) syllabus, he dismisses CEAP's potential to be central to EAP teaching. He claims that it is '(n)ot pure language analysis; not pure linguistic research; not arguing for rights, nor indeed challenging and trying to re-shape the entire raison d'être of our universities' but 'how to operationalise the language and skills needed for academic purposes' which is the aim of EAP pedagogy (ibid.: 5).

However, this restricted conceptualization of EAP does not seem to be serving students well. Pearson's (2020) review of UK-based studies on the effectiveness of pre-sessional EAP programs revealed that, whereas most students found the experience of studying EAP in the UK a rewarding experience and were able to pass the course, they displayed unremarkable progress in their language skills. Moreover, with many students starting their degrees with only borderline proficiency, the completion of EAP pre-sessionals did not preclude them from 'delayed degree completion, lower academic outcomes compared with direct entry students (both 'native-' and 'non-native speakers'), or failure, often by thesis non-(re)submission (in time)' (ibid.: 420). This failure to meet learners' EAP needs (Fedorova 2021) suggests that it is necessary to bring CEAP to the foreground as a means to enable EAP learners to negotiate more favourable conditions for themselves and to promote change in the way they are treated by the system.

This chapter will argue that CEAP should enter centre stage in EAP teaching and research. It will present and analyse the findings of a study of EAP practitioner attitudes to and experiences of applying CEAP in the classroom. It will also discuss the possible reasons for the lack of uptake of CEAP practices in mainstream EAP courses and its lack of representation in the academic literature. The purpose of this chapter is not to provide a comprehensive practical guide to implementing CEAP, but rather to revitalise interest in CEAP among colleagues and to promote further reflection in the industry.

A snapshot of the current state of CEAP

To consider the current state of CEAP and to what extent EAP practitioners viewed, understood and implemented CEAP in their teaching practice, we conducted a small-scale qualitative study to investigate EAP practitioners' attitudes to CEAP (Aspers and Corte 2019; Punch 2013; Braun and Clarke 2013). Participants were drawn from EAP tutors on the BALEAP and BALEAP Social Justice Special Interest Group mailing lists, and six UK-based participants (Table 3.1) were selected to capture the heterogeneity in the population (Maxwell 2013). Participants were provided with a clear set of instructions and guidance regarding the interview questions and how to submit their response. They were invited to inform themselves with relevant readings (Gibbs 1988; Fenton-Smith 2014) prior to responding to the interview questions. The questions were structured to encourage reflective responses, and participants self-administered

Table 3.1 Study participants in a small-scale qualitative study to investigate EAP practitioners' attitudes to CEAP

Participants	Gender	Institution	EAP Experience
1	Male	Private Company	less than a year
2	Female	University	3 years
3	Female	Private Company	4 years
4	Female	University	7.5 years
5	Female	University	10 years
6	Female	University	15 years

the interview. Four participants responded by typing their responses and two participants provided their responses via an audio recording.

The audio files were transcribed by Otter.ai software and independently checked by the researchers to ensure accuracy. To support the data analysis process, NVivo was utilized. The transcripts were transferred onto NVivo and read carefully to stimulate directions of interpretation (Maxwell 2013). Coding then positioned and connected extracts from across all the transcripts into nodes. Participant expressions and examples of their attitudes to and understanding of CEAP, implementation of CEAP in classroom practice and CEAP's connection to stakeholders were analysed. Subsequently, concept maps were produced as a visual representation of the data into emerging themes. Mapping, the rhizomatic expansion, assisted in generating new possible realities rather than singular representations and facilitated the exploration of connections within and across different experiences (Martin and Kamberelis 2013).

We conducted this analysis in a collaborative manner by following Braun and Clarke's six-step thematic analysis framework (2006, 2013). We were influenced by Braun and Clarke's (2019: 594) reflective thematic analysis which concentrates on 'the researcher's reflective and thoughtful engagement with their data and their reflexive and thoughtful engagement with the analytic process'. The transcripts were read from dominant and resistant perspectives – influenced by 'thick description' (Geertz 1973) and 'reading against the grain', with the aim to excavate beneath the surface responses to reach an insider's understanding by uncovering the silences and the absences. Nonetheless, the problematic nature of an interpretative analysis needs to be acknowledged.

Dominant reading

Understanding of CEAP

The six participants express diverse understandings of CEAP. A common theme is that CEAP promotes questioning and critical thinking: teachers questioning the role of EAP, their own role and the teaching materials, and raising students' awareness of their educational settings and empowering them to challenge the system. In relation to the latter, participants mentioned the issues of students' academic identities and unique backgrounds; their desires, purposes and aspirations; values and ideologies within HE; issues such as race, gender, class, and ethnicity. The positive views ranged from focusing on the role of CEAP inside the classroom in fostering individuality, autonomy (P2) and critical thinking (P1) to its wider role within the university and academia, e.g. the link between CEAP and decolonization (P5) and the idea that CEAP 'seeks to counter this (Western hegemony which marginalises non-Western academic discourse/literacies) by raising students' awareness of the extent to which the EAP education/syllabi construct their academic identities (wields power)' (P3). CEAP teaching is considered by these participants as more egalitarian, inclusive, dialogic, motivational and respectful towards students. In terms of the negative views, two participants (P2 and P5) placed CEAP into opposition to 'traditional' EAP due to its potentially disruptive or destabilizing effect. There was a strong feeling of perceived risk involved in challenging the status quo by employing CEAP. Participant 4 was notably critical of CEAP calling it 'patronizing' for positioning students as victims who 'don't know what they are paying for', and 'hypocritical' due to its alleged intention to impose certain political beliefs on students.

Overall, however, the data indicates that most of the participants do not have a deep understanding of CEAP, with four admitting to having a basic or incomplete understanding of the concept, demonstrated by responses such as: 'if I've understood it correctly'; 'perhaps I need a deeper understanding of CEAP to know if I am doing it or not'; 'my understanding of critical EAP is quite limited'. Participant 2 claims that there is no agreed definition of CEAP in the EAP community and that researchers should agree on a precise definition. Participant 6, the most experienced EAP teacher (fifteen years) within the sample, admits to not being familiar with Benesch's seminal work on CEAP. The least experienced EAP teacher (P1) admits that they do not know how to enact CEAP spontaneously or seamlessly into their lessons and would like 'training in this area'.

Implementation of CEAP

All except for one participant (P4) believe they do not implement CEAP sufficiently or at all in their teaching. The classroom practices which they believe represent CEAP to some extent are those encouraging students to develop critical thinking by means of reflecting and questioning: e.g. students reflecting on their skills and learning process, on the materials used in the classroom and on ideologies surrounding academia. This development of criticality is also manifested in the choice of texts including controversial topics as well as texts showing diversity and variation in the way academic writing was approached by the authors. In terms of the outcomes of such implementation, the majority assert that CEAP is relevant and has a positive impact on students: becoming 'more self-reflexive and more able to question or reflect on other ideologies' (P3), being encouraged to 'question their course, the materials and the discussions they have' and 'playing an active role in their own learning' (P2).

The only participant (P4) who was hostile towards CEAP feels strongly that CEAP should not be implemented in mainstream EAP teaching as it does not meet students' needs. A theme raised in some of the participants' responses was the role of EAP in addressing student needs and the role of the wider university. The role of universities, according to two participants, is to assist students develop their critical thinking so that they can question and critically approach their disciplines and the world outside the university. The role of EAP then, according to the participants, is, generally, to help students prepare for their degree. Participant 4 sees themself as helping level the playing field by giving students 'a fair chance of success'. This participant also believes they are raising social awareness by bringing in controversial topics into the classroom but sees students' needs as being limited to accessing the degree they are paying for and communicating successfully with tutors and peers. Some participants, however, see their role as going beyond simply helping students navigate their chosen university, to include developing learners into active agents of their learning rather than 'passive receivers'. One participant (P5) claims that EAP practitioners often operate under 'false consciousness': a 'well-intentioned belief' that they are helping learners to become successful.

In light of the tensions between the goals of traditional EAP and CEAP, the participants also discussed the challenges and risks of implementing CEAP. A prominent idea among the responses was that CEAP is 'disruptive', in the sense that it poses a risk to the students' academic studies and undermines the value of Western education by questioning it. Students 'want to believe in the credibility of the qualification that they are studying for' (P3). In this sense, the participants claim that CEAP does not meet students' needs: students have an interest in adapting to Western culture, have chosen their courses based on the high reputation of UK HE and may view obtaining a UK degree as merely pragmatic. Another view is that students' low level of English (P5) and their different cultural backgrounds may be obstacles to CEAP implementation. In addition, CEAP is seen by one participant (P5) as too cognitively demanding.

In terms of the teacher-related difficulties, the views are quite diverse, and include the time and effort involved and the lack of training opportunities. Teacher beliefs emerged in the view that academic norms should not be challenged and that teachers should not try to influence their learners' (political) beliefs (P4). The most frequent response (three participants) was teachers' perceived lack of job security and fear of 'disrupting' the system that provides them with employment. There may be feelings of powerlessness due to precarious contractual situations (Morgan 2009), or discomfort at reflecting critically on their own practices in teaching or materials design (Fenton-Smith 2014).

Resistant reading

Understanding of CEAP

CEAP is, generally, a branch of critical pedagogy, stemming from Freire's *Pedagogy of the Oppressed* (1972), of which Pennycook (1990) is one of the main proponents within EAP. Critical pedagogy, encompassing all teaching and not simply language teaching, is based on the belief that students should be challenged to analyse the power relations and various inequalities which define the status quo. Within this pedagogy, CEAP is seen by some researchers as a tool to revitalise the curriculum and to reconsider the power structures and hierarchies which play a role in shaping the curriculum in an institution (Helmer 2013). CEAP has the potential to show students that they have a choice when it comes to adopting the discoursal and linguistic dominant norms of their communities, and the right to challenge these norms.

Thus, at the centre of CEAP is the concept of rights analysis, as opposed to traditional needs analysis. Benesch (1996) asserts that EAP needs analysis is an ideological notion, as it imposes pre-determinants of the target situation. Learner needs are conflated with institutional needs, which leads to a deficit approach to teaching (Helmer 2013). Rights analysis, in contrast, can serve as a tool to challenge the distribution of power, can contribute to achieving equality in the learning and teaching conditions (Benesch 2001), and can enact social change both inside and outside the classroom (Benesch 1996).

The majority of the participants in our study articulated alignment with some of the CEAP principles. However, regardless of the level of the participants' EAP teaching experience, they revealed somewhat fragmented understandings of CEAP, displaying hesitancy and a lack of holistic (or deep) understanding. The language used by the participants shows a degree of perhaps not unsurprising (given how little CEAP is discussed in EAP circles) uncertainty over the exact purpose of CEAP and its importance. There is a degree of caution in the way the participants have approached the task of explaining their understanding. The words 'disruptive' and 'destabilizing' reveal the participants' fear of challenging the established system. This places CEAP in 'opposition' to mainstream EAP, suggesting that there is no place for CEAP in mainstream EAP without the risk of 'disrupting' the fixed order. The lack of understanding of CEAP shows in Participant 4's claim that it is 'patronizing' and 'hypocritical'.

The idea put forward by some participants – that students are fully aware of the neoliberal UK HE system and how it exploits international students – is not evidenced. There is a paradox: if typical EAP students are seen as novices (P4 and P6) and there is largely a consensus that they lack understanding of the culture and requirements of HE, why, by extension, are they not seen as lacking understanding of (or the need to understand) the (neoliberal) nature of the education system they are in? It seems illogical to claim that EAP students, the majority of whom come from very different academic cultures, would be well-informed of the capitalist ideological basis of their education. Dialogic interrogations, as proposed by Chun, could help such learners reflect on the issues surrounding the neoliberal nature of EAP and 'facilitate their interpretations and contestations of the ideological underpinnings of the discourses they draw upon in indexing their social identities and experiences' (2009: 119).

The view that CEAP proponents aim to impose their views on students is not evidenced either and may stem from a lack of understanding of CEAP. Neutrality is a pedagogical dilemma: do we have the right to impose on students certain social justice beliefs? Do we accept their views even when they may not align with ours (Morgan 2009; Fenton-Smith 2014)? How do we avoid influencing students with our own beliefs (Mortenson 2022)? Where do we draw the line on the controversial issues we raise? How far can we go in encouraging student activism? Fenton-Smith (2014) references much-criticised Chinese student protests in Australia against Tibetan independence to argue that student activism may be controversial, depending on the socio-political context in which student beliefs are expressed.

Another pedagogical dilemma is how to sustain the degree of criticality in one's teaching so that it turns into a meaningful rather than a one-off experience for students. Fischman and Haas (2008) suggest that a teacher aspiring to use critical pedagogy should have a high level of commitment, which short cost-effective pre-sessional courses often do not allow. It is also crucial not to fall into the trap of the 'narrative of redemption' which often surrounds the conversation about critical pedagogy. This narrative presents reality as a binary opposition (e.g. 'good versus evil' or 'evil neoliberalism' versus 'good social democracy'). This oversimplification breeds unrealistic ideas about heroic teachers and students and can lead to feelings of despair and depression in both, due to the impossibility of total success and the high perceived risk of failure (Fischman and Haas 2008).

Implementation of CEAP

There are many reasons why CEAP has never penetrated mainstream EAP research or practice, including neoliberalism, linguistic imperialism and native-speakerism, and issues of methodology and pedagogy. While neoliberalism purportedly has the noble aim of promoting resourcefulness and entrepreneurship in markets freed from government control, in practice it serves to re-establish the power and wealth of economic elites and stands in opposition to government spending on social welfare and support of the most disadvantaged, leading to an inequitable distribution of resources (Chun 2009). HE institutions in the countries where neoliberalism is woven into the fabric of the society are caught up in the cycle of sustaining this model, effectively turning them into businesses. HE institutions no longer serve democracy nor have as their goal the addressing of social problems (Giroux 2010). Chun (2009) provides vivid exemplifications of how neoliberalism plays out in the marketing of EAP courses in the US HE context, presenting such courses as a lifestyle and appealing to consumerist tendencies. Neoliberalism has, of course, brought benefits: the rise of EAP can, in part, be attributed to it and the subsequent rise in EAP jobs, albeit sometimes fixed-term and precarious, has offered career opportunities for EFL teachers. This makes CEAP's goals, which stand in opposition to neoliberal systems, harder to achieve.

Linguistic imperialism and native-speakerism may also play a role in resisting the changes proposed by critical pedagogies. Linguistic imperialism (Phillipson

1992) is also associated with issues of cultural superiority, prestige, influence and economic and political power. As English is the source of power, influence and the wealth it brings to the Anglophone countries, it is not surprising that such power is not surrendered easily. There is often resistance to the acknowledgment of Global Englishes in EMI institutions, with standard English still being the only acceptable variety (Garska and O'Brien 2019).

CEAP challenges the status quo of monolingualism and native-speakerism and promotes recognition of Global Englishes and such practices as translanguaging, which can empower students and support their linguistic rights (Akbari 2008). However, while NS norms continue to be used as a benchmark in EAP writing, learners, as in Garska and O'Brien's study (2019), will believe in the superiority of NS standards of writing against which their abilities in academic writing are measured. The same view is echoed by the ELFA scholar Jenkins (2014), who rejects the traditional genre approach to teaching EAP writing as conformist and native-speakerist.

Methodological and pedagogical considerations may also prevent a widespread use of CEAP. Bell (2022) hypothesises that the general neglect of issues of methodology in EAP research and practice may be due to EAP teachers being seen as already qualified to teach and the belief that there is nothing new to be said with regards to teaching methods. He also suggests that EAP may over-rely on general ELT methods such as task-based teaching and CLT. It may indeed be more comfortable and convenient to transfer these familiar methods into EAP practice, whereas the methods of critical pedagogy, by their nature dialogic and co-constructed with students (Jeyaraj and Harland 2014), may present challenges and stress to teachers. The diversity of approaches and strategies associated with critical pedagogy may also pose difficulty to a practitioner.

Participants' frank responses revealed the limits to their implementation of CEAP in their practice. Whilst the activities and teaching choices exemplified by the participants are valuable, there was not much evidence of encouraging students to think beyond their immediate surroundings towards the social mission of the university. Participants barely acknowledged the potential for CEAP skills to impact future employment and decision making. The possibility of student activism was questioned and no examples of such practice were provided. These responses, once again, reveal the extent to which the participants lack confidence in implementing CEAP. An emphasis on the need for top-down training and instructions from institutions and researchers, e.g. BALEAP, as a pre-requisite for wider implementation of CEAP may indicate the extent to which EAP practitioners feel the need for external validation and approval to use CEAP.

As for the student-related obstacles to CEAP implementation, whilst some of these ideas can be classed as legitimate challenges, most, again, synch with neoliberalism. The large fees paid by international students are used as an argument for not undermining the reputation of UK HE and disrupting this important stream of revenue. While the difference in fees for home and international students was mentioned by Participant 4, there was no recognition of HE's neoliberal positioning in the UK affecting home students too. With regards to the teacher-related challenges, lack of time and energy was noted by the participants: lessons are short and there is a large amount of material to cover. However, there is no reflection on why that is so. EAP courses are typically intensive and designed to cover areas of perceived need (i.e. academic study skills), with no room left for incorporating CEAP. There appears to be little recognition of the role neoliberal market forces play in this and in the precarious employment conditions for most EAP practitioners. On the contrary, what emerges is a sense of 'owing' the employment to the existence of EAP in its current form and a reluctance to challenge the status quo. Likewise, the participants in our research voiced no qualms about the overreliance on Chinese student numbers (Breen 2021) and how disruption in these numbers could impact the EAP profession. Generally, there was a noticeable lack of reflection on changing this situation.

As to the role of EAP and the wider university, some respondents in our study expressed doubts as to whether EAP actually does what it espouses: assisting students to navigate the UK HE environment. While there may be some understanding of the power differentials which require students to 'align their language use and by extension their identities, with a dominant Western form of academic English' (P3), there is hesitancy about advocating a 'decolonizing' of EAP practices. Except for Participant 4, all participants agree that the role of the university should be to prepare students to be critical and inquisitive about the world, especially in this post-truth era. However, connections are not drawn here between the potential of CEAP to assist the university to achieve this social goal. Participant 4 notably does not mention the social role of universities and instead uses capitalist/neoliberal language to describe what happens at university: the university provides 'services' to students, who receive the final 'product' (the degree). This participant was not alone in alluding to the importance of the marketization of universities, indicating the dominance of neoliberal constructs of HE in the participants' minds.

Conclusion

This chapter has reported and discussed the findings of a small-scale inquiry into the views of EAP practitioners on the subject of CEAP and the feasibility of wider CEAP implementation. The research demonstrates that EAP tutors are interested in implementing CEAP, as they consider it relevant and beneficial for students. There may also be practitioners who are reluctant to engage with CEAP as they do not believe that it addresses student needs. Our data suggest that there is a lack of in-depth understanding of CEAP among the practitioners. Barriers to implementation which emerged include this lack of understanding, institutional constraints, and perceived risks to tutor job security and to student academic achievement. These barriers can be considered as stemming from the lack of interest in CEAP in HE institutions and EAP communities of practice. This, in turn, reflects the dominance of the idea that the neoliberal marketization and financialization of EAP is inevitable.

In light of these findings, it can be seen that CEAP awareness should be raised among stakeholders if it is to be more widely implemented in mainstream EAP. CEAP can help challenge the deficit model of international students' needs and contribute to creating a critical and inquisitive mindset among young citizens, enabling them to contribute to creating a more equitable world. Continuing to dismiss CEAP as a viable alternative to traditional EAP is short-sighted in the current context of the ever more destructive forces of neoliberalism. It is hoped that stakeholders such as BALEAP will give greater prominence to CEAP and promote its implementation through increased CPD, sharing of best practice and organizing CEAP-focused conferences and symposia. Reiterating the question about the purpose of higher education raised at the beginning of this chapter, there is a clear case for dismantling traditional EAP orthodoxy and redesigning it to better address the humanistic aims of higher education.

References

Akbari, R. (2008), 'Transforming Lives: Introducing Critical Pedagogy into ELT Classrooms', *ELT Journal*, 62(3): 276–83. Available online: https://doi.org/10.1093/elt/ccn025 (accessed 14 August 2023).

Aspers, P. and U. Corte (2019), 'What is Qualitative in Qualitative Research', *Qualitative Sociology*, 42(2): 139–60. Available online: https://doi.org/10.1007/s11133-019-9413-7 (accessed 14 August 2023).

Bell, D.E. (2022), 'Methodology in EAP: Why is it Largely Still an Overlooked Issue?', *Journal of English for Academic Purposes,* 55: 101073. Available online: https://doi.org/10.1016/j.jeap.2021.101073 (accessed 14 August 2023).

Benesch, S. (1996), 'Needs Analysis and Curriculum Development in EAP: an Example of a Critical Approach', *TESOL Quarterly,* 30(4): 723–38. Available online: https://doi.org/10.2307/3587931 (accessed 14 August 2023).

Benesch, S. (2001), *Critical English for Academic Purposes: Theory, Politics, and Practice*, Mahwah, NJ: Lawrence Erlbaum Associates.

Benesch, S. (2009), 'Theorizing and Practicing Critical English for Academic Purposes', *Journal of English for Academic Purposes,* 8(2): 81–5. Available online: https://doi.org/10.1016/j.jeap.2008.09.002 (accessed 14 August 2023).

Braun, V. and V. Clarke (2006), 'Using Thematic Analysis in Psychology', *Qualitative Research in Psychology,* 3(2): 77–101. Available online: https://doi.org/10.1191/1478088706qp063oa (accessed 14 August 2023).

Braun, V. and V. Clarke (2013), *Successful Qualitative Research: A Practical Guide for Beginners,* Thousand Oaks, CA: Sage.

Braun V. and V. Clarke (2019), 'Reflecting on Reflexive Thematic Analysis', *Qualitative Research in Sport, Exercise and Health,* 11(4): 589–97. Available online: https://doi.org/10.1080/2159676X.2019.1628806 (accessed 14 August 2023).

Breen, P. (2021), 'Western Universities Need to Adopt a More Chinese-Friendly Pedagogy', *Times Higher Education,* 19 November. Available online: https://www.timeshighereducation.com/blog/western-universities-need-adopt-more-chinese-friendly-pedagogy (accessed 12 December 2022).

Charles, M. (2022), 'EAP Research in BALEAP 1975–2019: Past Issues and Future Directions', *Journal of English for Academic Purposes,* 55: 101060. Available online: https://doi.org/10.1016/j.jeap.2021.101060 (accessed 14 August 2023).

Chun, C.W. (2009), 'Contesting Neoliberal Discourses in EAP: Critical Praxis in an IEP Classroom', *Journal of English for Academic Purposes,* 8(2): 111–20. Available online: https://doi.org/10.1016/j.jeap.2008.09.005 (accessed 14 August 2023).

Fedorova, N. (2021), 'Questioning EAP: a Critique of The English for Academic Purposes Courses at University', *Journal of Teaching English for Specific and Academic Purposes,* 9(3): 401–8. Available online: https://doi.org/10.22190/JTESAP2103401F (accessed 14 August 2023).

Fenton-Smith, B. (2014), 'The Place of Benesch's Critical English for Academic Purposes in the Current Practice of Academic Language and Learning', *Journal of Academic Language and Learning,* 8(3): 23–33.

Fischman, G. E. and E. Haas (2008), 'Critical Pedagogy and Hope in the Context of Neo-Liberal Globalization', in W. Ayers, T. Quinn and D. Stovall (eds), *The Handbook of Social Justice in Education,* 565–75, New York: Routledge.

Freire, P. (1972), *Pedagogy of the Oppressed,* London: Penguin Group.

Freire, P. (1985), *The Politics of Education: Culture, Power, and Liberation,* Westport, Connecticut: Bergin and Garvey.

Garska, J. and O'Brien S. (2019), 'Power, Identity, and Culture in International Students' Perceptions of Academic Writing', *Trabalhos em Linguística Aplicada*, 58(1): 62–95. Available online: https://doi.org/10.1590/010318138653426454991 (accessed 14 August 2023).

Geertz, C. (1973), *Thick Description: Toward an Interpretive Theory of Culture. The Interpretation of Cultures*, New York: Basic Books.

Gibbs, G. (1988), *Learning by Doing: a Guide to Teaching and Learning Methods*, Oxford Polytechnic: Oxford.

Giroux, H. (2010), 'Bare Pedagogy and the Scourge of Neoliberalism: Rethinking Higher Education as a Democratic Public Sphere', *The Educational Forum*, 74: 184–96.

Harland, T. and N. Pickering (2011), *Values in Higher Education Teaching*, New York: Routledge.

Helmer, K. A. (2013), 'Critical English for Academic Purposes: Building on Learner, Teacher, and Program Strengths', *Journal of English for Academic Purposes*, 12: 273–87. Available online: http://dx.doi.org/10.1016/j.jeap.2013.08.003 (accessed 14 August 2023).

Hyland, K. and F. Jiang (2021), 'A Bibliometric Study of EAP Research: Who is Doing What, Where and When?', *Journal of English for Academic Purposes*, 49: 100929. Available online: https://doi.org/10.1016/j.jeap.2020.100929 (accessed 14 August 2023).

Jenkins, J. (2014), *English as a Lingua Franca in the International University: the Politics of Academic English Language Policy*, Abingdon: Routledge.

Lea, M. R., and B. V. Street (1998), 'Student Writing in Higher Education: an Academic Literacies Approach', *Studies in Higher Education*, 23(2): 157–72.

MacDonald, J. J. (2022), 'The Differing Discursive Constructions of EAP within the University: Contrasting Institutional and Language Centre Perspectives', in I. Bruce and B. Bond (eds), *Contextualizing English for Academic Purposes in Higher Education: Politics, Policies and Practices*, 131–48, London: Bloomsbury Academic.

Martin, A. D. and Kamberelis G. (2013), 'Mapping not Tracing: Qualitative Educational Research with Political Teeth', *International Journal of Qualitative Studies in Education*, 26(6): 668–79. Available online: https://doi.org/10.1080/09518398.2013.788756 (accessed 14 August 2023).

Maxwell, J. A. (2013), *Qualitative Research Design: An Interactive Approach*, 3rd edn, Thousand Oaks, CA: Sage.

Morgan, B. (2009), 'Fostering Transformative Practitioners for Critical EAP: Possibilities and Challenges', *Journal of English for Academic Purposes*, 8(2): 86–99. Available online: https://doi.org/10.1016/j.jeap.2008.09.001 (accessed 14 August 2023).

Mortenson, L. (2022), 'Integrating Social Justice-Oriented Content into English for Academic Purposes (EAP) Instruction: a Case Study', *English for Specific Purposes*, 65: 1–14. Available online: https://doi.org/10.1016/j.esp.2021.08.002 (accessed 14 August 2023).

Pearson, W.S. (2020), 'The Effectiveness of Pre-sessional EAP Programmes in UK Higher Education: a Review of the Evidence', *Review of Education*, 8(2): 420–47. Available online: https://doi.org/10.1002/rev3.3191 (accessed 14 August 2023).

Pennycook, A. (1990), 'Critical Pedagogy and Second Language Education', *System*, 18(3): 303–14.

Phillipson, R. (1992), *Linguistic Imperialism*, Oxford University Press: Oxford.

Pu, S. and H. Xu (2022), 'Resistance and Agency in Second Language Academic Discourse Socialization: Undergraduate Students' Experiences of an EAP Course', *Journal of English for Academic Purposes*, 58: 101122. Available online: https://doi.org/10.1016/j.jeap.2022.101122 (accessed 14 August 2023).

Punch, K. F. (2013), *Introduction to Social Research: Quantitative and Qualitative Approaches*, London: Sage.

4

Placing Assessment in the Vanguard of Social Justice in English for Academic Purposes

Jan McArthur

Introduction

The links between assessment and social justice are increasingly recognised in scholarship and practice (Ajjawi et al. 2023; Hanesworth et al. 2019; McArthur 2016, 2018, 2020; Tai et al. 2021). However, major challenges remain to firstly ensure better understanding of assessment's relationship to social justice, and secondly, to explore the best ways of realising this in our everyday practices. Assessment for social justice (McArthur 2016, 2018, 2020) is a concept that takes all we know about assessment for learning, and the pivotal role of assessment in shaping how and what students learn, and extrapolates this in the name of social justice. If assessment shapes learning, then surely our focus should be on ensuring greater social justice within and through our educational systems and practices. Yet, the field of EAP appears to have struggled at times with situating social justice within its sphere of activity, which in some instances is often remedial and reactionary to external demands.

One means of integrating a more purposeful sense of social justice into the activity of EAP teaching could be to develop a new philosophical perspective of socially-just assessment practices. Assessment's role in nurturing learning, as well as establishing standards, means it needs to be in the vanguard of EAP's commitment to social justice. Achieving the broad educational social justice ambitions that we are committed to, requires fundamental rethinking of our assessment values, practices and policies. Therefore, this chapter provides an introduction to assessment for social justice by exploring the importance of thinking of our students from the perspective of their whole self and their social membership. It argues that individual and social wellbeing are intrinsically aligned, as argued by many critical theorists (Honneth 2004), and this should influence how we think about assessment, and its relationship to diversity, inclusion and social justice.

Thus, the chapter combines the idea of assessment for social justice with an holistic sense of inclusion (McArthur 2021) that focuses not on discrete categories to label a student, but considers who they can become through the experience of engaging with learning; what sort of member of society and in what ways can they fulfil their own potential. Even well-meaning forms of support for different student categories, such as international students, can silo students into this one identity and obscure our understanding of the whole student, made up of many more experiences than simply being an international student (which of course, is itself a term that is based on a particular perspective).

Rejecting any deficit notions of language learning, we must embrace everything that a student brings with them when they enter an EAP context. This 'chameleon discipline' (Breen 2018) has been described as the poor relation to other academic disciplines in higher education (Hamp-Lyons 2011; Breen 2019). Undoubtedly related to this perceived status is the problem that what students lack (i.e. certain English language abilities) is foregrounded far more than in other disciplines. We do not think of a first year biology student as lacking knowledge, we think of them as here to gain knowledge. This perspective follows through to assessment systems, where EAP assessors are often forced into gatekeeping roles, reflecting the external standards set by government or institutions (Pearson 2021).

There are many social justice issues when we consider EAP in higher education, not least the fact that many universities have built business models based on the financial revenue from international students (Pearson 2021). EAP educators also know well the challenges of working in the context of English language dominance in global higher education. This can make a lack of English language appear to be aberrant behaviour; a moral failure. Instead, we must ensure we reinforce the legitimacy of students who come from different cultures and language traditions, while also supporting them to add English language to their many existing achievements. This must always be a two-way encounter, and thus it may require us to be responsive to different traditions and understandings of the English language. Many EAP teachers work in a broader context where they know that certain forms of English are regarded as more prestigious, often in conflict with other forms that are more accessible and attuned to local cultures (Alimi 2011). But the concept of prestige is exclusionary and serves little educational function. As we begin to understand assessment in terms of the student as a whole, and what they bring and learn, and not simply what they do not know, then the illusion of prestige is further dissipated.

My work on assessment for social justice is grounded in a belief in the cooperative nature of social life and of learning. This asserts the strong interrelationship between individual and social wellbeing, so that both are implicated in the realisation of the other. Assessment should cease to become a discrete task that generates an empty signifier of achievement in the form of traditional grades. Assessment for social justice connects the individual wellbeing of each unique student, with the sense of achievement they should gain as they learn and have that learning evaluated. In addition, at different stages of that learning students should be able to see their achievements in the context of their social membership; as representing different ways they contribute to the social whole, as this is also essential to their individual wellbeing. This may be through work, but it equally could be through bringing joy, happiness, kindness or care in other ways. EAP students often feel the need to reinforce their membership of their home society (which may be their inspiration for studying abroad) and a sense of belonging in the place they are studying; in both places the need for each individual to feel valued by others is fundamental.

Traditional forms of assessment can reinforce a sense of otherness, emphasising externally determined standards of English over which the international student has no control. Socially-just assessment celebrates the student as a whole person, and allows them to bring their experiences, culture, passions and creativity into the learning and assessment activities. This chapter will therefore explore how the idea of assessment for social justice can inform broader work to position the activity of EAP in line with such a philosophical perspective.

Assessment for social justice

As the phrase implies, assessment for social justice is born out of the hugely significant work on assessment for learning. Though hopefully we may now take the learning role of assessment for granted, this was far from the case going back even a few decades. Early significant writers in this field included Knight (1995), Samball and McDowell (1998), Hounsell (2003) Boud and Falchikov (2007). The work of such scholars did not just change our understanding of assessment, but they laid the way for us to *change* assessment even though work still remains to be done in this area. Traditional forms of assessment remain in place, often with little reflection or reconsideration of their purpose or validity. Even the huge disruption of the Covid pandemic did not really lead to the rethinking hoped for, as the rise of exam proctoring software demonstrates. Some desperately looked for an online solution to not having the traditional, time-limited exam in a huge hall, without ever reflecting on whether the assessment task was the right one in the first place. A sense of this is captured in the words drawn from critical theory in another context: it is simply 'the passive acceptance of what is merely the case' (Adorno 2001: 121).

My work in this field began simply enough with the thought: if assessment shapes learning and if we see learning through a social justice lens, then surely we need to think more about the role assessment plays in that social justice? The idea is not simply for 'just' assessment but also for assessment that nurtures a disposition to social justice: one that connects an understanding of knowledge learned with its social role and application. Also, assessment for social justice must be inclusive of all involved in the assessment processes: students, professional services staff and of course academics who are often employed on precarious contracts within the world of EAP, particularly in pre-sessional teaching situations.

With assessment for social justice, I draw, in different ways, on first and third generation critical theory (Habermas represents the second generation). From the first generation of Horkheimer and Adorno I take their visceral revelations of how so much injustice can be hidden in plain sight: what actions do we all currently do as teachers and assessors that we take for granted are just (or do not even think about it), when they may be quite the opposite? I also take a sense of what I term 'radical pessimism' from Horkheimer and Adorno. This may seem a strange idea when our aspiration is greater social justice, however, this reminder of how hard genuine, transformative change is, remains salutatory. It provides the safeguard against feel-good interpretations of social justice and wellbeing; tinkering initiatives that seem a good idea but ultimately do not address the fundamental issues of social injustice, and in some cases can make things worse.

To these influences I add that of third generation, Axel Honneth. Honneth is important because his work looks to provide a complex, yet relatively clear, conceptualisation of social justice that avoids the trap of a neat definition, and hence provides a really useful framework that, I argue, helps us avoid those well-meaning but pointless feel-good buzz words, terms and initiatives. Key to Honneth's understanding of social justice is its focus on mutual recognition and its plural nature, so that we do not say social justice is one thing, but rather understand it through a network of mutually reinforcing facets. Mutual recognition is a foundational idea in critical theory and has its roots in Hegelian philosophy. Such recognition emphasises the social nature of individual being, such that we truly become human when we are recognised as such by others, and as we recognise this in others. It leads to a strong sense of this mutual interconnectedness of individual and social wellbeing.

Honneth explores this through three dimensions that can be teased apart for purposes of discussion, but which are in reality deeply connected. The first is recognition of love. This is particular in nature, focusing on a basic sense of being loved and valued within individual relationships, such as that of father and son. Respect recognition is, by contrast, a universal form as it applies in the same way to everyone. This is the recognition born out of universal rights which we are able to understand and use, and in so doing, being meaningful members of civic society. In this sense, such a dimension could be applied to the participation of international students in the broader life of universities and the value accorded to their pre-existing linguistic or cultural experiences. Finally, esteem recognition is an individual form in that it relates to the knowledge, skills, dispositions and actions we each have as individuals, but which form our contribution to the wellbeing of others. Social justice requires forms of social organisation and interactions where all three forms of recognition can flourish, and where we minimise acts of misrecognition.

Assessment for social justice takes Honneth's realms of recognition and considers how they may apply in the context of assessment. The application of Honneth's thinking to a very specific area provides a framework through which we can reflect on how and why we assess through a social justice lens. Traditionally, assessment is known to serve at least three, if not many more functions: certification of a standard reached; promotion of learning; and the development of a capacity for future learning (Boud 2000). In the EAP context, the first and third are often those prioritised to the greatest extent perhaps.

Furthermore, while these purposes can be complementary, they are not always so, and hence we can see that what counts as 'just' in an assessment context is multi-faceted and varied. Similarly, when assessing for different purposes we may put more or less emphasis on different aspects of Honneth's plural theory of recognition. In order to demonstrate the ways this can be done, I have highlighted five values or commitments that should frame how we conceive assessment practices (see McArthur 2018). This is far from an exhaustive list, but is offered instead as an exemplar of how to rethink assessment through the lens of social justice.

Nurturing social justice through assessment in EAP

In this section I will demonstrate some possible ways of rethinking EAP assessment within a broader commitment to social justice. Assessment's relationship to social justice takes many forms, including justice of the marking system to students and staff and the dispositions of caring for others nurtured by the forms of assessment we choose. For example, highly competitive forms of assessment and grading reinforce a sense of educational achievement as an individual competitive one, rather than one of cooperation and learning through our interactions with others. IELTS for example is a highly individualised testing system, whilst such pedagogic approaches as the use of Academic Literacies in an EAP context are shaped around a sense of being part of a wider community. In the case of the latter, it is also not just a case of being socialised into that community but of being an active participant in the shaping and even transformation of it.

This sense of transformation also lies at the heart of social practice philosophical perspectives. Social practice theorist Theodore Schatzki (2002) uses an idea he calls 'general understandings' to describe the senses of worth that shape particular practices. For example, artisan craftspeople place a great sense of worth in crafting objects by hand, and this shapes the practices of how they make bowls or chairs, and the like. I suggest that in an assessment context, if we nurtured five senses of worth these would help shape transformations in our practices and contribute to greater social justice. My five concepts are not intended as the definitive list, but rather as examples of how nurturing a certain sense of worth could help nurture other ways of thinking about and doing assessment. These concepts should also be commensurate with the EAP context where there is a recognisable need to progress from a culture of deficit, remedy, correction and policing of error.

My five senses of worth are: trust, honesty, responsibility, forgiveness and responsiveness. These are not necessarily discrete concepts, and instead offer different and reinforcing perspectives on more socially just practices. For example, trust and honesty are, in some ways, opposite sides of the same coin, and each has links to love recognition in being the foundations of recognising a person as someone of basic worth; someone capable of honesty and trustworthiness. Trust and honesty relate to love recognition, by the intimate relational nature of what they imply. Assessment is a pedagogical relationship, and pedagogical relationships without any foundation in trust and honesty are fraught.

What particularly concerns me in an assessment context is that both these values have become largely one-directional: we ask students to trust us to mark their work, devoting the appropriate amount of time and resources, and yet we embed systems of obvious mistrust at the heart of assessment and call such distrust 'common sense'. We expect students to have integrity and academic honesty, and yet we are rarely honest with students about the real conditions under which we assess their work (unpaid teaching assistants, marking through the night to meet deadlines, etc.). Responsibility relates to respect recognition, with a focus on the capacity students have to learn about the processes by which they are assessed, and to exercise judgement and choice based on that knowledge. Forgiveness and responsiveness relate to esteem recognition, with a focus on how students are able to demonstrate their unique abilities to contribute to society, and to be recognised for this contribution by others and by themselves.

Trust

Communication is based on trust: we trust people to interpret our words in the ways they are intended, cognisant of accepted norms and practices. Without this trust, language breaks down, because if we explain the meaning of every word or phrase, they cease to have either utility or joy. Issues of trust are compounded when communicating in another language; there are gaps in the knowledge of those accepted norms and practices, years of socialisation into the language may be missing, and furthering one's learning will rely on being able to make mistakes. When viewed through an assessment prism, we have long known that students learn better in low stakes contexts rather than high stakes contexts (Knight 1995). There are many ways of creating the right environment, but crucial to all is this sense of trust, because if students do not believe it really is low stakes, then they inevitably acquire the stress of the high stakes environment. Trust is not an optional extra in any pedagogical or even human relationship, and does not become one just because of a formal assessment context. In previous work on assessment for social justice and trust (McArthur 2018), I focused on plagiarism software and the messages of institutionalised distrust that it embeds in the pedagogical relationship. Added to this, such software is an ineffective way of evaluating students' writing competency and understandings of academic integrity.

In the EAP context, plagiarism has taken on a particular significance (Abasi and Graves 2008; Divan et al. 2015; Merkel 2020), and not least because international/non-native speaking students are often positioned as more likely to plagiarise (Fatemi and Saito 2020). At the heart of this common, but not necessarily correct, view of EAP students, is a problem that has plagued higher education ever since we allowed software detection companies to lure us into a plagiarism detection approach to academic writing. This has meant that the term plagiarism has been over-used and wrongly used, and international and EAP students have been disproportionately affected. Plagiarism is an intentional act of passing someone else's work off as your own in order to deceive, and yet we report plagiarism, warn students and convene plagiarism panels when we often know that the student simply has poor writing and/or poor referencing skills. Add to that poor note taking when reading and collecting information for an assignment, and the student is in real trouble ensuring their writing approach meets our standards of attribution.

The entire higher education sector has done unspeakable harm by allowing the term plagiarism to be applied to well-meant but poor academic writing, where there is no intention to deceive. Indeed our responses to poor academic writing in the context of referencing, citations and working with the work of others, is entirely different to our response to poor analysis or a lack of critical interpretation. Neither of these academic problems get labelled with a term that implies almost criminal wrong-doing. And here the EAP student gets the double injustice of trying to establish their work within an unfamiliar context and being criminalised for making mistakes.

Calling for greater assessment trust, does not mean we cease to care about academic integrity. Indeed, I would argue that by getting rid of the distractions caused by multi-million pound plagiarism companies, we would be able to genuinely nurture greater integrity in our academic practices. What trust means in this context is firstly to trust that an international student's actions may credibly be based in their having different experiences to what they encounter as 'international' students. Trust transforms the issue of academic writing from one of policing to one of education. I am regularly dismayed by the depiction of certain nationalities as students who tend to collude, while we also have research and policies that promote peer learning and collaborative group work. We must ensure that similar practices are not viewed as peer learning when done by home students, but collusion when done by international students.

What I am suggesting here as a change in the way we think goes beyond simply providing more support for international students to help them avoid 'plagiarism'. Velliaris and Breen (2016), for example, outline an approach to academic integrity in an EAP context that helpfully makes a clear distinction between poor referencing skills and deliberate deception. This is welcome, and we need more of this within EAP assessment processes to ensure we can build the trust to nurture student learning and success – and to minimise fear. I am concerned, however, by approaches such as this one that are built around plagiarism detection software. In this case, despite the progressive distinction between poor writing and deliberate cheating, which then informs the academics' interpretation of Turnitin originality reports, there is a deliberate decision not to share such reports with students. Teachers are asking students to trust them in their interpretation of reports that exist because of a distrust of student approaches to study.

Trust has to be two-way. We ask students for trust when we assess their work: trust in our professionalism, work ethic and interest in their wellbeing. Poor academic writing (which can show up as so-called plagiarism) is an acknowledged problem in the field of EAP (Velliaris and Breen 2016). However, reliance on detection software puts us in an arms race we can never win or finish, and can be counter-productive. In the spirit of assessment for social justice, we build strong relationships of trust, which nurture student learning about academic writing and referencing, rather than terrorising them with fear of being caught doing something they poorly understand. This is not the only solution, and we still require work on deliberate cheating, as Dawson (2020) has outlined. But here too trust is essential in assessment: students should be able to trust us to demonstrate an understanding between not knowing how to do something unfamiliar and cheating.

Building trust in the pre-sessional contexts of EAP is particularly difficult, given that assessment sometimes works as a proxy for visa compliance (Pearson 2021). Students under threat of deportation are unlikely to settle easily into relationships of trust, nor move beyond the high stakes anxiety of assessment. In one instance, (Pearson 2017), a student named Kyle explains the situation: 'I cannot feel part of this city because I might be excluded any time I fail an exam' (ibid.: 173). Didactic approaches of telling international students about the evils of plagiarism also do nothing to explain to them what is really meant. It privileges a western value of individual ownership without providing any explanation (Pearson 2021). By focusing simply on not plagiarising, traditional assessment approaches offer little to help international students through the processes of working with multiple texts and sources. But use of developmental portfolios has enabled international students to learn for themselves, by the nature and importance of keeping a record of where ideas came from. This also helped them move beyond competitive notions of learning and enjoy the benefits of peer learning. The study also showed that this process of moving beyond ideas of competition took longer for some students, and most importantly that the benefits of peer feedback and/or assessment could only become evident once relationships of trust were already established.

Honesty

What is meant by the 'English' component of the acronym EAP, or even in the wider field of contemporary English language teaching in general, in a world of multiple Englishes? This is surely a fundamental question when we assess students on academic work written in the medium of English. It may seem a silly question to those outside the field, but within EAP the issue of what counts as English is well known as a heavily contested one. Moreover, the stakes are high in terms of what gets to count as English, with clear distinctions of prestige and opportunity often attached to different forms of written or spoken English. When we assess students we make decisions about which forms of English to privilege, and it is unjust not to be honest with students about the fact that we make such a decision. What is legitimised as appropriate English is not inevitable nor necessary – it reflects a choice we make.

Clearly this issue interconnects with the honesty required to acknowledge that English has been the language of colonisers and the language of epistemic violence. I will return to this, but want to focus first on a slightly different angle. Alimi (2011) discusses how English is both the language of colonisers and oppression, but also a language which different groups can, through the exercise of the agency they now have, make their own in many different ways. He argues that the standard English of many EAP exams in countries such as his own, Botswana, enable a minority to take up the privileges of a university education and other positions of prestige, but it is not the language that most students will go on to use and need to live their lives. Why do we assess students on a form of English which is not the form they need to communicate in their everyday lives (Alimi 2011)?

When I discussed honesty in my book on assessment for social justice, I emphasised honesty about how we grade, such as the illusion of precision generated by marking out of 100 per cent. Studies such as that by Romios et al. (2020) have raised similar issues in the EAP context, in this case looking at how honest we are with students about the use of high stakes, traditional, exams even when we know they have little pedagogical value. In the UK context, we have a further issue of honesty around the very purposes of EAP education and assessment. As Pearson (2021) explains, while many EAP educators have a progressive and inclusive approach that is about more than generic linguistic skills, they are forced to assess in a government-mandated way that simply looks to measure a basic competence. This completely ignores the rich learning experience that the EAP teacher may have nurtured. This point further highlights the important fact that assessment for social justice requires practices that are just for all involved, including teachers (McArthur 2018).

Responsibility

Respect recognition necessitates recognition of someone as a capable and informed citizen, cognizant of the rights they share with others. In an assessment context we can align this with what is often termed assessment literacy, although I find that term somewhat problematic. Put simply, we afford misrecognition if we place students in an assessment context in which procedures and practices of assessment are not clear to them and understood. Positioning this responsibility in terms of respect recognition ensures it is understood as a relational issue, as is the capacity to take an informed part in civic life. Thus, putting information in a handbook does not ensure we enable genuine responsibility in our students. What relationship do we build with students so that they feel confident that they understand how they are assessed, and can ask for clarification, or even change, when it is unclear?

I conceive assessment responsibility as about having the knowledge of processes and practices to genuinely make decisions about one's own assessment choices, and hence learning. My focus to date has therefore been on student responsibility. It is a key feature of assessment for social justice, however, that assessment must be just for all involved, including academic staff. Returning to Alimi's work on English language instruction in Botswana, he makes the point that the privileging of standard English has impaired many teachers' ability to take genuine ownership and responsibility for what they do: 'Hitherto, many educated Africans, including teachers of English, have been unable to take ownership of the African varieties of English primarily for lack of confidence' (Alimi 2011: 320).

If we think back to Honneth's three realms of recognition, the need to know the status and purpose of the form of language that is assessed is not only an issue of rights recognition, but also esteem recognition. Many student achievements may be under-valued or misunderstood because they do not conform to pre-determined decisions about English language. But esteem recognition is all about making unique contributions that nurture the wellbeing of others. As Alimi discusses, many of these contributions will be made possible through knowledge of local forms of English, not a remote standardised form.

In previous work, I considered responsibility also in terms of students' knowledge of how assessment works, and highlighted the crucial role that peer and self-assessment can play in growing understanding, hence confidence and responsibility. In an EAP context, Duque Micán and Cuesta Medina (2017) explain the importance of students being actively in control of their own learning, but highlight the problematic nature of this when students are given few chances to develop the abilities required to do so. Duque Micán and Cuesta Medina demonstrate how self-assessment is an important way of developing this sense of control, and hence in my terms, responsibility over their own learning. The authors argue that in language learning, self-assessment is particularly important for providing a safe place, with low stakes and less anxiety. As students set their own goals they are more likely, and easily, to develop control and responsibility over their learning, rather than in a high-stakes environment, where all the factors of success are externally imposed.

Pearson's (2021) study on using processfolios to emphasis the learning journey rather than outcome in assessment, also demonstrated a greater opportunity for students to make agentic decisions and choices about their learning along that journey. This includes some students being able to understand the marking criteria in order to make choices about what to do in their work. But Pearson also found that some others demonstrated what Torrance (2007) has named 'criteria compliance'. This demonstrates an essential aspect of Honneth's respect recognition. It comes not from simply knowing that one has certain rights, but in understanding the nature and meaning of those rights and being able to use them with freedom and agency. Put this in an assessment context, and having knowledge of marking criteria does not itself lead to responsibility or agency, if it simply engenders an attitude of compliance.

Understanding responsibility in an assessment context also highlights issues of power, and clearly in the field of language learning the colonial legacy of English impacts on power relationships. Welply (2022) found that students were particularly clear that assessment was an area in which 'the reproduction of forms of domination through institutional systems was particularly acute' (p. 76). He argues that the lack of attention to assessment in a decolonial/social justice context appears to arise from the complexity of bringing language assessment and mainstream assessment together. Indeed, Welply's analysis suggests that language assessment highlights many of the core shortcomings in mainstream assessment, particularly failure to account for 'multiple forms of literacy or oracy' (p. 78). This echoes the earlier work of Alimi (2011) and Nguyet Luu (2023) in this publication. EAP students will struggle to take responsibility for their own learning when the version of the language chosen for instruction differs from the norm where they have come from, and may well plan to return.

Forgiveness

The concept of forgiveness is particularly important in an English language context because learning a language, or a set of language conventions in the case of EAP, entails a lot of mistakes in the course of the journey. Our formal education systems, however, often stigmatise and penalise errors made in the process of learning. This is very unhelpful and self-defeating but it becomes particularly acute in an assessment context. While we as academics make clear distinctions between formative and summative assessment, they may not be so clear in students' minds, nor in their psyches that have been shaped by a competitive society where winning and getting things right are valorised over so much else.

Forgiving assessment approaches start by rejecting a deficit view of the fact that students do not know some things. An education is about acquiring learning, and lack of knowledge does not equate to weakness. This sense of moving away from expectations of students being fully equipped with a knowledge base at the outset is particularly pertinent to EAP. Pre-sessional courses in particular are front loaded and pre-packaged with very little personalised or tailored focus on individual student needs. However, such work as that of Pearson (2021) challenges these notions by focusing on the student journey as understood by the student themselves. By making an assessment about a journey over time and not one discrete moment of demonstrating a piece of knowledge, it embraces a culture of forgiveness in knowledge construction. As this study demonstrates, the culture of forgiveness is closely connected to one of low stakes approaches to assessment. Some of Pearson's students reported a reduction in stress/high stakes feelings once they realised their focus could be on the process and not a single end product.

Responsiveness

I conceive of responsiveness as both an understanding of what the student brings to an assessment task – so, responsive to the student – and a responsiveness to the social world where the student's learning takes meaning. Thus the interrelationship between individual and social wellbeing is also at the heart of this idea. The urgent challenge for EAP assessment practices is the recognition of the place of English in systems of linguistic domination. Indeed, Welply argues that English-speaking countries maintain a dual system of linguistic domination both internally and the perpetuation of colonialism through English as the lingua franca of capitalist systems (2022: 65).

Responsiveness in EAP assessment practices ought to be shaped by a stronger sense of how the assessment reflects the worlds in which the students exist. This might mean a shift in focus towards seeking out a more socially-just integration of their existing linguistic and cultural backgrounds. For example, Alimi (2011: 138) argues that if 'New Englishes benefit their users culturally and socioeconomically and they appropriately depict their experiences' then their use should be acceptable in learning and assessment situations. Surely students cannot reach their full potential if there is such a rigid communication demarcation between the place of study and the place of other life, with one seen as innately superior.

Mortenson (2022) challenges the EAP community to reflect more on their past complicity with colonial and Western-centric perspectives that unproblematically position English as the dominant language. She claims that 'historically EAP programs have tended to employ inauthentic, oftentimes outdated, materials' (p. 2). While acknowledging advances, she still contends that 'there has been minimal research into the adoption of critical, social justice-oriented content' (p. 2). To challenge this, she conducts an exploration of students' engagement with a text that powerfully challenges white, colonial perspectives. She places enormous emphasis on the pedagogy of teaching with this text and students' responses and perspectives. The context of the study *is* students preparing a piece of work for assessment, however it is worth noting that *nowhere* does Mortenson directly address the social justice implications of this being *assessed* work. One might reasonably say that assessment itself was not Mortenson's focus, and that is reasonable up to a point. But equally, approaches such as assessment for social justice emphasise the importance of always recognising the particular social justice implications in acts of assessment. For example, there are issues of power which can lead to compliance. While the students in this study magnificently challenged Western-oriented, colonial assumptions and began to see and understand suffering in a new light, as Mortenson herself concedes, they were not challenging her beliefs. To be clear, I am not criticising this exemplary piece of social justice research. I am, however, using it as an example of the tendency not to problematise assessment through a social justice lens, other than references to fairness, which themselves are often narrow and procedural (McArthur 2016, 2018).

Conclusion

EAP faces many challenges as it works to establish firmer foundations in social justice understandings of education and learning. Tackling assessment at the same time may seem a challenge too far, because in any context assessment is notoriously resistant to meaningful change. But really there is no choice. EAP teachers cannot ignore assessment when they seek to change teaching and learning, because the three are inextricably linked. Assessment carries messages to students about what teachers value. As such it can perpetuate stereotypes, ignorance, prejudice and misunderstandings. It is only when we think of our students holistically, and extend this to the realm of assessment, that we can truly understand how they behave and what they can achieve. Students enter EAP with rich histories and many achievements. We need assessment to celebrate this rather than try to obscure it in the name of uniformity as fairness. We need to think more about the aspirations of our students to understand how we design assessment practices to enable them to flourish.

None of this diminishes how difficult it is to change assessment practices and the sensitive position of EAP teachers where their work is linked to visa compliance and other external metrics. But the idea of what sense of worth we bring into our assessment practices is meant to demonstrate that small changes can have a huge significance for students, and teachers. Reinforcing pedagogical relationships in an assessment context and seeing the students as a whole person, move our practices on more than we realise. Greater social justice can seem an impossible goal, or we can try to find it in everyday practices and ways of learning and teaching – and assessing – together. If that can be done in such a specific context as EAP, then there are surely important lessons within this for the wider academy.

References

Abasi, A. R., and Graves, B. (2008), 'Academic Literacy and Plagiarism: Conversations with International Graduate Students and Disciplinary Professors', *Journal of English for Academic Purposes*, 7(4): 221–33. Available online: https://doi.org/10.1016/j.jeap.2008.10.010 (accessed 8 August 2023).

Adorno, T. W. (2001), *Kant's Critique of Pure Reason (1959)*, Cambridge: Polity.

Ajjawi, R., Tai, J., Boud, D. and Jorre de St Jorre, T. eds (2023), *Assessment for Inclusion in Higher Education*, London and New York: Taylor and Francis.

Alimi, M. (2011), 'Botswana English: Implications for English Language Teaching and Assessment', *Journal of Multilingual and Multicultural Development*, 32(4): 309–24. Available online: https://doi.org/10.1080/01434632.2011.574700 (accessed 8 August 2023).

Boud, D. (2000), 'Sustainable Assessment: Rethinking Assessment for the Learning Society', *Studies in Continuing Education*, 22(2): 151–67.

Boud, D., and Falchikov, N., eds (2007), *Rethinking Assessment in Higher Education*, Abingdon: Routledge.

Breen, P. (2019), 'Positioning an Academic Literacies Framework in an EAP Context: Case Study of a University Pre-sessional Course', *Journal of Learning Development in Higher Education* 15: 1–15. Available online: https://doi.org/10.47408/jldhe.v0i15.553 (accessed 8 August 2023).

Dawson, P. (2020), *Defending Assessment Security in a Digital World: Preventing e-Cheating and Supporting Academic Integrity in Higher Education*, Milton Keynes: Taylor and Francis Group. Available online: http://ebookcentral.proquest.com/lib/lancaster/detail.action?docID=6340937 (accessed 8 August 2023).

Divan, A., Bowman, M. and Seabourne, A. (2015), 'Reducing Unintentional Plagiarism Amongst International Students in the Biological Sciences: An Embedded Academic Writing Development Programme', *Journal of Further and Higher Education*, 39(3): 358–78. Available online: https://doi.org/10.1080/0309877X.2013.858674 (accessed 8 August 2023).

Duque Micán, A. and Cuesta Medina, L. (2017), 'Boosting vocabulary learning through Self-Assessment in an English Language Teaching Context', *Assessment and Evaluation in Higher Education*, 42(3): 398–414. Available online: https://doi.org/10.1080/02602938.2015.1118433 (accessed 8 August 2023).

Fatemi, G. and Saito, E. (2020), 'Unintentional Plagiarism and Academic Integrity: the Challenges and Needs of Postgraduate International Students in Australia', *Journal of Further and Higher Education*, 44(10): 1305–19. Available online: https://doi.org/10.1080/0309877X.2019.1683521 (accessed 8 August 2023).

Hanesworth, P., Bracken, S. and Elkington, S. (2019), A Typology for a Social Justice Approach to Assessment: Learning from Universal Design and Culturally Sustaining Pedagogy', *Teaching in Higher Education*, 24(1): 98–114.

Honneth, A. (2004), 'A Social Pathology of Reason: on the Intellectual Legacy of Critical Theory', in F. Rush (ed.), *The Cambridge Companion to Critical Theory*, 336–60, New York: Cambridge University Press.

Hounsell, D. (2003), 'Student Feedback, Learning and Development', in M. Slowey and D. Watson (eds), *Higher Education and the Lifecourse*, 67–78, Maidenhead: Higher Education and Open University Press.

Knight, P. (1995), *Assessment for Learning in Higher Education*, London: Kogan Page.

McArthur, J. (2016), 'Assessment for Social Justice: the Role of Assessment in Achieving Social Justice', *Assessment and Evaluation in Higher Education*, 41(7): 967–81.

McArthur, J. (2018), *Assessment for Social Justice*, London: Bloomsbury.

McArthur, J. (2020), Assessment for Social Justice: Achievement, Uncertainty and Recognition', in C. Callender, W. Locke and S. Marginson (eds), *Changing Higher Education for a Changing World*, 144–56, London: Bloomsbury.

McArthur, J. (2021), 'The Inclusive University: a Critical Theory Perspective using a Recognition-Based Approach', *Social Inclusion*, 9(3): 6–15.

Merkel, W. (2020), 'A Case Study of Undergraduate L2 Writers' Concerns with Source-Based Writing and Plagiarism', *TESOL Journal*, 11(3): Available online: https://doi.org/10.1002/tesj.503 (accessed 8 August 2023).

Mortenson, L. (2022), 'Integrating Social Justice-Oriented Content into English for Academic Purposes (EAP) Instruction: a Case Study', *English for Specific Purposes*, 65: 1–14. Available online: https://doi.org/10.1016/j.esp.2021.08.002 (accessed 8 August 2023).

Pearson, J. (2017), 'Processfolio: Uniting Academic Literacies and Critical Emancipatory Action Research for Practitioner-Led Inquiry into EAP Writing Assessment', *Critical Inquiry in Language Studies*, 14(2–3): 158–81. Available online: https://doi.org/10.1080/15427587.2017.1279544 (accessed 8 August 2023).

Pearson, J. (2021), 'Assessment of Agency or Assessment for Agency?: a Critical Realist Action Research Study into the Impact of a Processfolio Assessment within UK HE Preparatory Courses for International Students', *Educational Action Research*, 29(2): 259–75. Available online: https://doi.org/10.1080/09650792.2020.1829496 (accessed 8 August 2023).

Romios, L., Ashadi, A. and Purbani, W. (2020), 'High-Stakes Testing Policy and English Language Teaching: Voices of the Leftovers', *JEFL (Journal on English as a Foreign Language)*, 10(2): 193–221. Available online: https://doi.org/10.23971/jefl.v10i2.2005 (accessed 8 August 2023).

Sambell, K. and McDowell, L. (1998), 'The Construction of the Hidden Curriculum: Messages and Meanings in the Assessment of Student Learning', *Assessment and Evaluation in Higher Education*, 23(4): 391–402.

Schatzki, T. R. (2002), *The Site of the Social: a Philosophical Account of the Constitution of Social Life and Change*, University Park, Penn.: Pennsylvania State University Press.

Tai, J., Ajjawi, R., Boud, D., Bearman, M., Jorre de St Jorre, T. and Dawson, P. (2021), *What is Assessment for Inclusion? Problematising Inclusion, Equity, and Access in Higher Education Assessment*. Discussion Paper for CRADLE Symposium 2021, Deakin University, Australia.

Torrance, H. (2007), 'Assessment as Learning? How the Use of Explicit Learning Objectives, Assessment Criteria and Feedback in Post-Secondary Education and Training can come to Dominate Learning. 1', *Assessment in Education : Principles, Policy and Practice*, 14(3): 281–94. Available online: https://doi.org/10.1080/09695940701591867 (accessed 8 August 2023).

Velliaris, D. M. and Breen, P. (2016), 'An Institutional Three-Stage Framework: Elevating Academic Writing and Integrity Standards of International Pathway Students', *Journal of International Students*, 6(2): 565–87. Available online: https://doi.org/10.32674/jis.v6i2.371 (accessed 8 August 2023).

Welply, O. (2022), 'English as an Additional Language (EAL): Decolonising Provision and Practice', *Curriculum Journal*, 34(1): 62–82. Available online: https://doi.org/10.1002/curj.182 (accessed 8 August 2023).

5

The White Gaze and Translanguaging: Getting Multilingual Students' Voices Heard

Nguyet Luu

Western and non-Western academic heritages do not necessarily inhabit two ends of the same spectrum. Indeed, their somewhat diverse approaches lead to a variety of intellectual tactics and complementary skills, generating an increased number of opportunities for identifying and solving complex problems from distinctive standpoints within modern academia. Though there has been a great deal of discussion about social justice in the Western educational context, the east and southeast Asian experience often seems to be overlooked. Social justice is generally framed through a Western-centric lens in the same way as language pedagogy is also generally framed through such a lens.

Throughout my educational life and career, I have been angered by how Vietnamese and other east Asian students are perceived through the gaze of 'whiteness' as in Gillborn (2019). In such a definition, that 'whiteness' is differentiated from 'white people' as individuals by 'locating Whiteness in embodied actions, underlying prejudices, and biases that ultimately benefit white people' (Mortenson 2022: 2). Therefore, when looking at Vietnamese students, that whiteness is seen in perceptions of their Eastern collectivistic culture as hampering the structural efficacy of an autonomous learning environment (Murray 2022).

My past working experience initiated my curiosity for a more suitable position to better question the potential limitations of pervading theoretical concepts currently metaphorically tied to the ideology of individualism or Western philosophy. I have experience working in cross-cultural environments with the US Embassy in Hanoi and with Atlantic, a leading Vietnamese educational company, which allowed me to apply my knowledge base in academic literacy pedagogy and socio-cultural influences towards real-life scenarios (Lea and Street 1998). I have coordinated discourse between Anglophone educational specialists and Vietnamese teachers while proactively negotiating the differences between their two seemingly contrasting pedagogical viewpoints (Maha Sripathy 2007; Imada 2012).

The cultural lens of individualistic–collective cultures appear to problematise certain students' writing practices, generating negative internalised feelings for students of the non-prevalent culture. Acting in my leader position with Atlantic, I headed up an initiative to incorporate more cultural awareness lessons into the curriculum, which intended to better facilitate student understanding surrounding cultural identities. The initiative assisted with highlighting several drawbacks inherent within the current approaches. The principal identifiable element causing a combination of confusion and internalised inferiority amongst the students, was observed to be created through cultural-tagging teaching practices, and especially the linguistic-specific requests for students' writing practices. Interestingly, I also witnessed students being faced with similar occurrences when I was delivering English academic writing workshops at Thang Long University.

In hindsight, differences are among the root causes of inequality. It is well-exemplified in the UK's education-emigration context, where multilingual students are encouraged to leave behind their multilingual knowledge and academic skills to be better recognised. In detail, during the process, students, or more often multilingual students, are often given options to leave out parts of their identities and take up new linguistic repertoire. It happened to me when I read my Master's degree in TESOL in 2020; I was introduced to an exhaustive list of metadiscourse features and academic vocabulary, which were supposed to shape my academic voice.

Eventually, I found myself confused with a limited linguistic repertoire and ambiguous requirements upon projecting my academic voice. My autobiographical self as a collectivistic writer was problematised as potentially problematic via the cultural lens of individualistic–collective cultures. For example, Hyland (2002) posited that writers employ different rhetorical strategies to signal their presence and contributions, which accordingly constitute the authorial voice. Among these rhetorical choices, self-mention is first named as a powerful option for writers to claim their authorship yet constrained by disciplinary conventions. And pedagogical approaches, according to which students from collectivistic cultures, for example, who resort to employing self-mention, should be encouraged not to follow their writing practices (Hyland 2002) and would advocate the stratification of the individualistic and collective voice. This, accordingly, problematises cultural assumptions and possibly excludes second-language writers (Tardy 2016).

Additionally, it is important to acknowledge the interplay between writer-students and reader-assessors and the role reader-assessors play in constructing student-writers' identity (Matsuda 2015). Burgess and Ivanič (2010) share the same perspective via the concept of 'perceived writer'. This concept refers to the readers' impressions of the writers, created while reading. Such impressions could be constructed within microgenetic time (seconds, minutes, hours) and last for mesolevel time (weeks, months, years) or even persist over the lifetime of the readers who create them. In other words, the writers' representation depends significantly on the readers' interpretations, which could be multiple, based on the readers' selections of 'particular discoursal characteristics in the design of their texts' (Burgess and Ivanič 2010: 235). This, hence, could build up contradictory impressions of the writers (Ivanič 1998; Burgess and Ivanič 2010), especially when writers and readers are from different backgrounds with different discursive practices (Matsuda 2001), as in the case of multilingual students.

In the institutional context, international students' writing practices may expose themselves via their styles of writing and possible selections of certain discoursal characteristics, making them subject to marking bias (Fleming 1999). Similar circumstances were also observed in the case of senior academic writers when they sent their manuscripts to editors (Flowerdew 2000). Historically, up until now, non-native identities and non-conventional disciplines have been filtered and curated, which may negatively impact the evaluation of the presented content (Tardy and Matsuda 2009).

However, such metadiscourse pedagogical approaches could possibly reinforce the deductive and determinative pedagogy of teaching academic literacy (Bacon and Kim 2018). In that way, students' work is often curated or adjusted to the expectations of the readers and who their assessors are, generating the power relation gap attached to certain writing practices or certain linguistic features. In fact, pedagogical trends which encourage students to follow native speakers' writing norms have been challenged (Matsuda 2015; Lillis and Tuck 2016).

Moreover, that linguistic features are often simplified via a cultural lens as icons of either individualistic or collectivistic identity, as exemplified earlier, has worsened the situation. (Stapleton 2002; Zhao and Wu 2022). In other words, the ignorance of the varieties of English in the institutional context would feed into the multilingual students' feeling of inferiority (Phan and Baurain 2011) instead of empowering them, as suggested by Professor John Gray (2023) in the foreword section of this book. One example of difference in Eastern and Western thinking is in the sequencing and structuring of thoughts. In detail, the use of signposting – interactive metadiscourse (firstly, secondly, then. . .) to link ideas, and sentences and to create textual coherence and cohesion – is favoured in academic English over other approaches (Phan and Baurain 2011). In other words, the Vietnamese rhetorical strategy of constructing flows, according to which parts of the discussion held together would generate coherence and cohesion, is deemed non-academic and remedial in the Anglophone academic context. Hence, it could be argued that this practice of language remediation would give way to the privileging of English monolingualism, undermining the richness of multilingual students' linguistic repertoires and academic practices.

Hence, there has to be a movement or migration away from the ubiquitous idea of English as a second or foreign language as being a source of deficit. That migration perhaps needs to begin at a level of change in terminology. Often the labels of home student and international student are used in a way that places the latter outside of the mainstream higher educational community. By migrating towards a mindset of all students and all languages as having an equal place in higher education's teaching and learning environment, international students would become a main part of higher education's narrative and not just an appendix. This greater sense of inclusion would also enrich the overall resources of the higher educational community and would accordingly challenge the traditional approaches of how languages are contemporarily conceptualised as pre-determined practices and features linked with a bounded community (Blommaert and Rampton 2011). This also aligns with the current pedagogical trend that plurilingualism competence for language learners should be developed as positive values (Europarat 2020; García and Baetens Beardsmore 2009).

More effort should be made to challenge pedagogical approaches viewing Eastern students' linguistic repertoires as exotic or deficit. Lomer, Mittelmeier and Carmichael-Murphy (2021: 3) pointed out that international students, mostly Chinese students, are still more often tagged with deficit discourses as 'passive', 'lacking' or 'challenging', and less frequently with 'capable' in published literature. Such deficit narratives are impeding educators from performing inclusive pedagogic design, while other reasons for this delay in pedagogical innovation were said to be due to institutionally insufficient investment and support for research and experiments (ibid.). In this way, Eastern students, mostly Chinese, are often deemed the cash cow struggling to adapt during their study journey (Dong 2017), though they are contributing significantly to the UK's economy (Higher Education Statistics Authority (HESA) 2021).

At present, the hegemony of the deficit model means that even the term 'support' for international students is used in a corrective or remedial sense. However, a more meaningful and equitable form of support would be one of developing rather than correcting students' linguistic and cultural competence. That could be done/achieved via pedagogical approaches, such as translanguaging, which is reshaping the boundaries of languages (Wang 2022). Translanguaging in pedagogy and practice allows multilingual students to naturally and flexibly draw upon their entire repertoire embedded within their rich language, life and cultural experiences (Wei 2011). This, thus, empowers permeability across languages, and allows language users' to reinvent their multilingual repertoires to prioritise meaning-making in the knowledge acquisition process and facilitate social justice (Creese and Blackledge 2015; García and Leiva 2014).

However, it could be argued that the monolingual assessment system has made the provision of students' drawing in their experience of using other languages other than English, unwanted or not welcomed in the context of the Anglophone educational system (Costley and Leung 2020). Such a one-size-fits-all assessment approach has turned students' resources of languages other than English into a barrier to achieving 'good' performance (ibid.), resulting in multilingual students being 'exoticised' and encouraging feelings of inferiority, as mentioned above. Multilingual students' resources, on the other hand, could contribute equally in a more global and equitable discussion via a shift in assessment design. Accordingly, a greater emphasis on personalising the assessment – i.e. as simple as asking students to relate learning to their own national contexts wherever possible – may help cultivate related parties' realisation of different values. This, thus, promotes cross-institutional learning. In fact, such an approach is sometimes seen at PhD or Masters level, but more rarely at undergraduate level.

In practice, translanguaging would not necessarily mean employing all students' languages in both teaching/learning and assessment frameworks (Costley and Leung 2020). It could be as simple as encouraging students to engage with, and talk around, their own means of constructing knowledge, their textual practices and socio-cultural processes of writing (Lillis and Scott 2015). In this way, formative assessment approaches are recommended. These approaches require teachers to flexibly make responsive adaptations to students' learning progress as students elaborate on their dynamic and socially-constructed language practices (Ascenzi-Moreno 2018; McArthur et al. 2022). Students are, hence, given a safe translanguaging space to negotiate their comprehension and transform their knowledge, while revisiting their diverse linguistic repertoire in different parts of the assessment (ibid.).

Translanguaging is amongst the pedagogical approaches paving the way for the institutional effort to give values to non-prevalent languages (García and Leiva 2014). This is the first step for future changes in the nature of assessment in higher education, not subjecting Asian students to prejudices and Western-centric epistemologies. However, translanguaging is in its infancy and there are existing challenges to mainstream this pedagogy, particularly to accommodate students' wide multilingual language practices in an institutional context where linguistic diversity is high (Costley and Leung 2020). Hence, it is more urgent to call for more relevant parties' attention on assessment approaches due to the roles they play in shaping students and teachers' perception of multilingualism (ibid.). Likewise, questions about social justice should be raised about the prevalence of standardised tests like IELTS as gatekeepers for higher education in Anglophone universities (Hamid, Hardy and Reyes 2019). In sum, the use of sameness with a diverse group of students should be avoided as Anglophone universities should be encouraged to draw upon the rich resource of students' existing language repertoires instead.

References

Ascenzi-Moreno, L. (2018), 'Translanguaging and Responsive Assessment Adaptations', *Language Arts*, 95(6): 355–69.

Bacon, C. K. and Kim, S. Y. (2018) '"English is my Only Weapon": Neoliberal Language Ideologies and Youth Metadiscourse in South Korea', *Linguistics and Education*, 48:10–21. Available online: https://doi.org/10.1016/j.linged.2018.09.002 (accessed 15 January 2023).

Blommaert, J. and Rampton, B. (2011), 'Language and Superdiversity', *Diversities*, 13(2): 1–21.

Burgess, A. and Ivanič, R. (2010), 'Writing and Being Written: Issues of Identity Across Timescales', *Written Communication*, 27(2): 228–55. Available online: https://doi.org/10.1177/0741088310363447 (accessed 13 January 2023).

Costley, T. and Leung, C. (2020), 'Putting Translanguaging into Practice: A View from England', *System*, 92: 102270. Available online: https://doi.org/10.1016/j.system.2020.102270 (accessed 13 January 2023).

Creese, A. and Blackledge, A. (2015), 'Translanguaging and Identity in Educational Settings', *Annual Review of Applied Linguistics*, 35: 20–35. Available online: https://doi.org/10.1017/S0267190514000233 (accessed 13 January 2023).

Dong, Y. (2017), 'How Chinese Students Become Nationalist: their American Experience and Transpacific Futures', *American Quarterly*, 69(3): 559–67. Available online: https://doi.org/10.1353/aq.2017.0050 (accessed 15 January 2023).

Europarat, ed. (2020), *Common European Framework of Reference for Languages: Learning, Teaching, Assessment ; Companion Volume*, Strasbourg: Council of Europe Publishing.

Fleming, N. (1999), Biases in Marking Students' Written Work: Quality', in S. Brown & A. Glasner (eds), *Assessment Matters in Higher Education: Choosing and Using Diverse Approaches*, 83–92, Buckingham: Open University Press.

Flowerdew, J. (2000), 'Discourse Community, Legitimate Peripheral Participation, and the Nonnative-English-Speaking Scholar', *TESOL Quarterly*, 34(1): 127–50. Available online: https://doi.org/10.2307/3588099 (accessed 15 January 2023).

García, O. and Baetens Beardsmore, H. (2009), *Bilingual Education in the 21st Century: a Global Perspective*, Malden, Mass. and Oxford: Wiley-Blackwell.

García, O. and Leiva, C. (2014), 'Theorizing and Enacting Translanguaging for Social Justice', in A. Blackledge and A. Creese (eds), *Heteroglossia as Practice and Pedagogy*, 199–216, Dordrecht: Springer Netherlands. Available online: https://link.springer.com/10.1007/978-94-007-7856-6_11 (accessed 26 January 2023).

Gray, J. (2023), 'Foreword', in P. Breen and M. Le-Roux (eds), *Social Justice in EAP and ELT Contexts*, xvii–xxi, UK: Bloomsbury.

Hamid, M. O., Hardy, I. and Reyes, V. (2019), 'Test-Takers' Perspectives on a Global Test of English: Questions of Fairness, Justice and Validity', *Language Testing in Asia*, 9(1): 1-20. Available online: https://doi.org/10.1186/s40468-019-0092-9 (accessed 15 January 2023).

Higher Education Statistics Authority (HESA) (2021), 'Where do Students Come From?', *HESA,* 31 January 2023. Available online: https://www.hesa.ac.uk/data-and-analysis/students/where-from (accessed 15 January 2023).

Hyland, K. (2002), 'Authority and Invisibility', *Journal of Pragmatics*, 34(8): 1091–1112. Available online: https://doi.org/10.1016/S0378-2166(02)00035-8 (accessed 15 January 2023).

Ivanič, R. (1998) *Writing and Identity: the Discoursal Construction of Identity in Academic Writing*, Amsterdam: Benjamins.

Lillis, T. and Scott, M. (2015), 'Defining Academic Literacies Research: Issues of Epistemology, Ideology and Strategy', *Journal of Applied Linguistics and Professional Practice*, 4(1): 5–32. Available online: https://doi.org/10.1558/japl.v4i1.5 (accessed 11 January 2023).

Lillis, T. and Tuck, J. (2016), 'Academic Literacies: a Critical Lens on Writing and Reading in the Academy', in K. Hyland & P. Shaw (eds), *The Routledge Handbook of English for Academic Purposes*, 30–43, Routledge: Routledge Handbooks.

Lomer, S., Mittelmeier, J. and Carmichael-Murphy, P. (2021), *Cash Cows or Pedagogic Partners? Mapping Pedagogic Practices for and with International Students*, London: Society for Research in Higher Education.

Matsuda, P. (2015), 'Identity in Written Discourse', *Annual Review of Applied Linguistics*, 35: 140–59. Available online: https://doi.org/10.1017/S0267190514000178 (accessed 11 January 2023).

Matsuda, P. K. (2001), 'Voice in Japanese Written Discourse', *Journal of Second Language Writing*, 10(1–2): 35–53. Available online: https://doi.org/10.1016/S1060-3743(00)00036-9 (accessed 15 January 2023).

McArthur, J. et al. (2022), 'Student Perspectives on Assessment: Connections between Self and Society', *Assessment and Evaluation in Higher Education*, 47(5): 698–711. Available online: https://doi.org/ 10.1080/02602938.2021.1958748 (accessed 17 January 2023).

Phan, L.-H. and Baurain, B., eds (2011), 'The Writing and Culture Nexus: Writers' Comparisons of Vietnamese and English Academic Writing', in L.-H. Phan & B. Baurain (eds), *Voices, Identities, Negotiations, and Conflicts: Writing Academic English Across Cultures*, 23–40, Bingley: Emerald.

Stapleton, P. (2002), 'Critiquing Voice as a Viable Pedagogical Tool in L2 Writing: Returning the Spotlight to Ideas', *Journal of Second Language Writing*, 11(3): 177–90. Available online: https://doi.org/10.1016/S1060-3743(02)00070-X (accessed 15 January 2023).

Tardy, C. (2016), 'Voice and Identity', in R. M. Manchón & P. K. Matsuda (eds), *Handbook of Second and Foreign Language Writing*, 346–64, Boston: De Gruyter.

Tardy, C. M. and Matsuda, P. K. (2009), 'The Construction of Author Voice by Editorial Board Members', *Written Communication*, 26(1): 32–52. Available online: https://doi.org/10.1177/0741088308327269 (accessed 17 January 2023).

Wang, D. (2022), 'Translanguaging as a Social Justice Strategy: the Case of Teaching Chinese to Ethnic Minority Students in Hong Kong', *Asia Pacific Education Review*, 24(3): 473–86. Available online: https://doi.org/10.1007/s12564-022-09795-0 (accessed 13 January 2023).

Wei, L. (2011), 'Moment Analysis and Translanguaging Space: Discursive Construction of Identities by Multilingual Chinese Youth in Britain', *Journal of Pragmatics*, 43(5): 1222–35. Available online: https://doi.org/10.1016/j.pragma.2010.07.035 (accessed 17 January 2023).

Zhao, C. G. and Wu, J. (2022), 'Perceptions of Authorial Voice: Why Discrepancies Exist', *Assessing Writing*, 53: 100632. Available online: https://doi.org/10.1016/j.asw.2022.100632 (accessed 15 January 2023).

6

Becoming Socially Just Educators: A Trioethnographic Study of Exploring Professional Identity Through Dialogue, Ethics of Care and Creativity

Lorraine Mighty, Tomasz John and Iwona Winiarska-Pringle

Background

The initial idea for this research project emerged from critical incidents and subsequent discussions we experienced in our voluntary, public roles within the BALEAP English for Academic Purposes Social Justice Special Interest Group (EAP4SJ SIG). Examples of the critical incidents included receiving public and private challenges to what is meant by the term 'social justice', whether the concept is relevant to English for Academic Purposes and whether in some of the work we undertook we were centring the needs of one marginalised group over and above another. Some of these challenges were thoughtfully constructed and shared via email reflections on events we had hosted. Others manifested in anonymous mocking Padlet responses following an invitation for community members to respond to blog posts from colleagues sharing underrepresented perspectives within the field of English Language Teaching. All the challenges prompted reflection and discussion across our EAP4SJ SIG committee, and some acted as catalysts for further work.

In engaging with our work in the EAP4SJ SIG committee, we do so not from a position of being experts, but from a motivation to strive towards self-discovery and self-fulfilment professionally and personally. Our commitment to achieving this through public acts is underpinned by educational philosophies of scholarly activism which suggest that words, deeds and the responses to these can generate new and more socially just ways of being and doing in the world (Arendt 1998; hooks 1994; Kubota 2020; Lorde 2007). In addition, our work in this arena is one of our responses to a building call to action to EAP practitioners to step out of the margins and start to influence more widely within our higher education institutions and across the sector (Bond 2020; Ding and Bruce 2017).

Based on the above, we realise our work within the EAP4SJ SIG, and indeed this research project, could be perceived within the sphere of public pedagogy in that we seek to hold space for learning and unlearning situated beyond the formal structures offered by state-sanctioned education systems (Biesta 2012; Sandlin, Schultz and Burdick 2010). We are also mindful that public pedagogy can be conceptualised in many ways. Our interpretation aligns with that put forward by Biesta (2012) who suggests in his critique of differing interpretations that public pedagogy should reject the: '"politics of learning" i.e the tendency to turn social and political problems into learning problems, so that, through this, they become the responsibility of individuals rather than that they are seen as the concern of the collective' (ibid.: 693).

Instead, he positions pedagogy as the enactment of a concern for the public quality of human togetherness. Neither teaching nor learning are the aims of this approach. Instead, it is about creating space within which the spontaneity of public citizenship (Mihăilă et al. 2016) can manifest as a result of individuals feeling the freedom to share their opinions with their equals, and importantly, to be heard, in order to foster reflection, thought, judgement and action (Topolski 2008). The public pedagogue in such interactions is one who interrupts, with interruptions being a thought, experience, or event that challenges the homogeny of our being (Biesta 2012). It is such interruptions that have the potential to foster a citizenship of strangers within which plurality is preserved and actively pursued to ensure all members of the community feel recognised (Leubolt 2015, cited in Mihăilă et al. 2016) and free to disclose their distinct uniqueness in an effort to garner human togetherness in a common world (Gordon 2001, cited in Biesta 2012).

As a sub-group of the EAP4SJ SIG, three of us chose to explore our experiences as ELT/EAP practitioners focusing on critical moments in our careers which steered us towards social justice. When approaching this research project, we wanted to experiment with Biesta's (2012) interpretation of public pedagogy to see what it could offer us in our own learning and our educational practice. As a small group who have both convergent and divergent backgrounds and lived experience between us, we wanted to deepen our understanding of how the intersections of our personal identities have impacted on our professional identities and practice within the field of EAP and on our journey to becoming socially just educators.

Our guiding principles

At this point, we wish to transparently declare that this project was never driven by a quest for 'book knowledge'. To start from that point would have felt dehumanising on a project that is centred in the human togetherness of being, knowing and becoming. To truly understand the complexities of our identities, we knew very early on that we wanted to build our knowledge with and through each other using methods which would cultivate shared and individual understanding. With this in mind, and, building on the notion of an interrupter as key to a wholly democratic and ethical public pedagogy, we were immediately drawn to taking a dialogic approach (Bahktin 1981) to generating and analysing data.

Bahktin (1981), suggests that the opportunity for learning from and with each other presents itself because we each bring our own perspectives of the world, and all that is located within it, to our interactions. Consequently, our interpretations and associated articulation of the world are unique to us as individuals. A key reason for this is that the connotations of the language we use are derived from the specific historical, social, meteorological and physiological context within which our utterances take place, which Bahktin (ibid.) refers to as 'heteroglossia'. Bakhtin (ibid.) goes on to assert that this distinct language of each individual, will be seen by anyone else as *cuzoj*, which translates to 'alien' in English, and it is this 'alien-ness' to each other that makes dialogue possible. However, similar to the educational philosophies cited earlier, Bahktin (1981) suggests that to achieve active and engaged understanding of the *cuzoj* of others requires both listening and response as: 'Understanding comes to fruition only in the response. Understanding and response are dialectically merged and mutually condition each other, one is impossible without the other' (p.282).

Aligning our commitment to a dialogic approach, with a recognition that we were researching our emerging identities as social justice educators, we adopted duoethnography methodology in our research design. Developed by Sawyer and Norris (2013), duoethnography positions an ongoing dialogue between researchers at the centre of the research process. Similar to the notion of an interlocutor in public pedagogy, the dialogue is believed to generate opportunities for disrupting metacultural narratives, allowing the researchers to reconceptualise their life events. For reconceptualization to happen, the researchers are encouraged to explore the differences between their lived stories as they are seen as having the biggest transformative potential.

It is acknowledged, however, that critical dialogues can be uncomfortable, illuminate unexpected details and reveal deeply-held values the researchers can be unaware of. Such conversations can stimulate highly emotional responses, as was the case in our project too. Consequently, another key tenet of the methodology is that the researchers enter their dialogic research space with trust and ethics of care. Trust is needed to open up with one's own story and to accept the comments which can challenge one's values or worldviews, while care is necessary in the process of data collection and writing to ensure that researchers as well as those present in their stories are not the focus of the research. This is because duoethnography positions the researchers not as subjects but as sites of research placing the discussed social phenomenon, in this case the emerging socially just educator identity, at the heart of the research.

Another core tenet of duoethnography which appealed to us is its polyvocality. Rather than blending the researchers' voices into a single narration, the reader of duoethnography is welcomed to the dialogic research space by being able to 'hear' individual voices of the researchers in the published text. These typically take the form of reconstructed dialogues or stories/vignettes (e.g. Banegas and Gerlach 2021; Lawrence and Nagashima 2019; Lowe and Kiczkowiak 2016).

As a group of three researchers, we have used duoethnography tenets in our research design but are choosing to use the term trioethnography as is used by Hooper, Oka and Yamazawa in Lowe and Lawrence (2020). In communicating key outputs from our project, we have opted for extracts from our poems and associated stories to represent us, rather than dialogue. In other words, while we strived to enter into critical dialogues with each other's stories, we were equally keen to ensure the readers can have an insight into our respective *currere*, or lived experience (Pinar 1975, in Sawyer and Norris 2013).

Our methods

Inspired by an article by Dillabough (2020) which builds on the work of Hannah Arendt, Paul Ricoeur and Stuart Hall to illustrate the importance of storytelling with and in relation to others, our starting point was documenting our stories. We sought to reflect on our journeys within and outside the classroom, constructing an ecosystem of knowledge of our lived and professional experiences as English language teachers.

To trigger refection of the critical incidents in our professional careers, we decided to narrate our stories around the following themes: hurting place; joyful moments; and turning points/catalysts. We identified a structured approach to fostering deep engagement with, and reflection on stories shared in Edge and Olan's (2021) paper in which they utilised Langer's (2011) 'Five Stances'. The Five Stances encourages researchers to take an iterative approach to reading stories through different lenses. We interpreted the five stances to encourage us to move our thinking from individual responses to the stories we read, toward a collective, collaborative sense-making process that sought to understand the phenomenon being researched. Our process of implementing those five stances is as follows:

1. We responded to each other's stories after reading them for the first time (by adding comments, emailing each other back and forth, summarizing our reactions on our Teams Channel and our WhatsApp group).
2. We kept responding to each other's stories after subsequent readings.
3. We met on Zoom to make sense of each other's responses to help elaborate on our individual stories further; the meetings and the discussions were transcribed.
4. Some of us started journaling/editing/modifying our personal stories and the responses by generating Wordclouds summarizing the most frequent words and themes in our stories.
5. We redacted all outputs through the blackout poetry approach to produce final poems.

In addition to Olan and Edge's (2021) research, a further inspiration for exploring poetry as a method for sense-making is its strong tradition of exploring issues of belonging amongst academics we respect (e.g., bell hooks, Audre Lorde), including Adrienne Rich who speaks of the power of poetry in the extract below:

> It's potentially catalytic speech because it's more than speech:
> it is associative, metaphoric, dialectical, visual, musical;
> in poetry words can say more than they mean and mean more than they say.
> In a time of frontal assaults both on language and on
> human solidarity, poetry can remind us of all we are in
> danger of losing – disturb us, embolden us out of resignation
>
> Interview with Adrienne Rich – *Radcliffe Quarterly* (Fall 1998)

We wanted to experiment with the possibilities of what poetry could afford us in articulating the myriad of emotions that we anticipated would surface through the research process. To create a blackout poem a writer/poet takes a marker (usually black marker) to already existing text, such as a journal article and redacts words until a poem is created (Kleon 2010). We were inspired to use this method of inquiry not only by its use within Olan and Edge's (2021) research, but also by our attendance at workshops on the use of such poetry as an analysis and teaching tool. With a continued focus on ethics of care, we were also mindful that blackout poetry would give us the freedom to control what we were and were not willing to disclose within the process whilst allowing us to explore the various themes, intentions and messages within.

In the following section we each share an extract from one of our poems and offer our theoretical and personal reflections on the extract and the research process. These are followed by a joint discussion of the themes we have identified across our experiences related to the phenomenon of becoming a socially just educator.

Our stories

Lorraine's story

Extract from: **The Gift of Being Heard**

In this space we consciously and compassionately cultivated ▮, I felt no threat of rejection, no fear of exclusion, no apprehension of getting it wrong. ▮ in that ▮ space, ▮ I was able to give and receive the gift of being heard, of being listened to. ▮ ▮ Through sharing that gift I learned so much from you, both about you and about myself. ▮ we have much in common, yet ▮ have considerable differences in experience. ▮ the complexities of our identities mean ▮ at different times ▮ in different spaces we have and always will be structurally advantaged and disadvantaged in differing ways. ▮ ▮ Those differences are important to understand ▮ a reminder of where our power comes into being, ▮ when it is diminished ▮ ▮, when we may need an advocate to stand in solidarity.

As I sat down to muse on and share my career trajectory – including highs and lows – with Iwona and Tomasz, I had three realisations. The first was that it had been a long time since I had protected some time to critically reflect on my practice as an educator, the second was that I had rarely conducted that reflection before in conversation with others who were not observing my practice, and the third was that I really did not know Iwona and Tomasz very well! As our participation on the EAP for Social Justice Special Interest Group committee is voluntary, there tends to be limited time to get to know each other beyond that shared endeavour. Indeed, at the point of writing, we have yet to meet each other in person!

Against that backdrop it may seem like a brave or foolish endeavour to share moments of conflict and discomfort as well as successes with relative strangers; I am so pleased that we were all courageous. As is expressed in the extract above, sharing my story, hearing their stories, and coming together to retell our stories and sense-make collaboratively was a site of hugely transformative learning for me. Listening to Iwona's and Tomasz's stories highlighted significant gaps in my knowledge of historical, geopolitical contexts which occurred close to the continent I was living in, but were far outside my frame of reference as I grew up. Their experiences held a mirror up to privileges I was unaware that my second-generation immigrant, British-born, working-class background had afforded me. Everyday occurrences that I had taken for granted, such as having access to a range of fruits all year round and the ability to purchase Coca-Cola from the local shop, were illuminated as moments of rarity and wonder in Tomasz's and Iwona's childhood and adolescence.

Through our conversations, I realised that some of my ignorance was based in fear. A fear of asking questions. A fear wrapped up in the violence of the question we had each experienced in personal and professional contexts, 'Where are you from?' often followed by, 'No, but where are you really from?' or other iterations of follow up questions to indicate you had not provided the person asking with their desired response. A response that would satisfy their will to position you as 'other' in opposition to 'belonging'.

A key moment of learning for me in this project, was realising that my conscious determination to avoid interactions that may fall foul of othering the people I have met through my life, may have inadvertently resulted in many missed opportunities in broadening my global knowledge and further enriching personal and professional relationships. I continue to reflect on how systems and acts of oppression which seek to silence marginalised people, can also serve to deepen divides between marginalised and centred communities by discouraging conversations between them.

That said, as an educator who aligns with social constructivist epistemologies and critical methodologies, I have always held the learning I gain from my students as equally valuable to the skills development and insights I am able to provide them. I now realise that numerous colleagues along the way have also played an invaluable role in my process of becoming a socially just educator. Whether in my hurting places or moments of joyful resistance it has been a collaborative effort.

I am mindful that this realisation has emerged from a process that from the outset was steeped in a will to engage, a mutual respect and an approach centred in care. We each afforded each other the time and space that human-connectedness requires and deserves. In doing so, we cultivated nurturing conditions which served as an essential element of building trust amongst relative strangers. These conditions allowed us to move beyond the superficial, othering query of 'Where are you from?' and instead explore 'Where have you been? Who were you then? Who are you now? And where are you planning to go?' in the spirit of garnering mutual understanding of our shared and differing experiences.

Iwona's story

Extract from: On Privilege and Power

I had been oblivious to many privileges until I lost them initially this felt like freedom: be anyone, live anywhere, but conversations always inevitably steer towards my otherness. 'Where is home?' they ask, on a dog walk, in a shop, at the bus stop, outside school gate. Rarely tell me about theirs, though. Not belonging to one place, teaching language that's not mine a gift and a curse reminding me every day of privileges gone, privileges kept. Mine. Others. Teaching for me is about finding ways for my students to succeed dream big BUT also to look their privilege in the eye and realise it comes with a responsibility.

Becoming a socially aware educator has been a path of awakening for me. Growing up in politically enforced monocultural, monolingual and predominantly white country emerging from 50 years of communism, I perceived English as a language of everything I was denied: civic freedom, multicultural, multilingual and multi-ethnic diversity and richness. English was exciting until I started TESOL degrees where diversity was given lip service and where a very reductive view of English and its speakers was truly valued. For example, deviating from the RP accent was penalised and mocked by teachers, dissertation supervisors and sometimes peers. The colonial past was mentioned but not explored; only one particular type of linguistic native-like proficiency enforced. English became torturous and my second-class status cemented at the ELT workplace, where birthplace decided opportunities and pay. After four years, I desperately wanted to leave received pronunciation and ELT behind.

Moving to Scotland initially felt like freedom, but as described in the poem, in time it also brought challenges. Here, I became the 'other' mostly outside my profession. It was through the dialogues with Lorraine and Tomasz that I felt ready to explore (confront?) how this positioning had been affecting my identity and practice. Conversely to the experience of teaching English in Poland, and in the international EAP classroom at a Scottish university I feel at home, while outside of it very much a stranger. I am perceived and evaluated through the lens of what my interlocutor(s) believe, know or experienced about Poland and my fellow countrymen. Group identity, something also adopted towards international students in the UK, is not necessarily a negative experience if you come from a place/group which are familiar and/or desirable to your interlocutor, as one of my students said beaming with pride: 'I didn't know I was Italian until I came to Scotland!'. Yet, the seemingly neutral: 'Where is home?' can also forcefully position one as a stranger, despite their desire to belong. It can be a powerful reminder that those in power ask, and those without it, have to answer, not unlike in the classroom.

Reflecting with Lorraine and Tomasz on orienting myself towards social justice informed education, I realised that the experience of being othered, imposed or adopted (internalised?), has had a profound impact on me, much more than I was happy to admit prior to our discussions. The process of cyclical reflection and dialogue adopted in this research helped me understand how much the experience of displacement (even though not forced) set me on course to a more culturally, linguistically and socially responsible teaching practice. Becoming a migrant and then a parent transformed how I view the world around me and continues to determine what kind of teacher I want to be. These two powerful forces led to my engagement with the EAP for Social Justice Special Interest Group (SIG), which nurtured and extended opportunities to consider societal, political and cultural privileges beyond those bestowed by language: such as gender, sexuality, race or social class.

Many of those privileges, and/or lack of, emerged in our reflections for this chapter. Critical dialogues with Tomasz and Lorraine, full of emotions and insightful yet compassionate comments, resonated strongly with so much of the learning I have been doing for some time, but went beyond what I currently understand, leaving me with a desire to explore more. Discussions on power, privilege and injustice are not common in the field of EAP, and when they are discussed they often focus on the positionality of EAP students, precarious employment conditions of the teachers or their marginalised status within their institutions. Race, gender, class, sexuality, neurodiversity, native-speakerism and migration are not explored much, though. This project showed me how little I knew about my colleagues' struggles and achievements, and how much can be learnt by reflecting on those openly, with care and respect. Most of all, the collaboration with two creative and daring individuals helped me open up to uncertainty, which is no small feat for someone with a strong need to control everything. For that lesson, I am also very grateful.

Tomasz's story

Extract from: The English Language – my Saviour and my Oppressor

"I was 21, I had £50 in my pocket ▇▇▇▇▇▇▇▇▇▇▇▇▇▇▇▇▇▇▇▇▇▇▇▇▇▇▇▇▇▇▇▇ no fixed plans or expectations▇▇▇▇▇▇▇▇▇▇▇▇▇▇▇ feeling liberated ▇ not worrying about some mundane things ▇▇▇▇▇▇▇▇▇▇▇▇▇▇▇▇▇▇▇▇▇▇▇ I landed in London ▇▇ ▇▇▇, it was 20 July, one of the hottest days in the UK on record. The sun was shining bright, I put my tinted sunglasses on, ▇▇▇▇▇▇▇▇▇▇ I had dreams and I had… English." |

What you see above is an excerpt from my story of turning points and hurting places trying to deconstruct my identity as an English Language Teaching practitioner. My adventure with the English language started on a high, and for the first few years, I was definitely in the honeymoon phase with it. In the stories shared with Iwona and Lorraine, I initially struggled with revealing the more intimate moments from my professional ELT life. For example, instead of really reflecting on the critical incidents in my ELT career, I took a shortcut, and simply sent them my already submitted Senior HEA application thinking this would do the job: how naive was I!

It was the dialogic playfulness of Bahktin's (1981) heteroglossia that eventually opened me up. If I had not engaged with Iwona's 'alien-ess' as a privileged Pole, a woman and a mother, a feminist, another 'non-native speaker' with a different background story; Lorraine's narrative revolving around her never-ending fight with different forms of oppression and othering in ELT as a black woman; and the genuine support I had received from both of them, I would not have been able to come clean to fully reflect on my own trajectory.

My narrative revolved around the double-faced nature of the English language industry in my life – I presented it as a saviour, but also oppressor. While I glorified the English language as a 'door opener', a sort of capital enabling me social mobility moving away from my working-class roots, a gateway to liberate my sexuality as a queer person, a language allowing me to reimagine myself as whoever I wanted to be, it is also the same English language that later rejected me and bullied having a knock-on effect on my confidence, belief in my English language abilities, teaching skills, public speaking, writing and trust in general.

In her story, Lorraine talks about the ugly side of working for the ELT industry, and being treated as a sort of 'English language ambassador' whilst working abroad and how uncomfortable she felt being made to 'impose' awfully inappropriate English language rules/content on people hoping to use English as a commodity for social mobility. Lorraine's stories echoed with my own experiences of being a sort of English language ambassador when being sent away abroad on an English language assessment mission to interrogate and patronise 'the other'. I very quickly realised English and the ELT can be political. It was at that point that I understood my honeymoon phase with the English language was over. I suddenly felt incredibly uncomfortable working in an industry which to some extent legitimised colonisation and oppression. I realised what language as power meant – here English was used as a product to prevent, rather than enable, social mobility. So, is the English language and the whole bureaucracy around it used as a camouflage for what is actually a 'softer', continuous, and recycled colonisation of the oppressed, of the 'Oriental' others, non-Western people? What happened to English language sold as an enabler and saviour that is sometimes used to empower citizens to be conscious of their ability to form social bonds and work together to better the world?

I believe it was the very same English Language which 'saved me', and the industry that had gifted me with access to knowledge and power, that has sometimes transformed itself from Dr Jekyll to Mr Hyde and made me doubt myself, made me sick and made me feel like an imposter. But there is hope. The more secure jobs I have had over the years have allowed me to reimagine myself and steer more activism into my daily routine. In my current work I have developed a new module revolving around tackling native-speakerism ideology and promoting curriculum innovations building on global Englishes, and I supervise relevant, socially-just oriented PhD and Master's projects. I also started involving my students in volunteering placements, training them to teach vulnerable adults building on trauma-informed pedagogy. Furthermore, the work we have done together within the EAP4SJ SIG has also empowered me further to keep disturbing the status quo of the traditional role of an ELT practitioner. Having experienced the good, the bad and the ugly of the English language industry, I actively challenge the various obstacles, including representation in the ELT industry, I rewrite curricula to include 'the other' and weave in practical examples of activism, enabling students to become not just

English language users but active and proud global citizens. But is that enough to become a socially-just educator?

Discussion

We embarked on this research project wanting to deepen our understanding of how the intersections of our personal identities have impacted on our professional identities and practice within the field of EAP and explore the phenomena of an emerging socially just educator identity. Based on our conversations and on reviewing each of our choices in poem extract and stories – which we each wrote independently – an evident core theme is that our experience of being marginalised in our personal and/or professional life has acted as a catalyst for centring social justice in our professional practice. It is our deeply personal experiences of being othered that mobilise us to try to foster belonging in the educational spaces we facilitate.

Being othered

Our stories of hurting places pivoted around moments of being othered. These included examples of direct comments from colleagues which indicated they felt we did not belong in the professional space, witnessing unethical practices within programmes we have worked on and/or feeling complicit in systems that uncritically use English Language Teaching and English for Academic Purposes as a method of enforcing power over others. In our reflective conversations, we realised that those moments of hurting often consciously or unconsciously threw us back to our personal experiences of feeling like we did not belong, and thus mobilised us – when we felt safe to do so – to use our agency to foster belonging within our teaching practice. We acknowledged these as moments when we chose to challenge the ways in which we may have unconsciously reinforced systems of oppression in our professional lives and reminded ourselves that, 'the classroom remains the most radical space of possibility in the academy' (hooks 1994).

The issue of safety was something that we discussed frequently in this research project. We recognised in the early stages of designing our approach that our personal experiences of being marginalised, along with some of the critical incidents that acted as a catalyst for this research project, were moments of feeling unsafe. It was important to us to ensure that we each felt safe throughout the project, hence our commitment to the ethics of care which are embedded within the trioethnography methodology.

Ethics of care

However, we would argue that we went beyond ethics of care in our approach, and that we adopted what hooks (2001) describes as a 'love ethic'. She describes this way of being in the world as one which rejects ideologies underpinned by systems of domination and notions of pitting groups against each other. Instead, living by a love ethic embraces love and care for oneself and others as a means of casting out fear and building human interconnectedness (hooks 2001). It may seem far from academic to speak of love in a research project, but if we use hooks' understanding of love 'as the will to extend one's self for the purpose of nurturing one's own or another's spiritual growth' (Peck 1978, cited in hooks 2001: 10), you can see from our poems and stories that love was an essential ingredient for establishing the trust required for the transformational learning we each speak of.

In reflecting on our turning points and moments of resistance, we recognised that we were affording similar love and care in our EAP practice. This resulted in fruitful discussions within which we reassured ourselves that it is vital our work as socially-just educators prioritises empathy, compassion, and understanding in the education process. This echoes with Bali's 'Pedagogy of Care' (2021), which recognises that as we come from different backgrounds, experiences and perspectives, we should actively seek to create a supportive and inclusive learning environment that nurtures our growth and development. The Pedagogy of Care emphasises building relationships and creating a sense of community in the classroom, where teachers act as facilitators, guides and caretakers of the learning process. 'Committed acts of caring let all students know that the purpose of education is not to dominate, or prepare them to be dominators, but rather to create the conditions for freedom. Caring educators open the mind, allowing students to embrace a world of knowing that is always subject to change and challenge.' (hooks 2003: 91).

Regarding an emerging socially just educator identity, we recognise that we have just started to scratch the surface of what that process of becoming entails, and that this will be unique for each individual. However, what we have learnt through this project is that our decision to adopt a trioethnographic methodological framework, which centred a dialogic approach in the data collection and analysis, encouraged us to listen attentively to one another and be in meaningful conversation with each other. Through our discussions, we challenged our biases, confronted differences, crossed boundaries and recognised sites of solidarity, and in doing so we realised the potential noted by hooks (1994) of meaningful dialogue as an essential tool for building community and enriching our individual and collective research and teaching practice. Our loving, creative, dialogic approach undoubtedly fostered a sense of community, of belonging to a shared endeavour of understanding. There was no expectation that we would fully understand each other's direct experience, but we wholeheartedly committed to listening to, and hearing each other's experiences to gain a better sense of ourselves in relation to others and to identify sites of shared and differential power. Our attention and intention fostered a dialogue which allowed us to move beyond reductive concepts of identity such as class, race, gender and sexuality, and instead welcomed the plurality of our experiences (Dillabough 2020).

Conclusion

This trioethnographic study strengthened our communal sense of belonging and fostered a sense of accountability and interdependence. Exercising ethics of care, empathy and respect for each other and ourselves, helped us create a supportive and inclusive research environment with shared responsibility towards the well-being and needs of all involved. In her book *Belonging: A Culture of Place*, bell hooks (2008) writes: 'a beloved community is formed not by the eradication of difference but by its affirmation, by each of us claiming the identities and cultural complexities that shape who we are and how we live in loving and supportive ways that enable us to develop a strong sense of collective belonging.'

In our journeys to become socially-just educators, we connected with each other to create a solidified base and community through which we practised, but also engaged more deeply with learning and unlearning about our own individual epistemological biases. As we engaged with public pedagogy (Biesta 2012) through learning and unlearning and making sense of the injustices observed in the ELT/EAP sector (public spaces and cultural institutions), it was the other critical observers/interlocutors with whom we interacted and communicated that played a key role in the process of interrupting the homogeny, or uniformity, of our experiences. This interruption of homogeny challenged our existing understandings and beliefs, leading to transformation in our thinking and learning.

We feel grateful to have created the time and space to both give and receive insights into our experiences through our personal life and professional career. To listen to someone – really listen to someone – and to be afforded a precious insight into their experience, and in turn to be truly heard and know that you have each afforded each other space and perspective for sense-making, well, that is a very precious gift. A gift that we rarely make time for, but a gift that we hope we have articulated through this piece, and that can be hugely transformational.

In EAP scholarship, as we desperately strive for legitimacy as a community within our organisations, we feel compelled to follow the 'rules' of what constitutes an illustration of 'quality' / 'serious' research and scholarship. Fearful that deviating from those rules will further hinder our collective pursuit for legitimisation of the discipline and profession, we often remain conservative in our scholarly efforts, which ironically can have the opposite effect by preventing EAP practitioners from developing wider knowledge of research methods and epistemologies. Certainly, as we took the decisions to engage in a research project adopting dialogic, creative, love-led approaches, we knew we were running the risk of ridicule and the validity of our work being undermined. There were moments throughout the process of doubt, and concerns around our professional and personal wellbeing. But, in the infamous words of Susan Jeffers (2007), we chose to feel the fear and do it anyway. If any of what you have read has resonated or inspired you, we would encourage you to diverge from the norm and build and share knowledge through creative, collaborative, compassionate experimentation as you continue on your journey to becoming a socially just educator.

References

Arendt, H. (1998), *The Human Condition*, 2nd edn, Chicago, University of Chicago Press.

Bahktin, M. M. (1981), *The Dialogic Imagination: Four Essays*, ed. M. Holquist, trans. C. Emerson and M. Holquist, Austin: University of Texas Press.

Bali, M. (2021), 'Creating Equitable, Caring Communities Online'. Unpublished conference paper. BALEAP Biennial Conference 2021: Exploring Pedagogical Approaches In EAP Teaching. Glasgow, UK.: 6–10 April, 2021.

Banegas, D. L. and Gerlach, D. (2021), 'Critical Language Teacher Education: A Duoethnography of Teacher Educators' Identities and Agency', *System*, 98: 102474. Available online: https://doi.org/10.1016/j.system.2021.102474 (accessed 25 August 2023).

Biesta, G. (2012), 'Becoming Public: Public Pedagogy, Citizenship and the Public Sphere', *Social and Cultural Geography*, 13(7): 683–97. Available online: https://doi.org/10.1080/14649365.2012.723736 (accessed 1 April 2017).

Bond, B. (2020), *Making Language Visible in the University: English for Academic Purposes and Internationalisation*, Bristol: Multilingual Matters.

Dillabough, J. A. (2020), 'Identity as Other and the Promise of the Narrative Imagination in Educational Theorizing: Arendt and Ricoeur', in W. Veck and H. M Gunter (eds), *Hannah Arendt on Educational Thinking and Practice in Dark Times,* pp.63–78, London: Bloomsbury.

Ding, A. and Bruce, I. (2017), *The English for Academic Purposes Practitioner: Operating on the Edge of Academia*, Switzerland: Springer International.

Edge, C.U. and Olan, E.L. (2021), 'Learning to Breathe Again: Found Poems and Critical Friendship as Methodological Tools in Self-Study of Teaching Practices', *Studying Teacher Education*, 17(2): 228–52. Available online: https://doi.org/10.1080/17425964.2021.1910807 (accessed 20 May 2022).

Freire, P. (2014), *Pedagogy of Hope: Reliving Pedagogy of the Oppressed*, New York: Bloomsbury Academic.

hooks, b. (1994), *Teaching to Transgress: Education as the Practice of Freedom*, New York: Routledge.

hooks, b. (2001), *All About Love: New Visions*, New York: Harper Perennial.

hooks, b. (2003), *Teaching Community: A Pedagogy of Hope*, New York: Routledge.

hooks, b. (2008) *Belonging: A Culture of Place*, New York: Taylor and Francis.

Hooper, D. Oka, M. and Yamazawa, A.: Not all Eikaiwas (or Instructors) are Created Equal: A Trioethnography of 'Native Speaker' and 'Non-Native Speaker' Perspectives on English Conversation Schools in Japan in Lowe, R. J. & Lawrence, L. (2020). Duoethnography in English Language Teaching: Research, Reflection and Classroom Application. Multilingual Matters.

Jeffers, S. J. (2007), *Feel the Fear and do it Anyway*, revised and updated edition, London: Vermilion.

Kleon, A (2010), *Newspaper Blackout,* New York: Harper Perennial.

Kubota, R. (2020), 'Confronting Epistemological Racism, Decolonizing Scholarly Knowledge: Race and Gender in Applied Linguistics', *Applied linguistics*, 41(5): 712–32.

Lawrence, L., & Nagashima, Y. (2020). The intersectionality of gender, sexuality, race, and native-speakerness: Investigating ELT teacher identity through duoethnography. *Journal of Language, Identity & Education*, 19(1), 42–55. Available online: https://doi.org/10.1080/15348458.2019.1672173 (accessed 1 March 2023).

Lorde, A. (2007), *Sister Outsider: Essays and Speeches by Audre Lorde,* revised edition, Berkeley: Crossing Press.

Lowe, R. J., & Kiczkowiak, M. (2016). Native-speakerism and the complexity of personal experience: A duoethnographic study. *Cogent Education*, 3(1), 1264171. Available online: https://www.tandfonline.com/doi/full/10.1080/2331186X.2016.1264171 (accessed 1 March 2023).

Mihăilă, R., Popescu, G. H and Nica, E. (2016), 'Educational Conservatism and Democratic Citizenship in Hannah Arendt', *Educational Philosophy and Theory*, 48(9): 915–27.

Sandlin, J. A., Schultz, B. D. and Burdick, J. (2010), 'Understanding, Mapping, and Exploring the Terrain of Public Pedagogy', in J. A. Sandlin, B. D. Schultz and J. Burdick (eds), *Handbook of Public Pedagogy: Education and Learning Beyond Schooling*, p. 338–75, New York: Routledge.

Sawyer, R. D. and Norris, J. (2013), *Duoethnography*, Oxford: Oxford University Press. Available online: https://doi.org/10.1093/acprof:osobl/9780199757404.001.0001 (accessed 1 March 2023).

Topolski, A. (2008), 'Creating Citizens in the Classroom, Hannah Arendt's Political Critique of Education', *Ethical Perspectives* 15(2): 259–82.

7

What Silence Tells Us

D. Tran

In a qualitative study exploring multicultural competency and counsellor trainees' reactions to difficult dialogues, Watt et al. (2009: 86–7), referencing Watt (2007), note, 'A difficult dialogue can be defined as an exchange of ideas or opinions between individuals that centers on an awakening of potentially conflicting views of individual beliefs or values on social justice issues, for example, racism, sexism, or heterosexism/homophobia'. If you have ever initiated or been part of a conversation centred around a sensitive and complex area of discussion, it is very likely you would have experienced, as part of that conversation, moments of silence. Ranging from short pauses to much longer periods of quiet, the hesitancy which individuals and groups often have towards engaging or sharing thoughts and feelings relating to social justice issues can be difficult, partly due to the silences that often dominate conversational spaces. My own experience of being part of and facilitating similar conversations, or rather what has sometimes felt like facilitating silences, is what has motivated and informed this reflection.

This reflection tries to learn from these experiences by questioning possible meanings behind difficult silences, and how these may be navigated and negotiated within a teaching and learning space. It takes on an action-oriented lens to support practical ways of transforming silences. Commenting on the advancement of social justice and the value of related conversations, Love et al. (2016: 7) emphasise, 'It is important to remember that participation and self-reflection are key'. This short piece aims to highlight the value of personal reflection to help empower facilitators of varying experience and confidence levels to step into the silence and be creative with how they may work with the space. Working with and within these spaces can involve critical listening. In their article, 'Critical Listening and Storying: Fostering Respect for Difference and Action Within and Beyond a Native American Literature

Classroom', San Pedro et al. share that through 're-centering relationships through critical listening and storying, we are better suited to co-construct our shared truths and realities in the space between the telling and hearing of stories' (2017: 667).

It may be helpful to begin by considering the varying effects which silences can have on a conversation. For any individual, the choice to *invoke* silence affects themselves and those around them differently to if they are *met* with silence. If someone invokes silence, they choose to implement an active pausing of conversation. Even if the individual does so out of a form of discomfort, there is nevertheless a form of control that can be expressed through the conscious decision to invoke silence. If someone is met with silence, they can feel pressure to fill the silence, to change the subject, or continue with silence. Out of silence therefore comes choices for all those in the room, to either continue with or influence the outcome of the silence. The effect which silences can have on the session environment can quickly influence the tone and dynamic of a conversation, and potentially lay the foundation of expectations for participants moving forward. How silences are responded to can therefore play an important role in managing the present and signalling expectations for future conversations. For a facilitator, part of the role is to ensure silences do not hinder progress or overwhelm discussion.

Before considering ways of responding, it can help to explore possible reasons behind the occurrences of silences. Furthermore, the allowances of silences can also be revealing of listener intentions. If the topic of conversation is not only sensitive and multifaceted, but unfamiliar to an individual too, they may find comfort in silence. Some may choose quiet with the intention to create space for those who already have understandings of particular issues to share their knowledges. The space to listen becomes part of their learning journey to find out more about a subject until feeling able to contribute a valuable point. There may be fears of being embarrassed if their comments point to a lack of knowledge about the subject. The intersectionality of social justice issues can be intimidating for many, and increasing fears around being 'cancelled' can increase anxieties. Toler (2022) explains cancel culture as 'a form of boycott [. . .] to be cancel[l]ed means that a person or group decides to stop supporting someone or something based on a transgression that is either actual or perceived', which can impact the mental health of both the 'cancelled' and 'canceller' (ibid.).

Another influencing factor can be an individual's positionality. For some participants who identify with a dominant group, there can be concern that any criticism they may want to express towards ongoing injustices might come across as inauthentic due to their benefiting from the privilege of being part of a dominant group. For a facilitator, silences can create opportunities for new questions to be posed. Gayles et al. note, 'Individuals are more likely to contemplate or think deeply about social justice and diversity issues as exposure to ideas of privilege and power increases' (2015: 4). But as Love et al. (2016: 3), referring to Pease (2010), note, 'attempts to avoid difficult conversations inevitably reinforce systems of privilege and oppression'. Although the latter focuses on race and colour blindness, it can be applied to a range of social justice issues. For some participants who identify as being part of a marginalised or minoritised group, silences may also be deliberately employed. This is because sharing experiences of injustices, or parting knowledge to others can simultaneously situate individuals as carrying the weight of responsibility to move agendas forward. There are many reasons behind why a person may choose to take solace in silence, and it is a challenge for facilitators to straddle the line between respecting potential individual reasons and not allowing silence to derail or hinder learning objectives.

When faced with silences, the role of a facilitator can be made more challenging. But seeing the opportunities these silences can afford mean they can be used for the benefit of both the facilitator and participants. For example, a short pause or moment of silence offers a facilitator brief time to 'read the room'. Depending on whether the conversation takes place in person or online, the process of reading the room offers a chance to check the behaviours, expressions, chat threads, and back channels to see how participants are reacting individually and collectively. The pause in conversation creates space for the facilitator to assess in real time the situation unfolding before them, helping them to respond rather than react to silences. Based on the outcome of the assessment, the facilitator is able to choose the most appropriate path for the conversation to grow, not simply navigating the silence but *using* it productively.

Silences can be used by a facilitator to check participant understanding, create space for complex points to land and briefly considered in the moment. They can be used to reframe a question and even be prolonged further to inform participants that the silence is not the responsibility of the facilitator to fill. By stepping into and managing silence in a productive way, the facilitator can work with, rather than against the silence. This enables them to use it for the benefit of participants instead of allowing it to dominate the conversation. This can in turn help to manage expectations around participation and engagement for future sessions.

There is a contradiction in the process of writing a reflective piece about silence. Whether these experiences have been difficult or positive, there is always learning to be gained and applied to support individuals endeavouring to navigate silences within educational spaces. An embracing of silences enables the opportunity for a developmental discussion. Often the expectations versus experience of challenging conversations can be conflicting. But whether a facilitator is new to supporting such discussions or not, it does not make the role of facilitator any easier. These silences do not disappear for those who are experienced in facilitation.

Silences can point to gaps – whether these be gaps in knowledge, in experience, familiarity or something else. These gaps can be overcome individually and collectively through entering the silent space. The emotional and intellectual challenge of discussing difficult topics can be triggering, stressful, and daunting for any participant or facilitator. Often the facilitator is looked to as the person providing expertise and steer, placing them in a position where they are expected to 'know the answers'. Managing expectations around this plays a role in managing the dynamics in the room. The facilitator is there to be as open to learning from the conversation as other participants, and in many ways, they too are a participant.

References

Gayles, J. G., Turner Kelly B., Grays S., Zhang J. J. and Porter K. P. (2015), 'Faculty Teaching Diversity Through Difficult Dialogues: Stories of Challenges and Success', *Journal of Student Affairs Research and Practice*, 52(3): 300–12. Available online: https://doi.org/10.1080/19496591.2015.1067223 (accessed 17 August 2022).

Love, J. M., Gaynor T. S. and Blessett B. (2016), 'Facilitating Difficult Dialogues in the Classroom: a Pedagogical Imperative', *Administrative Theory and Praxis*, 38: 227–33. Available online: https://doi.org/10.1080/10841806.2016.1237839 (accessed 7 August 2022).

San Pedro, T., Carlos E., and Mburu J. (2017), 'Critical Listening and Storying: Fostering Respect for Difference and Action Within and Beyond a Native American Literature Classroom', *Urban Education*, 52(5): 667–93. Available online: https://doi.org/10.1177/0042085915623346 (accessed 21 January 2023).

Toler, L. (2022), 'The Mental Health Effects of Cancel Culture', *Verywellmind*, 14 April 2022, https://www.verywellmind.com/the-mental-health-effects-of-cancel-culture-5119201 (accessed 7 August 2022).

Watt, S. K. (2007), 'Difficult Dialogues, Privilege and Social Justice: Uses of the Privileged Identity Exploration (PIE) Model in Student Affairs Practice', *College Student Affairs Journal*, 26: 114–26.

Watt, S. K., Curtis G. C., Drummond J., Kellogg A. H., Lozano A., Tagliapietra Nicoli G. and Rosas M. (2009), 'Privileged Identity Exploration: Examining Counselor Trainees' Reactions to Difficult Dialogues', *Counselor Education and Supervision*, 49: 86–105.

Adopting a Social Justice Lens in EAP: The Application of Cognitive Skills of Compassionate Communication (CSCC) in Online Task-focused Group Meetings

J.M.P.V.K. Jayasundara

Introduction

The Covid-19 pandemic has affected drastically every aspect of human life all over the world. One of the major changes was the sudden shift from face-to-face teaching and learning to online forms, already a feature of Higher Education (HE) but now accelerated. Even though this shift facilitated the continuation of academic programmes, the challenges cannot be disregarded as they appeared to affect students' learning as well as social experiences. Researchers have highlighted the difficulty of online communication and engagement (Afrouz and Crisp 2021), the increased disconnection of students (Bauer et al. 2020; Stanford University 2020), and lack of motivation, understanding of the material, decrease in communication levels between the students and their instructors and their feeling of isolation caused by online classes (Alawamleh et al. 2020). These challenges have become common for students, irrespective of their demographic, social, educational or economic backgrounds, and have contributed to increased feelings of social isolation or loneliness. In studies of students as indicated by Aleman and Sommer (2022), Cacioppo and Hawkley (2009) and Hawkley and Caccioppo (2010), this has had negative psychological consequences, such as weaker overall cognitive functioning and a decline in quality of life. The students' isolation, particularly during the pandemic, is further intensified by the now widely reported hesitancy of students to turn on their cameras and thus be visible to one another during their online educational settings (Castelli and Sarvary 2021; McBrien, et al. 2019).

There has been little discussion of the role of the science of compassion as a cognitive, psychobiological motivation (P. Gilbert 2019) in enhancing one's own and others' social and learning experiences while facilitating social justice in online group work/teamwork. Hence, this chapter discusses the relevance of the science of compassion for addressing the above issues in online learning. Research on group work/teamwork in higher education has led to the development of compassion-focused pedagogy (CfP) used offline (e.g. a physical face-to-face class) to improve learning and social cohesiveness in task-focused teams. Inclusive eye contact – a key component of CfP (Katchen 1992; T. Gilbert 2019; T. Gilbert et al. 2018; T. Gilbert and Bryan 2019; Harvey 2020) – is not possible in online group meetings. In the online environment, 'screen-gazing' is the measure. In order for students to co-manage their group work meetings compassionately in both online and offline settings, they must feel at ease expressing and observing their own as well as other people's non-verbal communication, which they can only do if they actively look at the screen. If students do not turn on their webcams this capability of comprehending and conveying nonverbal signals during online group work meetings is significantly hindered and negatively affects group communication, interactions and engagement. Additionally, instructors might not be able to tell who is speaking, prompting, or possibly supporting the speaker if students' webcams are not turned on. Hence, it is essential for students, tutors, and examiners to be able to view every student throughout their online group sessions in order to communicate effectively and engage in authentic teaching and learning. The study reported here examined whether and, if so, how students may be inspired to turn on their webcams during their online group meetings by learning about the Cognitive Skills of Compassionate Communication (CSCC). This in turn advantageous for all participants to fully present online and especially notice one another's non-verbal signals and provide the necessary support (e.g. encouragement, repeating, rephrasing, etc.) whenever needed to the group. Thus, this equal presence by all members and their noticing of one another's behaviours allows everyone to have equal participation which is also represented through the sharing of equal virtual spaces enhancing the aspects of social justice.

Theoretical background

The psychobiological paradigm for Compassionate Mind Training (CMT), designed by the Compassionate Mind Foundation (2005), serves as the theoretical underpinning of the present investigation. Humans alternate between three mood-regulating systems: the threat, the drive and the soothing systems: 'Each system is associated with different brain regions and different brain chemistry. Distress is caused by imbalance between the systems, often associated with underdevelopment of the soothing system.' (Mindfulness and Clinical Psychology Solutions 2019: 4). Over-activation of the threat system that is hardwired into our brains for survival may render the brain incapable of higher-order thinking, including problem-solving and decision-making (Cozolino 2013). The drive mood-regulatory system gives us the ability to work hard to get what we want or need. Giving or receiving care from others or ourselves activates the soothing system, the third mood-regulating system in the brain, which helps us think more clearly, logically and with more focus. It is possible to train the brain's soothing mechanism such that it helps keep these three systems in balance (P. Gilbert et al. 2009). People who tend to oscillate primarily between the first two systems endanger the equilibrium between these three systems (P. Gilbert et al. 2009) and may become caught up in cycles of brooding, ruminating, and concern (especially anticipatory), trying to deal with perceived threat(s). The current pandemic has caused students to become socially isolated from their peers, and this isolation can lead to worry about perceived inadequacies, such as the ability to prosper in comparison to others (T. Gilbert 2018).

The study and the findings

In task-focused group meetings, compassion can be understood as the intention to notice (not normalise) one's own or others' distress or disadvantage, and then to take (wise) action to reduce or prevent this (T. Gilbert 2018). This approach was created and was intended specifically for the face-to-face context, not for online group work meetings. The purpose of the current study is to determine whether this Compassion focused Pedagogy (CfP) may be utilised to improve students' capacity to manage online groups of peers facilitating the adoption of a social justice lens. This intervention study aimed to explore the possibility of developing cognitive skills of compassionate communication among UK-based Sri Lankan HE STEM students in their online group work meetings. Student-led group meetings were conducted before and after the CSCC training that was given to the students concentrating on how to share knowledge with one another and so foster learning (in this case, from self-selected, peer-reviewed publications relevant to their STEM subjects) online. Further, CSCC intervention also sheds light on how students manage their group projects. Analysis of the pre-and post-CSCC intervention quantitative and qualitative data results indicated a statistically significant increase in students' screen gaze attentiveness to each other, and their motivation to switch their cameras on during the post-intervention online group work meetings. Moreover, the findings highlight how and why screen gaze helped others in the group, including strangers, and their influence in promoting social justice.

The Wilcoxon Signed-Rank Test results for screen gaze timing data in pre-and post-intervention for each group of $n = 4, p < 0.001$ indicated an improvement in all group members' sustained screen gaze after the CSCC training intervention. Further, R plots were created to analyse and then to graphically show the screen gaze behaviour of individual group members during each individual presentation and then every follow-up discussion before and after the intervention. Simultaneously, Jupyter in Python analysis was conducted to explore each group's average screen gaze behaviours before and after the intervention. Findings through the quantitative analysis showed an increase of sustained screen gaze by all group members during the follow-up discussion (after the intervention).

The micro-ethnographic analysis of all group members' behaviours during their journal article presentations and then again in their follow-up group discussions in each group indicated more prosocial behaviours of group members (verbal and non-verbal) during their post-intervention compared to their pre-intervention group meetings.

Overall, it was evidenced that screen gaze was better sustained across the groups during post-intervention group meetings than pre-intervention during the group presentations and discussions.

Adopting the lens of social justice

The findings suggest that training the students in CSCC motivated them to use practical compassionate communications to manage their group/teamwork interactions irrespective of their ethnic, religious or mother tongue differences. This may be the result of compassion being a valued concept cross-culturally (Van der Cingel 2014; Davidson and Harrington 2012; Goetz, et al. 2010; Immordino-Yang and Damasio 2007; Schwartz and Bardi 2001; Harrison and Peacock 2010). Thus, the findings are relevant for addressing the current tendency toward ethnic and religious polarization in student communities (Butt 2016; Subramanian 2015; Turner 2009; Leask 2005; Haigh 2002) and working towards a more socially just pedagogy and practice.

Equal participation and inclusivity (through non-verbal communication)

As revealed through both quantitative and qualitative findings of the study, there was a lack of screen gaze by the group members when they fulfil their roles as presenters, listeners as well as discussants. However, this lack of screen gaze contrasts with 'noticing' distress or disadvantage of group members, the first component of compassion without which the whole group is unable to observe one another's distress or disadvantage if encountered during their group meetings. The research of Vertegaal et al. (2002, 2003) is consistent with the current findings. Their eye-tracking study investigated the function of eye gaze in group work via video conferencing, finding that the distribution of eye gaze increased the effectiveness of problem-solving and decision-making and equalised involvement or participation among group members. It was particularly interesting to note that although the group's ability to maintain inclusive eye contact during in-person meetings (T. Gilbert 2016; T. Gilbert et al. 2018) was not possible online, there was an increase in camera use and, consequently, sustained screen gaze attention during the group's post-intervention meetings. The fact that the cameras are turned on during these discussion meetings is crucial to note because it appears to considerably improve screen gaze attentiveness and facilitate the equal participation of every group member. Thus, this ability to practice equal participation supports safeguarding social justice in online group meetings.

Moreover, the findings also revealed the enhancement of inclusivity through screen gaze attentiveness. If a speaker or presenter fails to look at the screen while speaking or presenting, they might fail to observe the non-verbal cues/signals made (even unconsciously) by the listeners to signal that they do not understand parts of the presentation, whether that is conceptual, or because of spoken English language errors or accent, or difficulties of English comprehension, such as from a speed of others' speech. Even a small frown or moving/turning of the head may signal to the speaker that they should repeat or/and rephrase a point. Observing these signals is useful in particular if listeners do not wish to verbally interrupt the presentation. Furthermore, if listeners do not understand and cannot signal potential difficulties non-verbally to a presenter who is not looking at them, a follow-up discussion might prove difficult. Not attending to non-verbal cues will therefore not only affect the listeners trying to communicate their difficulties in following what is said but the whole group's learning experience, in terms of the quality of criticality of the discussion that follows because some members may lack the comprehension they needed to participate. Both groups experienced such a problem during the pre-intervention group meetings.

On the one hand, if the speaker breaks or avoids screen gaze with the listeners, this may cause the listening group members to dissociate from their compassionate role of supporting the current speaker; this is true for the screen gaze of all students in the group, but particularly for the speaker. This may lead to there being no perceived necessity for listeners to sustain their own screen gaze because evidence of their attention to a speaker is not noticed by that speaker; listeners may feel that their supportive behaviours are pointless. Furthermore, in the online group format, in particular, the listeners may then become more susceptible to distractions in their physical environment. Hence, this may lead to disconnection of the listeners from the speaker creating difficulties in inclusivity in the group.

On the other hand, if the speaker does not sustain screen gaze with the listeners, it is most likely to also miss other highly communicative non-verbal signals of engagement from the listeners. Nodding and smiling are useful signals of understanding and/or encouragement to the speaker to continue. Turning/ moving heads from side to side, frowning or expressions of puzzlement or blank looks may be useful signals to the speaker that he/she is not communicating successfully at this moment, and should repeat, and/or rephrase, and/or slow down or simply stop and check understanding around the group. This also affects matters negatively, creating difficulties in securing the inclusivity of the group, as listeners might feel that they were excluded if the screen gaze was avoided or broken by the speaker. This inability of noticing their own and others' behaviours does not allow group members to observe their behaviours in terms of achieving the group tasks and securing social justice within the groups.

In order to fulfil the second component of compassion – 'taking wise actions to decrease or prevent the distress or disadvantaging of self and others' – it is critical to put the first component of compassion into practice for the setting of group work/ teamwork, which is 'noticing'. The students' realisation of the benefits of turning on their cameras during their group/team meetings online was aided by their understanding of this phenomenon and the practical implementation of the CSCC during the post-intervention task-focused group work meetings. This was made even better by their realisation that by applying what they had learned about CSCC, they could provide a variety of support to their peers. Hence, this approach appears to help address the multi-factored issue of delayed or abandoned development of social relationships that could be remedied through even non-verbal exchanges in online group meetings (Bedenlier et al. 2021; Khalil et al. 2020; Gherhes et al. 2021a, b) while aiding social justice.

Psychological safety and increased interaction

The current findings are significant for addressing negative emotions, such as those of isolation, loneliness and/or helplessness felt by students who were required to use online platforms (Butz et al. 2015). This study on compassion as an intention (not an emotion) (Compassionate Mind Foundation 2005) offers innovative perspectives for strengthening the productivity and psychological security of online team meetings. For instance, if there are four people in a group and the cameras are on, each person may see the expressions of the other three members of the group simultaneously on one screen. This is a difference in spatial dimensions for 'reading' faces and their non-verbal indications and messages (such as confusion, acceptance, disagreement and encouragement) throughout the meeting compared to when a group sits around a physical table. Further investigation into how the social brain responds in compassionate situations when oxytocin can aid in group cohesion, may be warranted by this finding alone (Colonnello et al. 2017). This is significant in light of studies like Greenfield's (2010) investigation into how children's brain architecture in digital societies is being altered by the pervasive demand for daily digital multi-focusing. According to her, 'you couldn't infer the nature and context of the game if you only concentrated on the behaviour of one player' (in a game of football, for example).

Similar to offline meetings, if students simply pay attention to the speaker during group meetings, they might not pay attentive attention to the other group members' instant facial reactions. For example, S6 in Group 2 explained the change of her previous perspective in a positive way after the CSCC intervention session.

> **S6:** I'm [I was] scared to make eye contact because I'm scared if they have this blank look on their faces like they don't understand what I'm saying. I'll have to repeat something. I'm scared of that. After this discussion, I think, I tried my best to look at everyone.
>
> Jayasundara et al. 2022: 17

However, this advantage of reading faces (in online group meetings) is only possible when attendees have their cameras are turned on.

Findings from Template Analysis conducted through NVivo (Pro 12) of transcriptions of group meetings and focus groups provided evidence for the enhancement of student interactions after the intervention. The importance of student communication, interactions and relationship building in the effective implementation of social justice, and the requirement of identifying the strategies to promote social justice through student interactions was highlighted (Guthrie and McCracken 2010).

Knowledge dissemination and critical perspectives

The analyses of the pre- vs post-intervention group meeting transcriptions indicated an enhancement of knowledge dissemination and critical perspectives during the post-intervention group meetings compared to the pre-intervention group meetings. For example, S6 in Group 2 highlighted how her group members started thinking and then contributing to the discussions after warmly inviting them (after CSCC intervention).

> **S6:** I invite someone into the discussion, um ... they might be sitting there and ... they don't understand what's going on.... by trying to be compassionate, like we have to invite someone to engage in the discussion. By that, they'll start thinking on that warm [sic] and then they will have thoughts like [to] implement, like giving ideas into that discussion.
>
> TR, PostIFG, G1

Further, group members' knowledge dissemination and critical perspective development were evidenced through the template analysis of the group meetings' transcriptions. Kolb (1984) has also indicated the significance of making a meaningful change with a learning experience that is powered through the enhancement of critical perspectives to ensure social justice.

Widening participation and community building

Moreover, students appeared to assess responses and overall reactions of the whole group to presentations or discussions more easily as they were looking at three other faces at once. Therefore, the increase of sustained screen gaze and students' tendency to look at all four faces during their post-intervention group meetings appeared to support intercultural communication and global citizenship as students from different ethnic backgrounds were found to be sharing the flow, knowledge, critical perspectives and friendship. This new possibility facilitates social justice through widening participation and community building too through the development of CSCC among online student groups. For example, S1 explained how this can be done through the application of CSCC.

> **S1:** So basically, using these strategies means that if a person is unfocused, ... using this strategy we can ask him or her to come and join the conversation or the discussion.
>
> TR, PostFG, G2

The verbal evidence for enhanced inter-student support of each other similarly aligned with the principles of non-verbal compassionate communications, as discussed in Section 4.1. Thus, the application of CSCC in groups facilitates practising social justice within and beyond the groups.

Teaching through compassion – compassionate task-design

The findings of pre-intervention focus group transcripts analyses highlighted a negative perspective of perceived social anxiety of students believing that they have limited background knowledge regarding others' journal articles. This idea led them to a negative feeling that they would not be able to contribute to the follow-up discussion due to their limited background knowledge. For example,

> **S4:** To ask questions, we should have some knowledge, the thing is this particular area, not very uh, friendly for us, for to me, ...
>
> TR, PreFG, G1

However, the analysis further revealed positive perspectives of the students regarding the overall group meeting. For example, students liked having self-chosen journal articles by each group member and four members in a group as evidenced below.

> **S3:** each one was given an equal opportunity to describe first and equal opportunity to question and answer time.
>
> TR, PreFG, G1

However, this feedback was due to two factors in the compassion-focused task design – to share knowledge and the task of criticality – not on the management of the group's communicative interactions, the third required factor of the task design, which was not evidenced.

This compassionate focused task design was also new to the students, as in their previous academic group work none of the students had experienced the task design used in this study (individual presentations and then group discussion of the content). Instead, their previous experience was of the whole class being given specific article(s) by the tutor that everyone should read.

Hence, a positive influence of the task design of this study to increase students' willingness to take part in group meetings, was evidenced through the analysis. This insight was supported by their understanding of the facilitation of such group designs/formats on enhancing their knowledge, interactivity and equal participation. Further, this task design allowed students to notice one another's non-verbal signals and to offer support to their group members when in need. Hence, the task designed for attention to compassion was also identified as an important factor that enhances students' sensitivity towards one another, encouraging social justice.

Education as transformation

As evidenced through the analysis, the CSCC appeared to support the students in transforming some of their negative group behaviours, that were apparent during the pre-intervention group discussion, into positive group behaviours during the post-intervention group meetings. For example, the students explained their previous experiences of the common group work behaviours such as inequality of sharing time, dominating behaviours, cliques, non-contribution of the group members, etc. For example:

> **S3:** What happens actually, sometimes the whole group is left out and one person is leading the whole group the whole time.
>
> TR, PreFG, G1

However, after the CSCC, students reported evidence of practising sharing equal time, sharing the notion of equal agency, a reduction of social anxiety, etc. For example:

> **S7:** after we present something, instead of asking 'any questions?', we could be more inviting.
>
> TR, PostFG, G2

The evidence above suggests the applicability of CSCC in education as a positive transformation that facilitates social justice too. The CSCC intervention session was found to increase students' sensitivity to the quality of others' social and learning experiences during the post-intervention group meetings and follow-up focus group meetings as well. Hence, the first component of compassion, *noticing*, and then *taking (wise) actions* were evident after the CSCC intervention session. Therefore, this ability to notice and take wise actions whenever self or others are in distress or disadvantaged, also facilitates students practising social justice within their group meetings. In this chapter, both quantitative and qualitative findings for verbal and non-verbal communications have indicated the development of students' social, learning and social experience have mediated with a learning experience after the CSCC intervention session.

What is discussed above provides evidence for adopting a social justice lens in EAP with the application of CSCC in online educational settings. This supports the view of providing students with tools to work towards the goal of action (Kincheloe 2004) where facilitation of cognitive skills of compassionate communication towards the practice of social justice is evidenced.

Conclusions

Current findings suggest the applicability of CSCC in online groups to facilitate promoting student interactions, equal participation, and inclusivity, ensuring psychological safety, knowledge dissemination, and critical perspective, widening participation and community building. These alterations, which every participant attributes to a fresh perspective on how to facilitate CSCC for oneself and others, point to the strengthened growth of a common, interdependent identity in each group that supports social justice. The results are also pertinent to the present focus in higher education on authentic evaluation of group/teamwork in EAP, and as preparation for adapting the lens of social justice in HE group meetings. In higher education, they guide group/teamwork activities for students, teachers, and curriculum developers. Overall, this research suggests that there are benefits for training students in CSCC for group/team meetings, which provides examples of how social justice can be practised. However, in the context of this study, future research will examine the sustainability of social justice among racially and socially divided student communities using the aforementioned CSCC-based training.

References

Afrouz, R and Crisp, B. R. (2021), 'Online Education in Social Work, Effectiveness, Benefits, and Challenges: a Scoping Review', *Australian Social Work*, 74(1): 55–67. Available online: https://doi.org/10.1080/0312407X.2020.1808030 (accessed 30 September 2022).

Alawamleh, M., Al-Twait, L. M. and Al-Saht, G. R. (2020), 'The Effect of Online Learning on Communication Between Instructors and Students During Covid-19 Pandemic', *Asian Education and Development Studies*, Vol. 11 No. 2, 380–400. Available online: https://www.emerald.com/insight/content/doi/10.1108/AEDS-06-2020-0131/full/html (accessed 18 September 2022).

Aleman, A. and Sommer, I. (2020), 'The Silent Danger of Social Distancing', *Psychological Medicine*, 1–2: pp 789–790. Available online: https://www.cambridge.org/core/journals/psychological-medicine/article/silent-danger-of-social-distancing/9CFFBF2802D6A6042A0707CD6D8E1052 (accessed 8 September 2021).

Bauer, C., Dicks, M., Holbrook, K. and Sarnell, C., 2020. 'All of My Students Turn Their Cameras Off. It's Making Class Miserable'. *Сайт журнала Slate*, 15. October 2020, https://slate.com/human-interest/2020/10/distance-learning-students-keep-cameras-on.html (accessed 20 December 2020).

Bedenlier, S., Wunder, I., Gläser-Zikuda, M., Kammerl, R., Kopp, B., Ziegler, A. and Händel, M., 2021. "Generation invisible?. Higher education students'(non) use of webcams in synchronous online learning. *International Journal of Educational Research Open, 2*, 100068 pp. 1–7 .

Butt, A. (2016) 'PEACEBRIEF210: Nationalistic Narratives in Pakistani Textbooks', United States Institute of Peace, July 16, 2016, http://www.usip.org/sites/default/files/PB210-Nationalistic-Narratives-inPakistani-Textbooks.pdf (accessed 18 January 2022).

Butz, N. T., Stupnisky, R. H. and Pekrun, R. (2015), 'Students' Emotions for Achievement and Technology Use in Synchronous Hybrid Graduate Programmes: A Control-Value Approach', Research in Learning Technology, 23: 1–16.

Castelli, F. R. and Sarvary M. A. (2021), 'Why Students do not Turn on their Video Cameras During Online Classes and an Equitable and Inclusive Plan to Encourage Them to do so', *Ecology and Evolution*, 11(8): 3565–76. Available online: https://onlinelibrary.wiley.com/doi/full/10.1002/ece3.7123 (accessed 17 February 2021).

Cacioppo, J. T. and Hawkley, L. C. (2009), 'Perceived Social Isolation and Cognition. Trends in Cognitive Sciences', 13(10): 447–54. Available online: https://www.sciencedirect.com/science/article/pii/S1364661309001478?via%3Dihub (accessed 10 August 2021).

Cozolino, L. (2013), *The Social Neuroscience of Education: Optimizing Attachment and Learning in the Classroom*, New York, NY: WW Norton & Company.

Compassionate Mind Foundation, (2005), see: http://www.compassionatemind.co.uk (accessed 12 September 2019).

Davidson, R., and Harrington, A. (2012), 'Visions of Compassion: Western Scientists and Tibetan Buddhists Examine Human Nature', *Oxford Scholarship Online*, March 2012, https://oxford.universitypressscholarship.com/view/10.1093/acprof:oso/9780195130430.001.0001/acprof-9780195130430 (accessed 1 January 2022).

Gherhes, V. and Para, S. S. I (2021a), 'Analysing Students' Reasons for Keeping Their Webcams On or Off During Online Classes', *Sustainability* 13(6), 3203. doi: 10.3390/su13063203. https://www.researchgate.net/publication/350091697_Analysing_

Students%27_Reasons_for_Keeping_Their_Webcams_on_or_off_during_Online_ Classes (accessed 5 January 2022).

Gherheș, V., Stoian, C. E., Fărcașiu, M. A. and Stanici, M. (2021b), 'E-Learning vs. Face-To-Face Learning: Analyzing Students' Preferences and Behaviors', *Sustainability*, 13: 13(8), p. 4381. Available online: https://pdfs. semanticscholar.org/2948/d853d384c92d3f3de9b8b41f9ff5a20ecf74.pdf?_ ga=2.190885610.1921795052.1648634848-36397666.1648634848 (accessed 12 January 2022).

Gilbert, P., McEwan, K., Bellew, R., Mills, A. and Gale, C. (2009), 'The Dark Side of Competition: How Competitive Behaviour and Striving to Avoid Inferiority are linked to Depression, Anxiety, Stress and Self-Harm', *Psychology and Psychotherapy: Theory, Research and Practice*, 82(2): 123–36. Available online: https://doi.org/10.1348/147608308X379806 (accessed 10 April 2020).

Gilbert, P. (2019), 'Explorations into the Nature and Function of Compassion', *Current Opinion in Psychology*, 28: 108–14. Available online: https://www.sciencedirect.com/science/article/pii/S2352250X18301222 (accessed 16 December 2021).

Gilbert, P. (2017), 'Compassion: Definitions and Controversies', in P. Gilbert (ed.), *Compassion: Concepts, Research and Applications*, 3–15,: Routledge/Taylor and Francis Group. Available online: https://doi.org/10.4324/9781315564296-1 (accessed 17 March 2020).

Gilbert, P. and Choden , (2013), *Mindful Compassion*, London: Constable and Robinson.

Gilbert, P., and Procter, S. (2006), 'Compassionate Mind Training for People with High Shame and Self-Criticism: Overview and Pilot Study of a Group Therapy Approach', *Clinical Psychology and Psychotherapy*, 13(6): 353–79. Available online: https://doi.org/10.1002/cpp.507 (accessed 20 June 2019).

Gilbert, P. (2005), 'Compassion and Cruelty: A Biopsychosocial Approach', in P. Gilbert (ed.), *Compassion: Conceptualisations, Research and Use in Psychotherapy*, 9–74, New York: Routledge.

Gilbert, T. (2016), 'Assess Compassion in Higher Education? Why and How Would We Do That?', *LINK*, 2(1), https://www.herts.ac.uk/link/volume-2,-issue-1 (accessed 12 July 2019).

Gilbert, T., Doolan, M., Beka, D. S., Spencer, N., Crotta, D. M. and Davari, S. (2018), 'Compassion on University Degree Programmes at a UK University: the Neuroscience of Effective Group Work', *Journal of Research in Innovative Teaching and Learning*, 11(1): 4–21.

Gilbert, T. and Bryan, C. (2019), 'Developing and Accessing Inclusivity in Group Learning. Innovative Assessment in Higher Education: a Handbook for Academic Practitioners', in C. Bryan and K. Clegg (eds), *Developing and assessing inclusivity in group learning*, 2nd edn, 151–62, Oxon: Routledge.

Gilbert, T. (2018), 'Embedding and Assessing Compassion in the University Curriculum', *Compassion in Education*, [blog], https://compassioninhe.wordpress.com/, accessed 9 December 2018.

Gilbert, T., (2017), 'When Looking is Allowed: What Compassionate Group Work Looks Like in a UK University', in P. Gibbs (ed.), *The Pedagogy of Compassion at the Heart of Higher Education*, 189–202, Cham; Springer.

Goetz, J. L., Keltner, D. and Simon- Thomas, E. (2010), 'Compassion: an Evolutionary Analysis and Empirical Review', *Psychological Bulletin*, 136(3): 351–74.

Greenfield, S., (2010), 'Neuroscience of Consciousness', *YouTube,* 27 November 2012, https://www.youtube.com/watch?v=WN5Fs6_O2mY&ab_channel=ANUTV [00:16:56] (accessed 8 September 2020).

Guthrie, K. L. and McCracken, H. (2010), 'Promoting Reflective Discourse Through Connectivity: Conversations Around Service-Learning Experiences', in L. Shedletsk and J. E. Aitken (eds), *Cases on Online Discussion and Interaction: Experiences and Outcomes*, 66–87, Hershey, PA: IGI Global.

Haigh, M. J. (2002), 'Internationalisation of the Curriculum: Designing Inclusive Education for a Small World', *Journal of Geography in Higher Education*, 26(1): 46–66.

Harrison, N. and Peacock, N. (2010), 'Cultural Distance, Mindfulness and Passive Xenophobia: Using Integrated Threat Theory to Explore Home Higher Education Students' Perspectives on 'Internationalisation at Home,' *British Educational Research Journal*, 36(6): 877–902.

Harvey, C., Maratos, F. A, Montague, J., Gale, M., Clarke, K. and Gilbert, T. (2020), 'Embedding Compassionate Micro Skills of Communication in Higher Education: Implementation with Psychology Undergraduates', *Psychology of Education Review*, 44(2): 68–72.

Hawkley, L. C. and Cacioppo, J. T. (2010), 'Loneliness Matters: a Theoretical and Empirical Review of Consequences and Mechanisms', *Annals Behavioural Medicine*, 40(2): 218–27.

Immordino-Yang, M. H. and Damasio, A. (2007), 'We Feel, Therefore we Learn: The Relevance of Affective and Social Neuroscience to Education', *Mind, Brain and Education*, 1(1): 115–31.

Katchen, J. E. (1992), 'Using the Video Camera to Improve Speaking and Performance Skills', in M.C. Yang (ed.), *Eighth Conference on English Language Teaching and Learning in The Republic of China*, 531–40. Available online: http://mx.nthu.edu.tw/~katchen/professional/Using%20the%20video%20camera.htm (accessed 6 January 2022).

Kolb, D. (1984), *Experiential Learning: Experience as the Source of Learning and Development*, Upper Saddle River, NJ: Prentice Hall.

Leask, B. (2005), 'Internationalisation of the Curriculum: Teaching and Learning', in J. Carroll and J. Ryan (eds), *Teaching International Students: Enhancing Learning for all Students*, 119–29, London: Routledge Falmer.

McBrien, J. L., Jones, P. and Cheng, R. (2019), 'Virtual Spaces: Employing a Synchronous Online Classroom to Facilitate Student Engagement in Online Learning', *International Review of Research in Open and Distance Learning*, 10(3): 1–17. Available online: https://doi.org/10.19173/ irrodl.v10i3.605 (accessed 18 November 2021).

Mindfulness and Clinical Psychology Solutions (2019), https://mi-psych.com.au/your-brains-3-emotion-regulation-systems/ (accessed 20 October 2019).

Schwartz, S. H. and Bardi, A. (2001), 'Value Hierarchies across Cultures: Taking a Similarities Perspective', *Journal of Cross-Cultural Psychology*, 32: 268–90.

Stanford University (2020), 'Cameras and Masks: Sustaining Emotional Connections with Your Students in an Age of COVID19 (Part 2 of 2): Tomorrow's Teaching and Learning.' Available online at: https://tomprof.stanford.edu/posting/1814 (accessed 12 January, 2021).

Subramanian, S. (2015) *This Divided Island: Stories from the Sri Lankan War*, London: Penguin Books Limited.

Turner, Y. (2009), 'Knowing Me, Knowing You, Is There Nothing We Can Do? Pedagogic Challenges in Using Group Work to Create an Intercultural Learning Space', *Journal of Studies in International Education*, 13(2): 240–55.

Van der Cingel, M. (2014), 'Compassion: The Missing Link in Quality of Care', *Nurse Education Today*, 34(9): 1253–7.

Vertegaal, R., Weevers, I., Sohn, C. and Cheung, C. (2003), 'Gaze-2: Conveying Eye Contact in Group Video Conferencing Using Eye-Controlled Camera Direction', in *Proceedings of the SIGCHI Conference on Human Factors in Computing Systems*, 521–8. Available online: https://dl.acm.org/doi/abs/10.1145/642611.642702 (accessed 24 January 2020).

Vertegaal, R. and Ding, Y. (2002), 'Explaining Effects of Eye Gaze on Mediated Group Conversations: Amount or Synchronization?', in *Proceedings of the ACM Conference on Computer Supported Cooperative Work*, 41–8, doi: 10.1145/587078 (accessed 24 January 2020).

Vertegaal, R., Weevers, I. and Sohn, C. (2002), 'GAZE-2: An Attentive Video Conferencing System', in *Conference on Human Factors in Computing Systems – Proceedings*, 736–7, Minneapolis, MA, doi: 10.1145/506443.506572 (accessed 24 January 2020).

English for Academic Purposes for Students in Fragile Environments

Yvonne Fraser

Introduction

The primary aim of this chapter is to discuss the academic and non-academic obstacles preventing more students from challenging contexts from being accepted onto overseas Master's programmes. This has been an area of personal interest and concern for several years, since working on teacher training and IELTS preparation programmes in Syrian refugee camps and host communities in Jordan, with underprivileged Egyptians on academic English programmes, on reform projects with English departments at universities across Libya, and most recently coordinating and teaching online academic English programmes for students from Afghanistan, Iran, Syria and Tajikistan.

Investigation into this area is essential for several reasons. Firstly, there is an increasing need for greater understanding of the predicaments and needs of people living in conflict zones and fragile environments, internally displaced people (IDPs) and refugees. By the end of 2021, there were 89.3 million forcibly displaced people globally (UNHCR 2021) and programme designers and educators should be more aware of learners' unique challenges (Nelson and Appleby 2015). Secondly, this chapter is an important contribution to the academic field; the fluid situations in some of these countries and absence of data in key areas concerning the difficulties faced by people still living in challenging contexts necessitates further investigation. Finally, in my experience, non-academic considerations are sometimes lacking in project/programme design, and interventions can cause additional and unnecessary stress to students already living in extremely difficult situations. It is hoped this chapter provides some insight into individual country situations, and the non-academic considerations that came through my research: trauma informed pedagogy, resilience, motivation and investment, and community and identity. Although my experience is of specific countries and programmes, the themes explored are relevant to students from other fragile environments applying for a range of postgraduate programmes overseas.

Higher education in fragile environments

Firstly, I believe it is important to discuss the term 'fragile environment'. Different terms are used by writers, for example, 'challenging context' (MacRae 2017), 'conflict zone' (Harvey and Delaney 2017), 'fragile state' and 'failed state' (Nay 2013), all of which denote subtle or significant differences in meaning and situation. In this chapter, I use 'fragile' and 'challenging' interchangeably with 'environment' and 'context' as they are more general terms applicable to the contexts I discuss.

A variety of aspects can contribute to an environment being defined as fragile, and it is vital to understand how these aspects interplay, alongside the dynamic nature of these contexts, which make working in such environments even more challenging. The Fragile States Index (n.d.) subdivides twelve risk indicators into four categories (cohesion, economic, political and social), used to measure a state's improving or deteriorating situation. Such frameworks can help avoid generalisations (Scollon 2011), and recognise the unique situations in different regions, countries, cities, towns and villages. The contexts I discuss suffer from a complex mix of political instability, extreme poverty, conflict and violence, persecution of ethnic and religious minorities, and gender inequality to name a few. Furthermore, an understanding of the educational contexts is vital for effective and empathetic programme planning and delivery. Several themes are common to the countries featured in this chapter: academic quality in general and lack of teacher training; challenges in higher education and the effects of conflict; university entrance requirements; complex language mixes; and hostility towards English. However, considerable differences obviously exist, which must be considered when programme planning for mixed nationality groups.

One of the main themes applicable to some of these countries is academic quality in general. Several papers on Afghanistan, including Alamyar (2017), report that ineffective and outdated teaching methodology is widespread. This is also arguably the case in Egypt, Libya and Syria. In Egypt and Libya I witnessed the use of traditional teaching methods and my Syrian students discussed teacher-centred approaches, which is also my experience of working with Syrian teachers. Building on the theme of academic quality, is teachers' low levels of English. Coleman's (2019) extensive British Council study, which surveyed 5,000 teachers at schools, madrasas and universities in fifteen of the thirty-four Afghan provinces, provides a useful background on English. The main findings were teachers' and students' extremely low levels of English, averaging A1 CEFR (Common European Framework of Reference for Languages) (2018). However, another significant finding was considerable variation across the country (Coleman 2019), also applicable to other areas in this chapter.

Regarding higher education in particular, the Afghan system suffered significantly under the Taliban regime, and problems remain of severe staff shortages, underqualified staff and poor academic quality (Tobenkin 2014). Data on education in Tajikistan echo this, and describe teacher shortages and unqualified teachers (DeYoung et al. 2018); however, significant differences exist between east and west Tajikistan. In Syria, the effects of conflict on education and higher education have been devastating (Dillabough et al. 2018; Milton 2019; Shaban 2020). Effects also differ vastly by region, but include the politicisation of higher education, destruction of infrastructure, displacement and de-credentialisation of staff, detention of staff and students, emotional trauma, and the end of government funding (Dillabough et al. 2018; Shaban 2020). Education is more stable in government-controlled areas, however IDPs have added pressure to these institutions (Al Hessan et al. 2016), and approximately one-third of professors have left Syria (Milton 2019). Several small-scale studies on English in higher education report significant issues: professional development for inexperienced teachers and resources are concerns at Aleppo and Sham Universities (Abdulkerim et al. 2022), and poor English language skills at Tezpur University are blamed on inadequate teaching and absence of academic skills (Mohapatra and Khoja 2017). Conversely, Al Hessan et al. (2016) describe Ministry of Higher Education training activities; however, these may have lapsed due to significant pressures on the system and competing priorities. For the students the results are significant: literacy problems in Arabic, lack of study skills, learner nonconfidence, and, significantly, language as a barrier to higher education abroad (Capstick and Delaney 2018).

In Afghanistan and Iran, university entrance requirements play a key role in students' English levels. Because English is not included in the *kankor* (university entrance examination) in Afghanistan, students lack motivation for English (Coleman 2019) and enter university with low proficiency. A qualitative study of students' English proficiency at Kandahar University also blames English exclusion from the *kankor* and ineffective teaching for low English levels (Sahibzada et al.

2018). Unfortunately, English levels at Kandahar University are among the highest, so the situation at other governmental universities may be worse, resulting in under-utilised overseas scholarships (Coleman 2019). A host of new, private universities filled this gap after the US invasion (Tobenkin 2014), and evidence indicates students who attended these institutions have higher language proficiency (Alamyar 2017). However, with recent changes in government, these partnerships with overseas universities may end. In contrast to Afghanistan, in Iran, English is a requirement in the *kankor*, perhaps accounting for higher English levels at universities (Moharami and Daneshfar 2022). However, centralised policymaking where educators were not consulted, has resulted in English curricula lacking appropriate content (Atai and Mazlum 2012).

Like Afghanistan, Tajikistan's complex language mix – the official national language (Tajik), the former common language (Russian), and the first language of most people in Gorno-Badakhshan in the east (Shughni) (Bolander 2016; DeYoung et al. 2018) – can disadvantage minority language speakers in education (Bahry 2016). Adding to this, significant Aga Khan Development Network investment in English education since the 1990s (Bolander 2017; Mostowlansky 2017), notably at the University of Central Asia, has elevated English (rather than Russian) to second language status (Bolander 2017), and in 2001 English Medium Instruction (EMI) was introduced specifically to facilitate international higher education (ibid.). Echoing concerns in some literature (Bolander 2016, 2021; DeYoung et al. 2018), my Tajik students discussed the challenges of learning multiple languages, rather than feeling empowered by the 'dual identity' discussed by Tadayon and Khodi (2016: 131). Different alphabets (Persian and Cyrillic) compound reading and writing issues in English even at higher levels, which is relevant to the other contexts, particularly Afghanistan, where students also learn multiple languages (Coleman 2019). It would be interesting to investigate whether EMI at the University of Central Asia and Kabul University has actually disadvantaged students or resulted in significantly improved language levels.

A further explanation for low language levels is hostility towards English, partly due to Taliban rule in Afghanistan (Coleman 2019) and post-2005 government policy in Iran (Farhady et al. 2010). Security concerns can result in high levels of student and teacher absenteeism, as in Afghanistan (Coleman 2019). For Afghan students wishing to take international entrance examinations, insufficient good private language courses represent a further obstacle, particularly in southern regions (Sahibzada et al. 2018), partly due to security issues around teaching and learning English (Alamyar 2017). In Iran this led to a 'purification' (Borjian 2013: 137) particularly in further and higher education, still relevant today (Moharami and Daneshfar, 2022), which resulted in the dominance of indigenised resources produced by local scholars, the closure of the British Council, the removal of international publishers, and the banning of private language institutions' foreign partnerships. Developing the theme of 'purification', a paper from the British Council's compilation on culture and learning English, claims Ministry of Education ESP-focused resources disadvantage university students taking international examinations, as they do not reference other cultures, teach students skills to manage authentic texts, or encourage critical/reflective thinking (Zandian 2015). Small-scale case studies undertaken at specific universities also discuss unsuitable course materials for a globalised world (Khajavi and Abbasian 2011; Samar and Davari 2011; Zohoorian and Pandian 2014), supporting Zandian's (2015) findings. To develop their academic English skills, the only option may be private courses, although these are only available to students who can afford the high costs (Aghagolzadeh and Davari 2017; Bolander 2017; Haghighi and Norton 2017). In my experience, successful students may have an academic culture shock and be overwhelmed by contrasting learning styles and very different academic demands in the UK.

Trauma informed pedagogy

Building on the themes in the previous section, it is essential to consider the most significant effects of instability and conflict on education: specifically language learning, and students' emotional well-being when planning interventions. For example, my Afghan students have discussed feelings of hopelessness, the psychological effects of the Taliban regime, and the effects on girls' and women's education. Less well reported by international media were government crackdowns in eastern Tajikistan which resulted in internet disconnection for several months and numerous arrests (Tondo 2022).

Moving to pedagogical interventions: similar to other areas of interest, most literature appears to focus on refugee education in host communities and camps, not education for students living in fragile environments (Capstick and Delaney 2018; Holmkvist et al. 2018; Ipek 2021; Palanac 2019; Shapiro et al. 2020). When planning and implementing pedagogical interventions, I believe of utmost importance is consideration of the principle of 'do no harm' (Active Learning Network for Accountability and Performance (ALNAP) 2018). The growing number of refugees and IDPs necessitates teachers (community-based and online) who have knowledge of how to support these students (Nelson and Appleby 2015).

I am aware of projects where there has been insufficient consideration of context, planning, risk assessment and continuing support after programme completion, and reports of such lessons learned are deficient in the literature. The most effective interventions build sustainability into the project design, commonly through training master trainers and cascade training programmes (Kennedy 2015), or through creating communities of practice (Wenger 1998), strengthening community cohesion and resilience (Capstick and Delaney 2018).

Another crucial consideration regarding additional support, is teacher training and professional development, absent in many fragile environments. A common literature theme is how supportive classroom environments can help address trauma (Capstick 2018), something personally witnessed with groups of Afghans, Libyans, Syrians and Tajiks. This highlights the importance of providing educators with specialised training in managing the results of instability, for example, trauma, mixed ability classes and lack of resources (Capstick and Delaney 2018). Crucial in these contexts are the psychosocial aspects of learning, which should be combined with language learning, not dealt with separately. Trauma can be addressed through creative activities in the safe space of a second language learning environment, and inclusion of psychosocial aspects into course materials (Capstick and Delaney 2018). Student counsellors are advocated by NGOs (UNRWA 2021); however, there should be consideration for online classes regarding platform security and student safety.

Discussion regarding the prioritisation of home languages, the predominantly negative impacts of EMI, and specific considerations for developing countries and fragile environments, are relevant and interesting considerations in the context of fragile states. A critique of several language initiatives in Bangladesh argues for the focus on literacy and numeracy in home languages, rather than English language education (Erling 2017b). Regarding Afghanistan, Coleman (2021) discusses the disadvantages of teaching English, and particularly the adoption of EMI. Firstly, most Afghan teachers do not have the language skills to effectively teach in English (Alamyar 2017). Secondly, in regions where Dari and Pashto (the official languages) are the medium of instruction, but not commonly home languages, English levels (and overall educational achievement) are lower, and introducing EMI could increase problems. Displacement in recent years due to conflict compounds the issue of children not being literate in the local languages of education, adding to vulnerabilities and absenteeism (Hatsaandh 2019). As part of their study into refugee resilience, Capstick and Delaney (2018) also stress the significance of the medium of instruction and importance of home languages, as these offer protection, community solidarity and a foundation for additional languages. Kester and Chang (2021) attempt to fill a knowledge gap concerning EMI in conflict afflicted areas, and go beyond language development to discuss the dangers of EMI due to the association of English with colonialism, epistemic injustice and Western-dominated curricula.

Resilience

The term 'language for resilience' has been used in recent years to describe educational projects in fragile contexts, particularly by the British Council regarding interventions in the Middle East, predominantly Iraq, Palestine and Syria (Capstick and Delaney 2018). Resilience is defined in various ways; conceptualised best in the 3RP Annual Report (2017: 9): 'resilience refers to the ability of individuals, households, communities, and societies to withstand shocks and stresses, recover from such stresses, and work with national and local government institutions to achieve transformational change for sustainability.'

Because resilience is a major theme in the literature, and highly relevant to the contexts considered in this chapter, a separate section is warranted. Two interconnected aspects of resilience are relevant: academic and emotional (Capstick 2018). Academic resilience describes increases in educational and employment opportunities for individuals, enabling them to positively impact household and community resilience through increased economic resources (Capstick 2018; Nelson and Appleby 2015), particularly in host communities. A central theme is the importance of language for building intercultural understanding and positive community relationships (Erling 2017a; Imperiale et al. 2017), especially for communities learning together (Capstick and Delaney 2018). Furthermore, combining home languages with the host community language (or second/third languages), can result in Tadayon and Khodi's (2016) empowering 'dual identity', and enable intercommunity communication.

Emotional resilience, that is, how people can improve their wellbeing, deal with trauma, tell their stories, and be empowered through language learning (Capstick 2018; Capstick and Delaney 2018; Palanac 2019), is of particular interest. Promoting wellbeing through alternative teaching methods and providing psychosocial support, is mandated by the United Nations Relief and Work Agency for Palestine Refugees' Education in Emergencies programme (UNRWA 2021). Developing the notion of emotional resilience, reports evidence that foreign language learning, particularly English, can provide people with a voice (Kramsch 2015) so their predicaments can be understood at an international level. The significance of English as a political tool is highlighted by a Palestinian teacher training programme (Imperiale et al. 2017). Participant feedback emphasised the importance of 'critical hope' (Freire 1994, cited in Imperiale et al. 2017: 34), namely, increased feelings of awareness, empowerment and resistance to better their situation, and ability to communicate their situation to the world through teaching and learning English. A context warranting further investigation is where movement is prohibited, and therefore monolingualism and 'enforced monoculturalism' (Imperiale et al. 2017: 33) are the norm, which is the case in Gaza and with girls' and women's education (or lack of) in Afghanistan.

Focus groups with various students, predominantly from Afghanistan, Syria and Tajikistan, echoed the themes in the literature. Students discussed additional resilience, commitment and motivation to succeed due to the possible positive impact on their communities after completing their studies. Their responses evidence academic and emotional resilience, and the empowering nature of language learning (Capstick 2018). Moreover, some students described actually being emboldened by conflict, leading to increased motivation, investment and resilience (Imperiale 2017; Shakhshir 2011), themes discussed in the following section.

Learner motivation and investment

Substantial research attests to the link between learners' motivation and engagement, and academic success (Gettinger and Walter 2012), underlining the significance of these factors. Furthermore, the specific nature of language learning and growth of communicative teaching methodologies necessitate engagement, the meaningful use of language and interaction (Hiver et al. 2021). When examining online programmes for students in fragile environments in particular, understanding of the interconnected themes of motivation, engagement, investment, learner identity, the role of community and online learning, is essential.

Firstly, in distinguishing between motivation and engagement, I concur with Reschly and Christenson (2012), who define motivation as an unobservable intent, and engagement as an observable action. Therefore, engagement is more measurable because it can be more easily monitored. Moreover, motivation can be a precursor and an effect on engagement, although I agree with Appleton et al. (2008) that motivation does not always result in engagement. Therefore, engagement in particular tasks, activities and modules may vary, indicating motivation is more constant and engagement fluctuating, depending on different factors, including workload, teacher-student relationships and external pressures (Muir et al. 2019). In my experience, students do not lack motivation, but varying engagement may be due to their previous learning experiences and styles, and certainly practical and emotional contextual influences (Nelson and Appleby 2015).

Developing the theme of motivation, it is relevant to consider investment in learning, a more sociological framework than the psychological construct of motivation (Norton 2016). The difference between motivation and investment is important, as students may be motivated to learn, but not invested in the teaching methodology or community, affecting outcomes (Norton 2013). This notion of investment was previously described as cultural capital, gained through education and qualifications, which should lead to better career opportunities (Bourdieu 1991; Norton 2016). Furthermore, in line with poststructuralist theory, Norton (2013) argues by investing in language acquisition, learners understand that symbolic and material resources can increase their future social standing and power, something particularly prized in some communities (Bolander 2018, 2021). This link between cultural capital, investment and future opportunities, is supported by several project reports which highlight the importance of language for learners in fragile environments (Ameen and Cinkara 2018; Capstick and Delaney 2018; Tadayon and Khodi 2016; Kester and Chang 2021). However, research also highlights students' ambitions to return to their countries after their studies and to work to bring positive changes to their home countries and communities, arguably specific to students from more challenging contexts. Students also discussed being motivated to become strong community leaders, respected in their communities as graduates from renowned UK universities. Literature on investment is corroboratory regarding investment in education and language learning to increase social standing (Norton 2013; Bolander 2018, 2021).

Regarding engagement specifically in online learning – commonly the only option in fragile contexts – practical considerations are essential. In unpredictable and unstable environments, there can be copious distractions (Mercer and Dörnyei 2020), amplified when studying from home in places with frequent power cuts and unstable internet connections, highlighted in Gray's (2016) report on online learning in Libya. These practical challenges have affected many of my students, particularly when entire programmes are delivered online. Issues are mainly due to internet connectivity, internet cost and quality in Afghanistan and Iran, while Syrian students also struggle with only two hours of electricity per day. More consideration into the timing of classes and consistently recording lessons could partly overcome some of these issues. Furthermore, studying from home rather than at a university or workplace, can create additional challenges. Some students are unable to find quiet places to study, and some cannot afford laptops so attempt to study using their phones. Students also discussed the emotional toll from constantly dealing with these issues, affecting engagement. Literature corroborates these discussions, and outlines the distress that can be caused by the learning environment (Hatsaandh 2019; Kester and Chang 2021). A much greater awareness of situations in-country is therefore vital for programme designers and educators, particularly for those outside the students' environments.

Furthermore, students' (and support staff's) digital literacy and acquaintance with platforms also affect engagement (Grey 2016), and so a pedagogical foundation in using educational technology is vital. Without sufficient training, students (and teachers) can be overwhelmed and actually disengage (Bedenlier et al. 2020). It would be useful to research the implementation and success of such training for students isolated at home, rather than at an educational institution. Furthermore, following the recent upsurge in online learning, innovative uses of learning technology have been developed to promote engagement, documented by several project reports. For instance, Akbari et al. (2016) report on the higher TOEFL scores and engagement levels of a Facebook group compared to a face-to-face class, and two British Council projects, PRELIM (Aylett and Clarke 2021) and B-MELTT (Orsini-Jones et al. 2018), demonstrate imaginative blends of synchronous and asynchronous learning using WhatsApp, Zoom and Massive Open Online Courses (MOOCs). My experiences, specifically in Jordan and Libya, also show platform combinations and flexibility for different contexts are essential in promoting engagement. Furthermore, my students described how the different platforms had facilitated their learning and made their online programmes collaborative, beneficial and enjoyable. They discussed using Zoom to socialise after classes and how they found commenting on each other's work on Moodle collaborative and motivating.

Community and identity

Closely linked to motivation, investment and commitment is learner identity (Dörnyei 2009; Bourdieu 1991; Norton 2013). Dörnyei (2009) discusses motivation as driven by learners' aspiration to move from their actual selves to ideal selves, described as the 'L2 Motivational Self System' (Dörnyei 2009: 9). Of additional importance are influences from the learning experience including the immediate learning environment (Dörnyei 2009), and more broadly the effects of culture and context on 'identity content' (Galliher et al. 2017: 2011). Language learning can be described as a 'social practice' (Norton 2016: 426) where identity is realised through unequal relationships, and as 'the way a person understands his or her relationship to the world, [...] and possibilities for the future' (Norton 2013: 4). Research into specific groups supports Norton's identity theories, Hobsbawm's discussion of identity as 'multi-dimensional' (1996: 1067), and Arnett's 'bicultural identity' (2002: 777). For example, studies into language learning effects on immigrants discuss identity changes as unavoidable, but dual or multiple identities can be empowering and increase opportunities (Tadayon and Khodi 2016; Dörnyei 2010).

Regarding community identity, there are two overarching aspects: identity within a community, and identity in external host or wider communities. Data appears to be lacking on vulnerable, marginalised people living within their own fragile contexts, while literature focuses on immigrant/refugee communities. These studies discuss the importance of common language to reduce hostility and intercultural misunderstanding (Scollon 2011), and broadening conventional language teaching boundaries to prioritise communicative practice better equipping refugees for the globalised world (Baker 2022). Considering community identity in fragile contexts, shared language can foster feelings of belonging and safety, important in identity construction, and can strengthen group solidarity (Capstick and Delaney 2018). Furthermore, research into the complex mix of languages in Central Asia highlights the importance of language for maintaining identity within multilingual communities (Bahry 2016). Literature from the region also discusses the additional influence of religious identity on community and English language learning (Beben 2019), which transcends national borders, ethnicity and home languages (Bolander 2018, 2021). Echoing the literature, my students are generally very positive about the support they receive from their wider communities and describe technical help, support with internet connectivity and emotional support.

To link motivation, identity and community, it is essential to discuss where students live, and their learning communities. The socio-educational model of language acquisition emphasises integrative (second language culture/community insights) and instrumental (practical reasons, for example, work) motivation (Gardner 2002). Developing the notion of integration, in addition to this culture/community aspect, learners' conditions and contexts (Dörnyei

2003), or 'person-environment fit' (Reschly and Christenson 2012: 13), are crucial to understanding factors influencing engagement, and means of increasing it. Of additional importance is consideration of the interrelated aspects of learners' environments, including family, community and culture (Shernoff 2013). The broader context of countries is also vital, especially when discussing fragile environments.

Regarding learning/classroom communities, social interactionism theory (Williams and Burden 1997) supports Gardner's (2002) 'integrativeness' by stressing the importance of the social aspect and inclusion of L2 culture in the learning process. Access to other languages and cultures, building classroom relationships and supportive learning activities can increase group and individual resilience, lessen feelings of isolation, and increase wellbeing (Capstick and Delaney 2018). Dörnyei (2010) develops 'integrativeness' to self-identification as a global citizen through English language learning, which may increase instrumental motivation and investment, particularly for students in fragile environments. However, this integration can be lacking for students in their home countries, particularly online, who may feel detached from the L2 culture and classroom community. Collaborative activities and online discussions may promote engagement and integration (Robinson and Hullinger 2008), and the concept of virtual classroom communities or 'imagined communities' (Norton 2014: 160) can be perceived as integration. My students are overwhelmingly positive about their online learning experiences and discussed classrooms transcending national borders and the benefits of cultural diversity. In addition to classmate relationships, the student-teacher relationship is vital, and can be established through a strong teacher presence (Martin and Bolliger 2018) and a course designed specifically for online learning that connects students and teachers through engaging materials (Stone 2017). Teacher communication is also paramount (Muir et al. 2019), and could be achieved through more regular tutorials.

Conclusions and recommendations

To conclude, my experience and research highlighted the significance of the non-academic factors affecting students living in fragile environments, and the interconnectedness and importance of resilience, motivation, investment, community and identity to some of these students. In my experience academic factors are either the only or primary considerations and the non-academic factors are sometimes overlooked by programme designers and educators. Interestingly, for some students, fragile home environments seemed to bolster their motivation and resilience, perhaps giving them greater impetus to serve and better their communities. These findings highlight the importance of not only understanding students' academic needs, but also their unique motivations, contexts, and resulting emotional and practical needs.

My overarching recommendation for programme designers is thorough needs analysis. This may sound obvious; however, due to the lack of data and students' differing academic backgrounds and needs, greater understanding is essential before programme design and any financial investment. Furthermore, non-academic factors are essential and individual student situations and contexts must be included when analysing needs. Additionally, I would strongly advise regular individual tutorials, perhaps with a trained counsellor. My students discussed the benefits of one-to-one academic support, and a non-academic aspect would allow greater understanding of students' challenges and needs. Through tutorials, possible psychosocial needs could be more easily identified, which may necessitate external expertise. I would also recommend specific training for teachers in working with students from fragile environments and conflict zones.

Based on my findings and experience in this field, there are clear directions for future research. The focus of current research is on education and non-academic interventions for refugee and migrant populations, while there is a significant gap in data regarding the situations of people still living in fragile environments. Another aspect noticeably absent in the literature was students' voices and individuals' feedback on their experiences and perspectives of interventions. I addressed this to some extent, however there is a need for a more substantive understanding of learners' needs in challenging environments, so their complex situations can be more thoroughly accounted for when designing and delivering programmes.

Finally, further research into the motivation and engagement of learners in fragile environments and their resilience would be extremely worthwhile and interesting for programme designers and educators. My work highlights the huge challenges these students must overcome to acquire proficient English skills. Investigation and greater understanding of whether the worsening situations in Afghanistan and Tajikistan, and adverse conditions in other countries, provide learners with additional motivation and investment in helping their communities, could direct programme planning, and influence this vital provision of student support.

References

3RP Annual Report (2017), available at: https://reliefweb.int/sites/reliefweb.int/files/resources/63530.pdf (last accessed 01-09-2023).

Abdulkerim, A., Nasır, A., Parkinson, T., Marais, D., Altaha, R. and Shaban, F. (2022), 'Enhancing Higher Education Teaching and Learning in Northern Syria: Academic Development Needs of Teaching Staff at Free Aleppo and Sham Universities', *International Journal of Education Research Open*, 3: 100143.

Active Learning Network for Accountability and Performance (ALNAP) (2018), *Incorporating the Principle of "Do No Harm": How to Take Action Without Causing Harm*, available from:https://www.alnap.org/system/files/content/resource/files/main/donoharm_pe07_synthesis.pdf (accessed 30 September 2021).

Aghagolzadeh, F. and Davari, H. (2017), 'English Education in Iran: From Ambivalent Policies to Paradoxical Practices', in R. Kirkpatrick (ed.), *English Language Education Policy in the Middle East and North Africa*, 47–62, Cham: Springer.

Akbari, E., Naderi, A., Simons, R-J. and Pilot, A. (2016), 'Student Engagement and Foreign Language Learning Through Online Social Networks', *Asian-Pacific Journal of Second and Foreign Language Education*, 1(4): 1–22.

Alamyar, M. N. A. (2017), 'Emerging Roles of English in Afghanistan', *INTESOL*, 14(1): 1–24.

Al Hessan, M., Bengtsson, S. and Kohlenberger, J. (2016), 'Understanding the Syrian Educational System in a Context of Crisis', *Austrian Academy of Sciences*, 9: 1–44.

Ameen, R. F. and Cinkara, E. (2018), 'The Impact of Language Learning on Internally Displaced and Refugee Resilience', *European Journal of Educational Research*, 7(3): 529–38.

Appleton, J. J., Christenson, S. and Furlong, M. J. (2008), Student Engagement with School: Critical Conceptual and Methodological Issues of the Construct', *Psychology in the Schools*, 45(5): 369–86.

Arnett, J. J. (2002), 'The Psychology of Globalization', *American Psychologist*, 57(10): 774–83.

Atai, M. R. and Mazlum, F. (2013), 'English Language Teaching Curriculum in Iran: Planning and Practice', *The Curriculum Journal*, 24(3): 389–411.

Aylett, R. and Clarke, M. (2021), *Partnered Remote Language Improvement (PRELIM) Project Report*, London: British Council.

Bahry, S. A. (2016), 'Societal Multilingualism and Personal Plurilingualism in Pamir Tajikistan's Complex Language Ecology', in E. S. Ahn (ed.), *Language Change in Central Asia*, 125–48, Berlin: De Gruyter.

Baker, W. (2021), 'From Intercultural to Transcultural Communication', *Language and Intercultural Communication*, 22(3), pp.280-293.

Beden, D. (2019), 'Religious Identity in the Pamirs: the Institutionalisation of the Ismaili Da'wa in Shughnan', in D. Dagiev and C. Faucher (eds), *Identity, History and*

Trans-Nationality in Central Asia. *The Mountain Communities of Pamir,* 123–42, Oxen: Routledge.

Bedenlier, S., Bond, M., Buntins, K., Zawacki-Richter, O. and Kerres, M. (2020), 'Facilitating Student Engagement through Educational Technology in Higher Education: A Systematic Review in the Field of Arts and Humanities', *Australasian Journal of Educational Technology,* 36(4): 126–50.

Bolander, B. (2016), 'English Language Policy as Ideology in Multilingual Khorog, Tajikistan', in E. Barakos and W. J. Unger (eds), *Discursive Approaches to Language Policy,* 253–74, London: Palgrave Macmillan.

Bolander, B. (2017), English, Motility and Ismaili Transnationalism', *International Journal of the Sociology of Language,* 247: 71–88.

Bolander, B. (2018), 'Scaling Value: Transnationalism and the Aga Khan's English as a "Second Language" policy', *Language Policy,* 17: 179–97.

Bolander, B. (2021), 'Voices of English: Language and the Construction of Religious Identity Amongst Ismaili Muslims in Pakistan and Tajikistan', *International Journal of the Sociology of Language,* 271: 87–106.

Borjian, M. (2013), *English in Post-Revolutionary Iran,* Bristol: Multilingual Matters.

Bourdieu, P. (1991), *Language and Symbolic Power,* Cambridge: Harvard University Press.

Capstick, T. (2018), 'Resilience', *ELT Journal,* 72(2): 210–3.

Capstick, T. and Delaney, M. (2018), *Language for Resilience The Role of Language in Enhancing the Resilience of Syrian Refugees and Host Communities,* London: British Council.

Coleman, H. (2019), *The Condition of English in Multilingual Afghanistan,* London: British Council.

Coleman, H. (2021), 'The Roles of English in Afghanistan', *World Englishes,* 41(1), pp.54–71.

Council of Europe (2018), *Common European Framework of Reference for Languages: Learning, Teaching, Assessment. Companion Volume with New Descriptors. Strasbourg: Language Policy Division.* Available online: https://rm.coe.int/cefr-companion-volume-with-new-descriptors-2018/1680787989 (accessed 8 June 2022).

DeYoung, A. J., Kataeva, Z and Jonbekova, D. (2018), 'Higher Education in Tajikistan: Institutional Landscape and Key Policy Developments', in J. Huisman, A. Smolentseva and I. Froumin (eds), *25 Years of Transformations of Higher Education Systems in Post-Soviet Countries,* 363–86, Cham: Palgrave.

Dillabough, J-A., Fimyar, O., McLaughlin, C., Al-Azmeh, Z., Abdullateef, S. and Abedtalas, M. (2018), 'Conflict, Insecurity and the Political Economies of Higher Education. The Case of Syria Post-2011', *International Journal of Comparative Education and Development,* 20(3/4): 176–96.

Dörnyei, Z. (2003), 'Attitudes, Orientations, and Motivations in Language Learning: Advances in Theory, Research, and Applications', *Language Learning,* 53(S1): 3–32.

Dörnyei, Z. (2009), 'The L2 Motivational Self System', in Z. Dörnyei and E. Ushioda (eds), *Motivation, Language Identity and the L2 Self,* 9–42, Bristol: Multilingual Matters.

Dörnyei, Z. (2010), *The Psychology of the Language Learner: Individual Differences in Second Language Acquisition,* London: Routledge/Taylor and Francis.

Erling, E. J., ed. (2017a), *English Across the Fracture Lines: the Contribution and Relevance of English to Security, Stability and Peace,* London: British Council.

Erling, E. J. (2017b), 'Language Planning, English Language Education and Development Aid in Bangladesh', *Current Issues in Language Planning,* 18(4): 388–406.

Farhady, H., Hezaveh, F.S. and Hedayati, H., 2010. Reflections on Foreign Language Education in Iran. *Tesl-ej,* 13(4), p.n4.

Fragile States Index. (n.d.), available at: https://fragilestatesindex.org/indicators/ (accessed 11 July 2022).

Galliher, R. V., McLean, K. C. and Syed, M. (2017), 'An Integrated Developmental Model for Studying Identity Content in Context', *Developmental Psychology,* 53(11): 2011–22.

Gardner, R. C. (2002) 'Integrative Motivation and Second Language Acquisition', in Z. Dörnyei and R. Schmidt (eds), *Motivation and Second Language Learning,* 2nd edn, 1–20, Honolulu: University of Hawai'i Press.

Gettinger, M. and Walter, M. J. (2012), 'Classroom Strategies to Enhance Academic Engaged Time', in S. L. Christenson, A. L. Reschly and C. Wylie (eds), *Handbook of Research on Student Engagement,* 653–74, New York: Springer.

Gray, B. (2016), 'Skype-Based Teacher Training Solutions in Libya', available at: https://www.teachingenglish.org.uk/article/ben-gray-skype-based-teacher-training-solutions-libya (accessed 3 November 2021).

Haghighi, F. M. and Norton, B. (2017), 'The Role of English Language Institutes in Iran', *TESOL Quarterly,* 51(2): 428–38.

Harvey, K. and Delaney, M. (2017), 'The Emotional Health of English Language Teachers Working in Tough Environments', in E. J. Erling (ed.), *English Across the Fracture Lines: the Contribution and Relevance of English to Security, Stability and Peace,* 81–90, London: British Council.

Hatsaandh, A. H. (2019) 'The Need For Bilingual Education in Afghanistan', available at: https://www.eurasiareview.com/23042019-the-need-for-bilingual-education-in-afghanistan-analysis/ (accessed 8 June 2022).

Hiver, P., Al-Hoorie, A. H., Vitta, J. P. and Wu, J. (2021), 'Engagement in Language Learning: A Systematic Review of 20 Years of Research Methods and Definitions', *Language Teaching Research,* 1–30.

Hobsbawm, E. (1996), 'Language, Culture, and National Identity', *Social Research,* 63(4): 1065–80.

Holmkvist, E., Sullivan, K. and Westum, A. (2018), 'Swedish Teachers' Understandings of Post Traumatic Stress Disorder among Adult Refugee-background Learners', in S. R. Shapiro, R. Farrelly and M. J. Curry (eds), *Educating Refugee-background Students: Critical Issues and Dynamic Contexts,* 177–90, Bristol: Multilingual Matters.

Imperiale, M. G., Phipps, A., Al-Masri, N. and Fassetta, G. (2017), 'Pedagogies of Hope and Resistance: English Language Education in the Context of the Gaza Strip,

Palestine', in E. J. Erling (ed.), *English Across the Fracture Lines: the Contribution and Relevance of English to Security, Stability and Peace,* 81–90, London: British Council.

Ipek, O. F. (2021), 'English Language for Refugees at Higher Education', *International Journal of Education,* 9(2): 77–87.

Kennedy, C., eds (2015), *English Language Teaching in the Islamic Republic of Iran: Innovations, Trends and Challenges,* London: British Council.

Kester, K. and Chang, S. Y. (2021), 'Whither Epistemic (In)Justice? English Medium Instruction in Conflict-Affected Contexts', *Teaching in Higher Education: Critical Perspectives,* 27(4): 437–52.

Khajavi, Y. and Abbasian, R. (2011), 'English Language Teaching, National Identity and Globalization in Iran: the Case of Public Schools', *International Journal of Humanities and Social Science,* 1(10): 181–6.

Kramsch, C. (2015), Language and Culture in Second Language Learning', in F. Sharifian (ed.), *The Routledge Handbook of Language and Culture,* 403–16, New York: Routledge.

MacRae, E. (2017), 'Promoting Intercultural Understanding through the British Council's Work in North Korea (DPRK)', in E. J. Erling (ed.), *English Across the Fracture Lines: the Contribution and Relevance of English to Security, Stability and Peace,* 123–8, London: British Council.

Martin, F. and Bolliger, D. U. (2018), 'Engagement Matters: Student Perceptions on the Importance of Engagement Strategies in the Online Learning Environment', *Online Learning,* 22(1): 205–22.

Mercer, S. and Dörnyei, Z. (2020), *Engaging Language Learners in Contemporary Classrooms,* Cambridge: Cambridge University Press.

Milton, S. (2019), 'Syrian HE During Conflict: Survival, Protection, and Regime Security', *International Journal of Educational Development,* 64(1): 38–47.

Minett, A. J. (2017), 'English Language Teachers on the Fracture Lines: Voices and Views from Afghanistan and Iraq', in E. J. Erling (ed.), *English Across the Fracture Lines: the Contribution and Relevance Of English to Security, Stability and Peace,* 23–30, London: British Council.

Mohapatra, D. and Khoja, B. (2017), 'The Real Story of English Language Teaching in Syrian High Schools and the Bumpy Transition into the University Level', English in South-East Asia Conference Talk: Thailand 2017.

Moharami, M. and Daneshfar, S. (2022), 'The Political Climate of English Language Education in Iran: A Review of Policy Responses to Cultural Hegemony', *Issues in Educational Research,* 32(1): 248–63.

Mostowlansky, T. (2017), 'Building Bridges across the Oxus: Language, Development, and Globalization at the Tajik-Afghan Frontier', *International Journal of the Sociology of Language,* 1–29.

Muir, T., Milthorpe, N., Stone, C., Dyment, J., Freeman E. and Hopwood, B. (2019), 'Chronicling Engagement: Students' Experience of Online Learning Over Time', *Distance Education,* 40(2): 262–77.

Nay, O. (2013), 'Fragile and Failed States: Critical Perspectives on Conceptual Hybrids', *International Political Science Review,* 34(3): 326–41.

Nelson, C. D. and Appleby, R. (2015), 'Conflict, Militarization, and their After-effects: Key Challenges for TESOL', *TESOL Quarterly,* 49(2): 309–32.

Norton, B. (2013), *Identity and Language Learning: Extending the Conversation,* 2nd edn, Bristol: Multilingual Matters.

Norton, B. (2014), 'Non-participation, Imagined Communities and the Language Classroom', in M. P. Breen (ed.), *Learner Contributions to Language Learning: New Directions in Research,* 159–71, Harlow, UK: Longman.

Norton, B. (2016) 'Identity and Language Learning: Back to the Future', *TESOL Quarterly,* 50(2): 475–9.

Orsini-Jones, M., Conde, B., Borthwick, K., Zou, B. and Ma, W. (2018), *B-MELTT: Blending MOOCs for English Language Teacher Training,* London: British Council.

Palanac, A. (2019), 'Towards a Trauma-Informed ELT Pedagogy for Refugees', *Language Issues,* 30(2): 3–14.

Reschly, A. and Christenson, S. (2012), 'Jingle, Jangle and Conceptual Haziness: Evolution and Future Directions of the Engagement Construct', in S. L. Christenson, A. L. Reschly and C. Wylie (eds), *Handbook of Research on Student Engagement,* 3–20, New York: Springer.

Robinson, C. C. and Hullinger, H. (2008), 'New Benchmarks in Higher Education: Student Engagement in Online Learning', *Journal of Education for Business,* 84(2): 101–8.

Sahibzada, J., Saeedi, K. H. and Hussaini, S. M. A. (2018), 'The Causes of English Language and Literature Students' Poor English Skills at Kandahar University', *International Journal for Innovative Research in Multidisciplinary Field,* 4(10): 1–14.

Samar, R. G. and Davari, I. H. (2011), 'Liberalist or Alarmist: Iranian ELT Community's Attitude to Mainstream ELT vs. Critical ELT', *TESOL Journal,* 6(5): 63–91.

Scollon, R. (2011), *Intercultural Communication: a Discourse Approach,* 3rd edn, Chichester: Wiley-Blackwell.

Shaban, F. (2020), 'Rebuilding Higher Education in Northern Syria', *Education and Conflict Review,* 3: 53–9.

Shakhshir, K. (2011), 'Palestinian Education under Occupation: Successes and Challenges', in I. Nasser, L. N. Berlin and S. Wong (eds), *Examining Education, Media, and Dialogue Under Occupation: the Case of Palestine and Israel,* 3–13, Bristol: Multilingual Matters.

Shapiro, S., Farrelly, R. and Curry, M. J., eds (2018), *Educating Refugee-background Students: Critical Issues and Dynamic Contexts,* Bristol: Multilingual Matters.

Shernoff, D. J. (2013), *Optimal Learning Environments to Promote Student Engagement,* New York: Springer.

Stone, C. (2017), *Opportunity Through Online Learning: Improving Student Access, Participation and Success in Higher Education (Equity Fellowship Final Report),* Perth, Australia: National Centre for Student Equity in Higher Education.

Tadayon, F. and Khodi, A. (2016), Empowerment of Refugees by Language: Can ESL Learners Affect the Target Culture?', *TESL Canada Journal/Revue TESL Du Canada*, 33(10): 129–37.

Tobenkin, D. (2014), 'Revitalizing Education in Afghanistan', *International Educator*, July-August 2014 23(4): 22–33.

Tondo, L. (May 2022) 'Twenty-five Ethnic Pamiris Killed by Security Forces in Tajikistan Protests', *The Guardian*, 19th May 2022. Available online: https://www.theguardian.com/global-development/2022/may/19/twenty-five-ethnic-pamiris-killed-by-security-forces-gorno-badakhshan-tajikistan-protests?CMP=Share_AndroidApp_Other (accessed 8 June 2022).

United Nations High Commissioner for Refugees (UNHCR) (2021), *Refugee Data Finder*, available from: https://www.unhcr.org/refugee-statistics/ (accessed 30 August 2022).

United Nations Relief and Work Agency for Palestine Refugees (UNRWA) (2021), *Education in Emergencies (EiE)*, available from: https://www.unrwa.org/what-we-do/education-emergencies (accessed 1 August 2022).

Williams, M. and Burden, R. (1997), 'Motivation in Language Learning: a Social Constructivist Approach', *Les Cahiers de L'apliut*, 16(3): 19–27.

Zandian, S. (2015) 'Migrant Literature and Teaching English as an International Language in Iran', in C. Kennedy (eds), *English Language Teaching in the Islamic Republic of Iran: Innovations, Trends and Challenges*, 111–20, London: British Council.

Zohoorian, Z. and Pandian, A. (2014), 'An Evaluation of Authenticity: a Case of EAP Textbooks in Iran', *International Journal of Languages and Literatures*, 2(1): 91–113.

10

Contesting Narratives of the Deficit Writer: A Writing for Publication Workshop Programme for Displaced Syrian Academics

Marion Heron and Tom Parkinson

Introduction

[The face-to-face workshop] showed me the importance of collaboration and teamwork, and the need to support others just as the UK-based colleagues are volunteering to support us. I gained better understanding of what academic writing is and how to select and meet the requirements of journals.

Syrian researcher

While I understand that the aim of the scheme [Cara Syria Programme] is to advance the careers of the mentees by facilitating their work in the Anglo/European academy, it does mean that they are coerced into producing a certain KIND of essay; one that they might not produce otherwise.

UK-based mentor

The first quote above is from a Syrian participant and the second one is from a UK-based mentor, both provided after completing a writing workshop programme offered to Syrian research teams on the Council for At-Risk Academics (Cara) Syria Programme, which we facilitated. Taken together, these reflections depict some of the tensions and issues inherent to 'North-South',[1] 'centre-periphery' researcher development initiatives, which are the focus of this chapter. The first explicit aim of the writing workshop programme (and of the

---

[1] We use these descriptors on the basis that they have currency within discourses surrounding global higher education, but in acknowledgement that they are reductive and unsatisfactory.

Cara Syria Programme more broadly) is capacity building, and the second is output production. While the former might appear *prima facie* to promote success in the latter, through our ongoing action research we have discovered that these two aims can also be at odds with each other, particularly, as highlighted by the UK-based mentor, when the norms of a writing genre exclude writers with different genre knowledge, and the 'academy', as a community of scholars and marketplace of ideas, becomes impenetrable (Tusting 2018). The questions we engage with in this chapter are: how can we best support academics in a centre-periphery context characterised by structural inequalities, epistemological marginalisation and precarity? How do Syrian academics position themselves in this context? How can we develop capacity and produce academic outputs whilst ensuring the Syrian academics' voices are heard? We also take a critical stance on social justice norms which appear to foreground marginalised voices, but in so doing further reify the positioning of the periphery academic as one who lacks agency and authorial voice.

The challenges associated with writing for publication have been well documented (Heron et al. 2021; Nygaard 2017), though the literature is dominated by studies of resource-rich, Anglophone centre contexts. In such contexts, the phrase 'publish or perish' is often used to describe 'the pressure in academia to develop and sustain a research career by disseminating research findings in peer-reviewed journals' (Doyle and Cuthill 2015: 671). This pressure is heightened and fuelled by the drive for outputs (Johnson et al. 2017), and can often result in certain types of genres being valued over others (Tusting 2018) and puts additional pressure on academics to publish according to established norms and markers of prestige. For example, Murray (2013) reports that many academics juggle their written outputs in terms of what will be published in high impact journals and what will contribute to their field. In the context of the Cara Syria Programme, Syrian academics experience further challenges as they struggle to secure jobs in exile (Parkinson 2019), jobs which are often dependent on publication of peer-reviewed outputs. In Turkey, where the majority of academics on the Cara Syria Programme are domiciled and where many are employed in universities, academic career progression is dependent on a system whereby points are awarded for different forms of academic output (e.g., Web of Science indexed research articles = 40 points; papers presented in scientific meetings such as international congresses, symposiums, panels = 4 points, see UAK 2022). To maintain their professional status or to be eligible for promotion to Associate or Full Professor, academics must accrue the requisite number of points. In such a context therefore, adherence to academic writing genre norms becomes a direct matter of professional survival. Other genres of writing, which individuals may be intrinsically motivated to work in, and which may hitherto have constituted their scholarly practice and output, are implicitly devalued.

These challenges are exacerbated when academics must write in a second language (Flowerdew 2019; Hanauer, Sheridan and Englander 2019; Hyland 2016) and when they are unfamiliar with the publishing and review process of journals in the second language. Jiang, Borg and Borg (2017) found that English as an additional language (EAL) scholars in China experienced difficulties with language and believed they faced discrimination from reviewers in the publication process. In some non-Anglophone contexts, writers may experience further challenges and barriers, such as poor infrastructure, lack of internet and lack of access to journals (Salager-Meyer 2014).

Following Lillis, Magyar and Robinson-Plant (2010), we identify the UK-based mentors, workshop leaders, academic developers and EAP specialists participating in the Cara writing workshop programme as representatives of the academic 'centre' (i.e. Anglophone, global North), while the Syrian academics represent the academic periphery (i.e. non-Anglophone, global South[2]). Notwithstanding the Cara Syria Programme's aim of supporting Syrian academics to overcome structural barriers and to succeed in the international academy, centre-periphery encounters of this kind arguably reify structural inequalities in terms of resources, power and authority: the resource-rich Anglophone North-based academics bring greater linguistic resources and social and linguistic capital. The power imbalances inherent in these encounters can affect the writing process (Heron et al. 2022; Lillis, Magyar and Robinson-Pant 2010; Trahar et al. 2019). For example, Khuder and Petric (2020) found that tacit knowledge on academic writing held by the centre academic impeded the periphery academic's authorial voice.

Mitigating for and working through these power imbalances can be hazardous. Over several years of facilitating and observing writing collaborations, we have identified two contradictory but equally problematic tendencies that can arise in collaborative writing encounters between centre and periphery academics. The first of these entails the tacit belief that the knowledge of the

---

[2] We acknowledge that the categories of 'global South' and 'global North' are themselves reductive and contested, but they nonetheless have currency in international research management, not least in relation to research funding. The British Academy Writing Workshop scheme is funded through the Global Challenges Research Fund (GCRF), which explicitly seeks to benefit countries in 'the global South' in receipt of UK Overseas Development Assistance (ODA) (REF). The GCRF is funded via a combined contribution from the UK's research and aid budgets.

centre is self-evidently superior, and that relinquishing centre control would ultimately jeopardise publication success. Our research has revealed that this tacit belief can be held on either side of the centre-periphery binary (Heron et al. 2022). The second tendency is to interpret the enterprise of periphery academics' pursuing publication according to the norms of the centre as *first and foremost* a capitulation to and manifestation of imperialist injustice. This second tendency may seem more closely aligned with a social justice agenda due to its postcolonial orientation, however it risks positioning periphery academics as inevitably coerced and thus lacking in agency, regardless of the desires, choices, motives and perspectives of the academics themselves. As we have demonstrated elsewhere (Heron et al. 2022), neither of these conceptualisations reflects the nuanced reality of writing for publication in centre-periphery contexts.

Notwithstanding the layered tensions inherent to interdisciplinary collaborative writing, in this chapter we outline how, through iterative cycles of observation, reflection and adjustment, we have refined a programme design that mitigates for some of the issues above and supports more equitable partnerships, while addressing the Syria Programme's dual aims of capacity building and publication success. Of particular significance to our workshop design and facilitation are attention to relationships within and across the writing groups, and the approaches taken to allow for participants' authorial voices to be heard. We envisage that the discussion and issues presented in this chapter will resonate with those who work with 'less heard' marginalised academics in a range of different contexts. It is also our hope that the design of the workshop programme will be of use to others working with academics from different demographics and in different contexts. In the following section, we describe the context in which our workshops take place, namely the Cara Syria Programme.

Overview of the Cara Syria Programme and setting context

The Council for At Risk Academics Syria Programme (hereafter Syria Programme) was established in late 2016 to support Syrian academics living in the Middle East region to sustain their academic work, networks and identity in exile. In practice, the majority of participants enrolled on the Syria Programme are based in Turkey, where over 3.5 million displaced Syrians are domiciled. Following early consultations with the Union of Free Syrian Academics and a roundtable event at Bogazici University in late 2016, the programme was initially set up across three main strands of activity: English for Academic Purposes (EAP), Academic Development (AD) and Research Incubation Visits (RIV). Participant-led workshops followed in March 2017 to determine priorities and set the agenda for the first phase of delivery (2017–18) (see Parkinson 2019). Following an iterative action research approach, the Syria Programme's AD priorities and agenda have been revisited, revised and updated for subsequent phases of the programme as the cohort has grown and the participants' needs and realities have changed.

Developing research capacity and profiles through active research and publication in English has consistently been identified by participants as a priority (see Hanley 2019; Parkinson, McDonald and Quinlan 2019) and has been addressed across all strands of the programme. Although most Syria Programme participants hold doctorates in their field, many have limited experience of writing for publication, as it was not required by Syrian universities, whose priority was teaching (Heron et al. 2021). Very few have prior experience of writing in English for peer-reviewed journals.

On the AD strand, for which we are Steering Group members and workshop facilitators, key areas of support include a competitive grant scheme that funds small-scale research projects, research mentoring by experienced researchers (usually based at UK universities) and writing workshop programmes on which research teams are introduced to different aspects of the academic writing experience (such as the typical peer review cycle, choosing journals, responding to reviewers) and given a structured environment in which to write collaboratively and to prepare manuscripts for publication.

Based on an analysis of participatory workshop discussions and personal development plans, Parkinson et al. (2020) identified three dilemmas that problematise planning and delivery on the Syria Programme as a whole. These are: a) the challenges of balancing individuals' needs with those of the Syria Programme community at large; b) whether to take a needs-based approach or an asset-based approach;[3] and c) the balancing of a radical *transformative* agenda that challenges the structural barriers that contribute to scholars' marginalisation, with a pragmatic, *alleviating* agenda that 'emphasises self-management capacities but does not challenge political-economic structures' (Parkinson et al. 2020: 196). As they explain:

---

[3] Assets here refer to all forms of tangible and intangible resource that the academic community already possess and can leverage to support development and address challenges.

> this dilemma is exemplified in academic publishing norms, where Anglophone dominance in academic publishing both derives from and reinforces an Anglophone academic centre (Lillis, Magyar and Robinson-Plant 2010). Non-Anglophone, peripheral academics stand greater chances of achieving purchase at the centre by developing their English and normative academic literacies, but this does little to redress the balance of power at a structural level. [Furthermore], The [global North Anglophone academic's] position at the centre affords access to social, cultural, and material capital, which they can distribute outwards [...]. Yet this approach arguably capitulates to structural inequalities inherent to international academia, reinforces the centre's authority over the periphery, and effects structural dependency. On the other hand, challenging the norms of the academic centre might ward against dependency, but would likely inhibit participants' access to power.
>
> Parkinson et al. 2020: 196–7

Dilemmas are decision-making encounters where all the options available are imperfect and carry negative outcomes (or carry the risk thereof) as well as positive outcomes, and where decision-making therefore requires cost-benefit analysis. However, while dilemmas can present as a single decision-making encounter, they can also linger as defining conditions of a context such as the Syria Programme, to be revisited, engaged with and negotiated on an ongoing and case-by-case basis. The design, facilitation and mentoring of the writing workshops are in large part framed by the challenges of balancing the needs of all participants, the tension of a needs-based or assets-based approach and the dilemma of a transformative vs alleviating agenda (Parkinson et al. 2020). In particular, the third dilemma prompts us to consider what a social justice approach to supporting writing for publication might entail, what risks and negative consequences might accompany such an approach, and how these risks and consequences might be mitigated. In the following section we summarise the development and refinement of our writing workshop programme, before outlining the key concepts underpinning the design.

The writing workshop programme: design and development

Our approach has developed iteratively over several writing workshops between 2018 and 2022. The first face-to-face (F2F) workshops were held in 2018 and 2019 in Istanbul, each lasting four days. They were attended by research teams working in the social sciences who had all undertaken data-driven empirical research. Few of the participants had prior experience of publication in peer reviewed journals, and not all groups were accompanied by mentors. According to pre-workshop progress reports submitted to Cara, all groups were at a similar stage in the research process, having undertaken literature review and data collection, and planned an outline of their research paper, but not yet started their write-up. Accordingly, we designed the workshop programme to coach participants through each section of their articles, in linear 'lock-step', following the Introduction, Methodology, Results and Discussion (IMRaD) structure and using a move analysis approach for each section. We also provided process-level input, introducing participants to the peer review process and guidance on choosing an appropriate journal according to a range of factors, including aims and scope, audience, impact factor/ranking and access.

While this approach was successful for many who attended, problems emerged where groups' progress reports did not reflect their actual progress, or where participants arrived late or missed sessions. This led to some groups falling behind in relation to the wider cohort, which in turn, in some cases, led to demotivation, isolation and inertia. For some groups with mentors, the writing dynamic ceased to be collaborative; the Syrian participants deferred to the UK-based mentor, who took responsibility for writing the article while the group observed. This arguably reflected a tacit belief in the superiority of the native speaker's knowledge and ability, and drew our attention to the tension between capacity-building and output production discussed earlier. Here, the production of the output was prioritised at the expense of skills development, collaboration and the centring of Syrian researchers' authorial voices. It also alerted us to the vulnerability of this writing workshop model to differences between groups.

To address these problems, for later workshops we moved away from the 'lock-step' approach towards a model rooted in goal-setting and reflective practice. Following this model, each group establishes their own goals from the outset, in discussion as a team, and follows a systematic reflection process to identify where the knowledge and expertise lies in the team, how this can be leveraged effectively in the writing process, and where more capacity is needed. As workshop facilitators, we hold groups accountable to their self-identified goals at collective feedback points, elicit individuals' and groups' reflections on their development as research writers, and deliver tailored support at individual group, rather than cohort level. Although this approach is more labour intensive, it allows for differentiation while maintaining cohort culture and rapport, and ensures that all members of writing groups participate in goal setting.

The most recent iteration of the writing programme was a hybrid design, largely due to the restrictions imposed by the pandemic. However, although initially frustrating, the hybridity in fact became a valuable core feature of the programme. Meeting online prior to F2F meetings afforded opportunities for preparation, focused input and drafting. The on-site workshop focused on fine-tuning papers and, significantly, allowed participants to meet in person.

This programme therefore comprised two parts. The first part was a seven week series of writing workshops which were conducted online (see Appendix A). The second part was a four-day workshop held in person (see Appendix B). The aim of the first part was to develop skills, knowledge and awareness in preparation for the intensive, on-site workshops.

The two main aims of the programme were: a) to ensure an output of quality research articles from the projects undertaken by each research group; and b) to develop the academic and writing skills of participants as part of the capacity building remit of Cara. This dual purpose inevitably resulted in certain tensions as described above. Participants were expected to have submitted their Cara reports prior to Part A, and were expected to submit their draft manuscripts six weeks prior to the on-site workshop, for initial review and comments by the Syria Programme Peer Review College. Their revised drafts would constitute the texts for completion and refinement at the workshop. The activities were designed to foster collaboration between Syrian and international academics. They were also developed to ensure knowledge and resource sharing, mutual interest and support networks, and support the presence of Syrian voices within international academic discourse. The objectives of the programme were:

1. To build research writing capacity among early career researchers, and facilitate their engagement in professional and scholarly networks.
2. To develop four areas of writing expertise: content, process, rhetorical and formal knowledge.
3. To develop working relationships and professional networks with mentors and other Syrian colleagues.
4. To develop an understanding of how different publication formats can contribute to a broader dissemination strategy.
5. To develop the academic skills of writing rigorous, targeted and persuasive grant proposals.
6. To develop the academic writing skills of genre awareness and linguistic skills.
7. To develop skills in presenting and discussing their research in an academic conference context.

The overall programme aimed to focus on written outputs from research projects funded through the Cara Research Grants scheme. It was structured to offer a range of support that would be of value to participants at all stages of their research journeys. One UK-based mentor noted these features of the design in their evaluation: 'I think the workshop was brilliantly organised – mainly because we were left to self-organise. Help was there if needed, but it wasn't too structured.' Participants benefited from group-level input from experts in relation to grant proposal writing, journal selection and academic writing, and worked closely with their discipline mentors and EAP tutors to finalise manuscripts for submission to peer reviewed journals, or prepare new applications for forthcoming grant opportunities. Reflecting on the process knowledge the mentors brought to the group in terms of familiarity with journals and the academy, one of the Syrian researchers commented: 'During the workshop, I successfully got the article ready for publication, through in-depth discussions with the mentors, who – based on the target journal – went through the text in detail'.

Writing for publication programme: principles and key concepts

Since 2019 we have approached the delivery of workshops as a formal action research project. We have drawn on and synthesised prior research in the fields of applied linguistics and educational psychology with our own empirical research in the workshop setting to better understand and theorise the collaborative writing process, to better explain the process of collaborative research writing to participants, and to make further evidence-based adjustments to our workshop design. In this section we outline the key concepts which underpin the design of the writing workshops: 'genre knowledge' (Tardy 2009) and 'relational expertise' (Edwards 2011). These concepts are discussed and illustrated through the voices of our participants and will be exemplified in practical terms in the section below.

Genre knowledge

An ability to communicate with a community of experts rests on the writer's ability to understand and demonstrate what Tardy (2009) referred to as 'genre knowledge'. According to Tardy (2009), genre knowledge comprises four distinct but overlapping domains: subject-matter knowledge; process knowledge; formal knowledge; and rhetorical knowledge. 'Subject-matter knowledge' refers to the disciplinary knowledge the writer brings to the act of writing. In the context of the Syria Programme writing workshop programme, writers come from a range of disciplinary backgrounds,[4] and each bring their theoretical and research expertise to their writing groups. 'Process knowledge' refers to an understanding of the writing process itself, such as the procedures for submitting for review, understanding and responding to review comments. 'Formal knowledge' refers to an understanding of the lexico-grammatical features of writing in a particular genre, such as what tense to use in writing the Results section, and 'rhetorical knowledge' refers to understanding expectations of the journal audience and what is considered 'knowledge' in this particular domain (Tusting 2018). Knowledge in these four domains results in writing expertise.

An awareness of genre is necessary for all writers, particularly for those who may be writing in a genre with which they are unfamiliar and / or uncomfortable (Lea and Street 2006). In order to instrumentalise the concept of genre knowledge in the design and facilitation of the workshops, we drew on genre pedagogy approaches. In particular, we coached participants in using the tools of genre analysis (Hyland 2007) to determine the features of writing genres and to understand how they relate to the four knowledge domains. The intention here was not only to develop participants' awareness of the genre expectations of an English language, peer-reviewed research article for the present task, but also to empower them to be able to apply the tools of genre analysis for further written and spoken output, across a range of genres, in the future. In this way it is hoped that participants can 'exploit the expressive potential of society's discourse structures, instead of merely being manipulated by them' (Hyland 2007: 150).

Although a genre pedagogy approach arguably does not empower writers in and of itself, taken together with an academic development approach the two can support linguistic and academic/research development by focusing on a key dimension of academic practice and normative expectation of international academic work. In a meta study of papers addressing teaching English for research publication purposes, Li and Flowerdew (2009) found that most pedagogic interventions were organised around the IMRaD (Introduction, Methodology, Results and Discussion) structure, used a genre pedagogy

---

[4] To date, disciplines represented include agriculture, biology, town planning, archaeology, Arabic language and literature, English language and literature, history, anthropology, geography and media studies.

approach, included genre analysis and genre awareness activities, and were often based on researcher articles as materials and exemplars. McGrath, Negretti and Nicholls (2019) used Tardy's (2009) framework in working with higher education practitioners to raise their awareness of the genre knowledge implicit in their assignments and assessments. Similarly, McGrath et al. (under review) discuss how higher education teacher development programmes (e.g. Post-Graduate Certificate in Learning and Teaching: PGCert) can incorporate a genre knowledge model into initial in-service teacher training. In the context of this writing programme, framing the task of writing in a second language in terms of genre helped to demystify Anglophone research literature, revealing it to be a matter of identifiable conventions as opposed to an impenetrable, esoteric and inherently superior domain.

Genre knowledge not only underpinned the design of the input and practical activities, but also served as a heuristic for self-evaluation and group reflections on the workshop in terms of both learning (capacity building) and writing (output production). At scheduled reflection points throughout the workshop, and in the final evaluation, Teams were asked to consider their collaboration in relation to the four knowledge domains; Resources were developed according to the four genre knowledge domains (see the section on programme design below).

It has been recognised that English L1 writers also experience linguistic challenges and lack of confidence in writing for publication (Hyland 2016a). This was confirmed by the value ascribed to these activities from our UK-based mentors, already established researchers and published authors. One participant commented: 'I found the exercise of writing an abstract / summary a great one. I was therefore wondering whether small exercises like that could be incorporated within each workshop day' (UK-based mentor).

In the context of a writing programme as described in this chapter, further myths about linguistic superiority and the expert / novice paradigm could be broken down through UK mentors sharing their own linguistic challenges with their Syrian colleagues. This could create more collaborative and collegial dynamics, as well as contribute to relational expertise, as outlined below.

Relational expertise

Interdisciplinary collaborative writing can be highly rewarding and beneficial (Storch 2019), but presents significant challenges. These have been discussed in the literature in general (Lowry et al. 2004) and in the context of working with displaced Syrian academics in a multilingual context (Heron et al. 2022). 'Relational expertise' refers to confidence in one's own area of expertise, combined with a willingness to recognise the expertise of others. Developed by Edwards (2008, 2011) in the context of multidisciplinary professional teams, we have found the concept to be hugely valuable in understanding the nature of collaboration in interdisciplinary writing contexts and in setting the conditions in which successful collaboration can occur. In order to develop relational expertise, it is essential that group members create common knowledge by explicitly articulating their own knowledge, recognising that of others and agreeing joint action. These processes are crucial to effective working practices in 'boundary spaces' (Edwards 2011), particularly where, as in this context, experts must work together at linguistic, cultural and disciplinary boundaries on a common goal (in this case an academic output).

In the context of academic writing, authorial voice and identity are key, to the extent that participants will invest in the collaborative writing process, and ultimately the finished product. Heron et al. (2022: 917) describe the challenges and benefits afforded by interdisciplinary collaborative writing and conclude that the 'the ability and willingness to compromise and synthesise one's expert knowledge with [that of] collaborators lies at the heart of this aspect of authorial identity'. The reflection below from a mentor exemplifies relational expertise in the context of the programme described in this chapter. It highlights how the UK-based mentor, a disciplinary expert and experienced academic writer, was able to recognise the expertise of their group members: 'By the end of the four days we had made progress towards turning the research report into a paper for a journal, but just as importantly, we (co-mentors) had a much clearer understanding of the social, political and historical context of the research.' (UK-based mentor).

Interestingly, opportunities for relational expertise to emerge and develop were contingent on the space in which the team members were working. The physical space was more conducive to this opportunity, as pointed out by the UK-based mentor below.

> The main benefits related to working side by side in a room after eighteen months of working together online. The lead Syrian researcher in our team took a really active role in this, and said he found it much easier to do in person (and over a few days) rather than in one-two hour zoom meetings spread over a number of weeks.
>
> UK-based mentor

The comment below also highlights the impact of shared understandings and respect of others' knowledge and expertise as part of constructing common knowledge (Edwards 2011). The same UK mentor described how understanding his Syrian colleagues' motivations and backgrounds was a valuable insight for the research. 'By the end I felt I had a better grasp of my Syrian colleagues' individual interests and motivations in relation to the research. I think this knowledge will help me be a better mentor in the future when we are discussing potential plans and activities.' (UK-based mentor).

What is of particular interest here is the insights we gain into the notion of life-long learning. Relational expertise rests on an awareness of one's own and others' expertise, and this awakening and growing awareness in this particular UK-mentor will continue to grow, suggesting that future collaborations either within the same context or beyond, can flourish.

Issues: benefits and challenges

Anglophone, Western, global North perspectives are vastly overrepresented in the international research space, resulting in biases, absences, and erasures in academic knowledge across the disciplinary spectrum. While scholars working in resource-rich contexts are steeped in/enculturated into 'international' writing norms, those without access to scholarly literature due to paywalls and other barriers have limited opportunity to develop genre knowledge, inhibiting their chances of publication success. As discussed at the outset of this chapter, North-South research writing collaborations and capacity-building interventions offer the potential to challenge and address these inequities, but without due care can also replicate them at the micro level. Tacit deficit perspectives – on the part of both global North 'centre' collaborators, mentors and facilitators *and* global South 'periphery' collaborators – can manifest in hierarchical writing dynamics where centre academics assume control over the writing process and authority over the finished product. At the same time, as discussed, we have also identified a countertendency on the part of centre academics to view those from the periphery as perennially and *above all else* structurally disadvantaged by an unjust academic system, which can also downplay their agency and invalidate their desire to participate and succeed *within* that system. A radical transformative orientation towards the unjust academic system may provide catharsis for centre academics and lead to more just conditions over time, but a pragmatic approach which capitulates to the systems norms and values can bring direct professional advantages in the here and now.

The approach adopted in our workshops since 2020, wards against both tendencies by formalising the establishment of shared goals as part of the writing process. In so doing, it ensures shared agency and promotes transparency, compromise, discussion, and collective ownership. Through discussion, participants develop relational expertise, gain a richer understanding of each other's values and perspectives, and work through this and other complex dilemmas together. This places capacity-building at the heart of the workshop but also increases the chances of producing collaborative outputs that authentically represent all authors' voices and values.

Implications and future plans

Although the context of this chapter has been the Cara Syria Programme, many of the issues we have discussed will resonate with groups in different contexts, and the design principles will be relevant to any group working together on an interdisciplinary, collaborative project.

The overall hybrid design, although not initially planned, was in fact an advantage for the reasons described above. However, the social and relational advantages of the on-site stage of the workshops cannot be underestimated. Many participants commented on the importance of meeting in person and working in a shared physical space. This was highlighted in the following comment from a Syrian participant: 'It saved us a lot of time and we have managed to make a remarkable progress especially opposed [to] the pace of progress in a virtual environment. Another important aspect is the in-person teamwork'.

Based on the underpinning concepts of genre knowledge and relational expertise we developed a number of features which we believe are the cornerstones of our programme design and approach. These include the following:

1. A focus on short-term and long-term goals and responsibilities by setting intentions at the beginning of the workshop programme.
2. Self-evaluation throughout the programme, focusing on the four domains of genre knowledge to foster an awareness of the skills, experience and expertise represented across the group members.
3. Focused input sessions to raise awareness of genre, e.g. rhetorical moves in writing an abstract.

4. Input to develop process knowledge, e.g. tips on getting published, how to choose your target journal.
5. Opportunities for sustained group writing sessions followed by regular reporting back, e.g. three hours writing time followed by thirty minutes of group feedback on achievements and short-term goals.
6. Guest speakers on specific areas, e.g. inviting a journal editor to give an editor's perspective on submitting for publication and answering questions.

Ultimately, our aim was to support the Syrian participants in their journey of writing for publication and to engage our UK-based mentors in this process. In this spirit, we conclude with their voices. The three quotes below speak to and reflect two key features of the workshop programme. The first reconciles the tension between capacity building and a demonstrable output. The second highlights relational expertise – recognising and accepting the different forms of knowledge each participant brings to the group and capitalising on this range to work towards a common goal. The third highlights the value that organisations such as Cara can play in supporting peripheral research writers to pursue their self-identified research goals and overcome structural barriers, and in so doing promote a more inclusive and socially just knowledge space.

> [It was a] very good and unique workshop. It was useful to me because its benefit is not limited to the current article, but it is useful to my work in research and publication.
>
> Syrian researcher

> Socially, it was extremely rewarding to finally meet with our team and build more personal connections, as well as understand better how different teams work together. In terms of our writing, I feel that it really made us mentors feel much more invested in the paper. It gave us a much better understanding of how our team members worked together, and where the gaps that we should be contributing were.
>
> UK-based mentor

> None of this would have been achieved so fast and easily online. I believe this workshop was the most successful and useful one ever held by Cara. Therefore, I suggest holding such workshops becomes the regular practice for teams working on drafting their reports and articles.
>
> Syrian researcher

References

Cara, (2019a), *Cara Regional and Country Programmes,* available at: https://www.cara.ngo/what-we-do/ (accessed 8 August 2023).

Cara, (2019b), *The State of Higher Education Pre-2011*, available at: https://www.educ.cam.ac.uk/networks/eri/publications/syria/190606-BC_SYRIA-REPORT-ENGLISH_HR.pdf (accessed 8 August 2023).

Doyle, J. and Cuthill, M. (2015), 'Does "Get Visible or Vanish" Herald the End of "Publish or Perish"?', *Higher Education Research and Development*, 34(3): 671–4.

Edwards, A. (2011), 'Building Common Knowledge at the Boundaries between Professional Practices: Relational Agency and Relational Expertise in Systems of Distributed Expertise', *International Journal of Educational Research*, 50(1): 33–9.

Flowerdew, J. (2019), 'The Linguistic Disadvantage of Scholars who Write in English as an Additional Language: Myth or Reality', *Language Teaching*, 52(2): 249–60.

Hanauer, D. I., Sheridan, C. L. and Englander, K. (2019), 'Linguistic Injustice in the Writing of Research Articles in English as a Second Language: Data from Taiwanese and Mexican Researchers', *Written Communication*, 36(1): 136–54.

Heron, M., K. Gravett and Yakovchuk N. (2021), 'Publishing and Flourishing: Writing for Desire in Higher Education', *Higher Education Research and Development*, 40(3): 538–51.

Heron, M., Parkinson, T., Alajaj, N. and Khuder, B. (2022), 'Interdisciplinary Collaborative Writing for Publication with Exiled Academics: the Nature of Relational Expertise', *Compare: a Journal of Comparative and International Education*, 52(6): 914–32.

Hyland, K. (2007), 'Genre Pedagogy: Language, Literacy and L2 Writing Instruction', *Journal of Second Language Writing*, 16(3): 148–64.

Hyland, K. (2016a), 'Academic Publishing and the Myth of Linguistic Injustice', *Journal of Second Language Writing*, 31: 58–69.

Hyland, K. (2016b), *Academic Publishing: Issues and Challenges in the Construction of Knowledge*, Oxford: Oxford University Press.

Jiang, X., Borg, E. and Borg, M. (2017), 'Challenges and Coping Strategies for International Publication: Perceptions of Young Scholars in China', *Studies in Higher Education*, 42(3): 428–44.

Johnson, L., Roitman, S., Morgan, A. and MacLeod, J. (2017), 'Challenging the Productivity Mantra: Academic Writing with Spirit in Place', *Higher Education Research and Development*, 36(6): 1181–93.

Khuder, B. and Petric, B. (2020), 'Academic Socialisation through Collaboration: Textual Interventions in Supporting Exiled Scholars' Academic Literacies Development', *Education and Conflict Review* 3: 24–8.

Lea, M. R and Street, B. V. (2006), 'The "Academic Literacies" Model: Theory and Applications', *Theory into Practice*, 45(4): 368–77.

Li, Y and Flowerdew, J. (2009), 'International Engagement Versus Local Commitment: Hong Kong Academics in the Humanities and Social Sciences Writing for Publication', *Journal of English for Academic Purposes,* 8(4): 279–93.

Lillis, T and Curry, M. J. (2010), *Academic Writing in a Global Context: the Politics and Practices of Publishing in English,* Abingdon: Routledge.

Lillis, T., Magyar, A. A. and Robinson-Pant, A. (2010), 'An International Journal's Attempts to Address Inequalities in Academic Publishing: Developing a Writing for Publication Programme', *Compare: A Journal of Comparative and International Education,* 40(6): 781–800.

Lowry, P. B., Curtis, A. and Lowry, M. R. (2004), 'Building a Taxonomy and Nomenclature of Collaborative Writing to Improve Interdisciplinary Research and Practice', *The Journal of Business Communication,* 41(1): 66–99.

McGrath, L., Donaghue, H. and Negretti, R. (under review), 'Fostering Subject Lecturers' Capacity to Develop their Students' Disciplinary and Professional Literacy: a Triadic Model', *Teaching in Higher Education.*

McGrath, L., Negretti, R. and Nicholls, K. (2019), 'Hidden Expectations: Scaffolding Subject Specialists' Genre Knowledge of the Assignments they Set', *Higher Education,* 78(5): 835–53.

Murray, R. (2013). '"It's not a hobby": Reconceptualizing the Place of Writing in Academic Work', *Higher Education,* 66(1): 79–91.

Nygaard, L. P. (2017), 'Publishing and Perishing: an Academic Literacies Framework for Investigating Research Productivity', *Studies in Higher Education,* 42(3): 519–32.

Parkinson, T. (2019), 'A Trialectic Framework for Large Group Processes in Educational Action Research: the Case of Academic Development for Syrian Academics in Exile', *Educational Action Research,* 27(5): 798–814.

Parkinson, T., McDonald K. and Quinlan K. M. (2020), 'Reconceptualising Academic Development as Community Development: Lessons from Working with Syrian Academics in Exile', *Higher Education,* 79(2): 183–201.

Salager-Meyer, F. (2014), 'Writing and Publishing in Peripheral Scholarly Journals: How to Enhance the Global Influence of Multilingual Scholars?', *Journal of English for Academic Purposes,* 13: 78–82.

Storch, N. (2019), 'Collaborative Writing', *Language Teaching,* 52(1): 40–59.

Tardy, C. M. (2009), *Building Genre Knowledge,* West Lafayette, IN: Parlor Press.

Trahar, S., Juntrasook, A., Burford, J., von Kotze A. and Wildemeersch D. (2019). '"Hovering on the Periphery"? Decolonising Writing for Academic Journals', *Compare: a Journal of Comparative and International Education,* 49(1): 149–67.

Tusting, K. (2018), 'The Genre Regime of Research Evaluation: Contradictory Systems of Value Around Academics' Writing', *Language and Education,* 32(6): 477–93.

Appendices

Appendix A: Online workshops

Table 10.1 Workshop for Cara Research Grant Winners: Writing for publication programme (online)

	Session topic	Aims	Materials / pre-session activities
1	Getting published	• Introductions and Warmer • Introduction to the workshop series • Stating goals • Getting published – tips, tricks and advice from an editor • Preparation for poster session • Reflections on writing expertise	Fill in a sheet on common goals and areas of expertise Identify a list of five preferred journals. Download and bring the author guidelines. Questions about peer review process
2	Presenting and summarising your work	• Poster presentations, discussion and feedback • Peer feedback • Evaluation criteria / panel • Recordings and formative feedback	Watch the two webinars on giving presentations Prepare a poster which reflects the structure of a paper
3	Genre knowledge and writing expertise	• Genre approach to writing for publication	Choose one paper from chosen journal. Read it before the session.
4	Writing retreat one: intensive writing and feedback	• To evaluate report as a text for a paper	Identify target journal(s) Identify sections from the report to be used in paper for writing retreat one.
5	Writing retreat two: intensive writing and feedback	• To evaluate, write and reflect on the introduction and literature review sections.	Draft sections of introduction and literature review to be completed before writing retreat two.
6	Writing retreat three: intensive writing and feedback Evaluation and feedback	• To evaluate, write and reflect on the methodology and results sections.	Draft sections of methodology and results to be completed before writing retreat three.
7	Final writing retreat Evaluation	• To finalise paper • To prepare for in-person writing retreat.	

Appendix B: Four day in-person writing workshops

Workshop for Cara Research Grant Winners: Writing for publication
Programme:
Day one

Time	Activity	Who?
9.15 – 10.30	Introductions, Plans Self-evaluation: writing expertise Group discussion: roles and responsibilities	All groups
10.45 – 11.00	Break	
11.00 – 1.00	Working in teams	All (support from TP, MH, MLR)
1.00 – 2.00	Lunch	
2.00 – 3.00	Working in Teams	All (support from TP, MH, MLR)
3.00 – 3.15	Break	
3.15 – 4.15	Working in Teams	All (support from TP, MH, MLR)
4.15 – 5.00	Taking stock Paper summary preparation	All
5.00	Close	

Day two

Time	Activity	Who?
9.15 – 10.30	Taking stock: feedback on day one Plans for the day Distribution of roles and responsibilities	All groups
10.45 – 11.00	Break	
11.00 – 1.00	Working in teams	All (support from TP, MH, MLR)
1.00 – 2.00	Lunch	
2.00 – 3.00	Working in teams	All (support from TP, MH, MLR)
3.00 – 3.15	Break	
3.15 – 4.15	Working in teams	All (support from TP, MH, MLR)
4.15 – 5.00	Taking stock Paper summary preparation	All
5.00	Close	

Day three

Time	Activity	Who?
9.15 – 10.30	Paper presentations Five mins per group plus translation	All groups
10.45 – 11.00	Break	
11.00 – 1.00	Working in teams	All (support from TP, MH, MLR)
1.00 – 2.00	Lunch	
2.00 – 3.00	Working in teams	All (support from TP, MH, MLR)
3.00 – 3.15	Break	
3.15 – 4.15	Working in teams	All (support from TP, MH, MLR)
4.15 – 5.00	Taking stock Paper summary preparation	All
5.00	Close	

Day 4

Time	Activity	Who?
9.00 – 10.00	Paper summary presentations	All
10.00 – 11.00	Working in teams	All (support from TP, MH, MLR)
11.00 – 11.15	Break	
11.15 – 12.30	Working in teams	All (support from TP, MH, MLR)
12.30 – 1.30	Lunch	
1.30 – 2.00	Taking stock • Reflecting on the workshop • What next? • How can Cara support you? Workshop evaluation	All (support from TP, MH, MLR)
2.00 – 3.00	Certificates and close	All
3.00	Close	

11

A Reflection on Social Justice in International EAP: Addressing (or Not...) Gender Inequality Through English Instruction

Magdalena Rostron

Social justice is a broad, multi-dimensional topic, inviting passion and controversy in equal measure. It becomes even more complex in conjunction with women's issues, leading to additional debates when positioned within the field of English language education. In this rather difficult context, various facets overlap, mesh and clash, producing both problems and solutions. The issue gives rise to a spiralling series of questions: to teach or not to teach social justice? How should it be taught anyway? How should it be taught in a Western classroom? How should it be taught in an English classroom abroad? And, in such a classroom, how should social justice for women be taught? Should it be taught at all? Why/why not?

Any attempt at reflecting on this set of related questions (even without aiming to provide definitive answers or resolutions) needs to start from presenting working definitions of the terms involved. The next step will be to examine to what extent these definitions can demonstrate mutual relationships between the issues and the character of those relationships. Finally, it seems fitting to offer a brief evaluation of the practical applications of ensuing pedagogical approaches, placing them in a specific academic and socio-cultural context to test their effectiveness. Thus, I will want to consider how the idea of teaching social justice for women might work in an English classroom in a Gulf Arab country. Immediately, a related question emerges, asking what social justice *does* mean to such women and what would need to be done to achieve it in this context. This question invites further research, firmly grounded in local parameters. However, it falls outside the scope of the current chapter, which will focus on the attempts to apply social justice-aligned pedagogy in a non-Western EAP classroom.

The concept of social justice is no longer as clear and unambiguous as it may have been in the not-so-distant, but pre-postmodern past. In traditional, conventional terms, it was a set of ideas and actions aimed at advancing general equality, liberty and tolerance, designed to usher in a fair(er), more humanised society. It stemmed from the philosophical and ethical thought that developed in Western Europe in response to the Industrial Revolution and new forms of social inequality it engendered. Grounded in Marxist ideology, social justice initially:

> emerged as an expression of protest against what was perceived as the capitalist exploitation of labour and as a focal point for the development of measures to improve the human condition. It was born as a revolutionary slogan embodying the ideals of progress and fraternity. Following the revolutions that shook Europe in the mid-1800s, social justice became a rallying cry for progressive thinkers and political activists. Proudhon, notably, identified justice with social justice, and social justice with respect for human dignity. By the mid-twentieth century, the concept of social justice had become central to the ideologies and programmes of virtually all the leftist and centrist political parties around the world, and few dared to oppose it directly. Social justice represented the essence and the raison d'être of the social democrat doctrine and left its mark in the decades following the Second World War.
>
> UN 2006: 12

The notion of social justice gradually evolved, expanding its focus from economy-induced social inequities to incorporate the wider-ranging issues of race, class and gender. It was women's issues in particular that came to the fore with the onset of the European and American suffragist movements in the nineteenth century whose significance grew exponentially in the next century resulting in new waves of feminist activity aimed at bringing broadly understood social justice to millions of oppressed women in the West (e.g. de Beauvoir 1949; Friedan 1963; Greer 1970; Firor Scott 2002; Grady 2018; Ware 2019, 2020).

Simultaneously, the question of social justice for women and related issues crossed over the boundaries of socio-political and economic domains and entered the field of Western academia, inspiring courses, theses, scholarly articles and books, and marking its presence in humanities, arts, and social sciences, usually under the banner of Women's Studies. In a similar vein, other social causes were adopted in the fight for social justice and subsequently taken up by political activists as well as academics, artists, social scientists and others.

Indeed, the UN document cited earlier states that 'of particular importance in the present context is the link between the growing legitimization of the concept of social justice, on the one hand, and the emergence of the social sciences as distinct areas of activity and the creation of economics and sociology as disciplines separate from philosophy (notably moral philosophy), on the other hand' (UN 2006: 12). These processes have increasingly affected the interpretation of what social justice is and how it should be achieved, whether in relation to women's issues or other pressing social problems to do with class, ethnicity, race, etc.

While remaining a crucial value embedded in many public declarations and charters, the notion of social justice has become increasingly visible in diverse areas of practical human activity. In fact, it no longer functions as a general socio-economic ideal: instead, it has been replaced with its more fragmented and radicalised understandings (Murray 2020: 51–63). Such new understandings not only steer our ideological attention towards particular goals in particular socio-political domains, but also seem to be growing in significance as an integral element of education.

These more recent perceptions of social justice have also become associated with Critical Theory and its various branches, such as Postcolonial Theory, Queer Theory, or Gender Studies, deriving from French-inspired postmodernist thinking, with its complex terminology and interpretations. As such, they offer much narrower, more 'specialised' perspectives, permeating academic discourse, philosophically nuanced, socially progressive, with strong left-wing leanings, action-oriented, incorporated into educational programmes and manifestoes, and radical in their demands.

Despite being hailed by many as transformative and effective in initiating social change, these new approaches to social justice are sometimes criticised as either detached from the reality of ordinary people, or 'woke': increasingly politicised, illiberal and rigid (Larsen and Newell 1993; Jahn 2021; Pluckrose and Lindsay 2021; Rauch 2021). Their disconnection from the prosaic experience of life as lived by most people tends to be blamed on the almost esoteric academic language used by social justice theoreticians, as exemplified in the writings by Judith Butler, Gayatri Spivak, and others. The 'woke' label can be as controversial as the contents it signifies. On the one hand, it is understood as 'a concept that symbolises awareness of social issues and movement against injustice, inequality, and prejudice' (Mirzaei 2019), which has gained traction since the BLM movement. But more critical definitions describe it as 'the fixation with identity, the bad faith assumptions, the aggressive historical vandalism, combined with moral superiority and absolutism' (Folarin Iman 2022).

A significant portion of criticism concerning the reinterpreted concepts of social justice also points out the irony of their irrevocable ties with Western ideas and ethics which some see as a form of Western cultural domination and yet another attempt to universally impose Western ways of thinking while claiming to reject them (Mohanty 2003; Hobson 2007; Murray 2020; Pluckrose and Lindsay 2021).

These shifting and jarring perceptions of what social justice is and how it should be achieved, together with their critical evaluations, are interesting to observe in academic settings, including TESOL. In teaching, social justice and its causes are increasingly seen as constituting ever stronger and more visible undercurrents in curriculum design and research, spilling over to pedagogical methodologies, approaches, syllabi, classroom materials and activities (e.g. Au et al. 2007), all designed to lead towards social change.

In the era of overseas branch campuses, internationalised schooling, and global dominance of English as the language of instruction, education thus understood and practised is typically exported in a one-directional mode, from the West to, well, everywhere else. In this, it assumes its own universality, which results in pedagogical and ideological complexities and opens floodgates of criticism from all sides, mainly because the very *raison d'être* of education is paradoxically dualistic. On the one hand, it is based on a generally acknowledged intention to instigate personal, cultural, economic and social change. On the other hand, its fundamental but latent goal is to maintain the status quo and produce compliant and cooperative members of society (Szyliowicz 1973; Atkinson 2002; Lauder et al. 2006; Marmolejo 2010; De Wit 2013). Hence, more questions arise: what kind of change should globalised education be initiating in local contexts? What types of social orders and codes, cultural regimes, and systems of values should globalised education strive to uphold in local contexts? Who should, and on what basis, make decisions in these matters?

Social issues are steeped in cultural values (Leung and Stephan 2001). How one views and implements principles of social justice is determined by one's understanding of its meaning in a specific cultural setting. This appears to be particularly notable in regard to women's issues, rights, and status, whose conceptual understandings and practical realisations vary greatly from one locality to another, determining their reception in different public discourses. It follows that, often, if a non-Western society is described as conservative and traditionalist in its outlook, then Western ideas of women's equality may be met there with suspicion or even resentment, rather than helping to further women's causes and engender socio-political transformations (e.g. Mohanty 2003; Golley 2004).

Given this multifaceted context of its globalised praxis, English language education which teaches or explicitly promotes social justice for women may only exacerbate the existing problems instead of solving them in places where the fundamental principles of gender equality (seen in Western perspective) have not been met, whether in socio-political or cultural terms. This is strongly linked to the political and cultural complexities of teaching English in non-Western settings, with related accusations of cultural imperialism and neo-colonialism (e.g. Said 1993; Atkinson 1999; Edge 2003, 2006).

At the same time, the inclusion of social justice in academic English instruction has not been sufficiently explored either in terms of its pitfalls or, indeed, benefits, especially in complex settings of cultural, social, and political forces interacting and clashing with each other. Qatar's Education City is an example of such a context. Located in the capital city, Doha, it hosts Western branch campuses with diverse faculty, administration, and student populations, coexisting and co-operating with established local cultures and values, in dynamic and not always easily predictable ways (Rostron 2009; Pessoa and Rajakumar 2011; Telafici et al. 2014; Woodworth 2014).

One of the most meaningful examples of how these forces result in social change and progress is the issue of gender equality in Qatar (Golkowska 2017; Rostron 2018). The changing parameters of women's role and position in Qatari/Gulf society are a result of multiple factors – including political and economic as well as social and cultural variables – but Western education with its English instruction is seen by many as remarkably influential in this respect (Findlow 2007; 2008, 2013; Pessoa and Rajakumar 2011; Golkowska 2017, 2018). Arguably, not only has it been striving to remodel theoretical approaches to women's issues in Qatar but has also altered perceptions of gender equality in practical terms, educating a new generation of female academics, entrepreneurs, diplomats, teachers, writers, scientists and 'doers', taking charge of their lives, discarding tradition and societal expectations, while striving for social justice for local women. These processes, however incomplete and still under construction, have raised praise and concern alike, inviting positive responses and objections in equal measure, and for several reasons. The applause and encouragement come from some Western sources (while many others remain critical of Qatar's insufficient progress in that area). Accolades can also be found in many official Qatari documents, articulated in an effort to enhance the international image of the country as modern and liberal (e.g. Felder and Vuollo 2008; MOFA 2021; The Borgen Project 2021; Women and the Community 2022). However, a degree of foreign praise and domestic image-building attempts are only part of the scene. The other part is less obvious and more subtle, mostly hidden from public view and only manifested through private discourses, off-the-cuff exchanges in the classroom, and spontaneous responses to teaching materials and texts assigned for class analysis.

The following vignettes, based on my own experiences as an EAP practitioner in Qatar's Education City or gleaned from conversations with colleagues, illustrate the undercurrents of vernacular thinking about social justice for women as promoted through Western education vis-à-vis local sensibilities. They tell a slightly different story, presenting a narrative of deep-seated reservations regarding the perceived attempts at changing traditional values rooted in religion and social conservatism by 'foreign teachers pushing their foreign agendas', as one Qatari student phrased it.

Vignette 1

After teaching a 1977 novel by Egyptian writer Nawal El Saadawi, *Woman at Point Zero*, to IB classes in a local school with an international curriculum, two North-American teachers found their contracts terminated. The decision followed protests by Qatari parents objecting to contextually inappropriate classroom materials, which were nevertheless an integral element of the IB literature syllabus.

Vignette 2

A Western-led and administered project aimed at recreating what was termed as a 'local female space' in a university setting came under harsh criticism from young Qatari women involved in it. Their criticism was focused on misrepresenting Qatari culture through attaching Western social justice ideas (i.e. women's equality) to indigenous traditions and customs and attempting to modify them to suit foreign academic purposes.

Vignette 3

After reading an article in a British broadsheet newspaper about the Hijab Day in Europe in solidarity with Muslim women, a discussion developed in an academic English class collectively rejecting Western interpretations of the hijab as generalisations and stereotypes.

Vignette 4

During a literary analysis of Ibsen's *A Doll's House* (1879), voices were raised in class criticising 'Western ways' of liberating women from male dominance. Local students stressed the importance of traditional values related to women's role as mothers and wives, caregivers and homemakers, with their male counterparts seen as main breadwinners and protectors of the family.

Vignette 5

In a class presentation of Virginia Woolf's *A Room of One's Own*, a female Qatari student expressed an opinion in favour of Woolf's 'old-fashioned feminism', stating that contemporary versions of it, as taught by some Western faculties, were generally seen here as too culturally controversial to gain any traction amongst local women.

Based on these vignettes, it appears that the idea and practice of teaching social justice (at least as illustrated through its one aspect, namely women's issues) is far from straightforward or effective in an English language classroom with instruction for non-native speakers. It is therefore reasonable to propose that teaching *for* social justice might be a more promising option. Losing its transitive character, the verb 'teach' acquires a more flexible quality, allowing for slow and culturally appropriate processing of values related to social justice and gender equality, without imposing their immediate Western readings and applications, which only turn off many non-Westerners.

Furthermore, including social justice as part of graded coursework in an English language class is akin to forcing students to perform voluntary work in order to gain an academic credit. It would be more desirable to make sure that non-native students gain sufficient linguistic proficiency to be able to deal with more complex and subtle texts, enhancing their awareness of the complex and subtle layers of many contemporary issues and developing their grasp of the multitude of voices and options. Such an approach could be more effective in fostering a more organic understanding of social justice, leading to tailor-made, specific forms of social activism applicable in the context.

That said, familiarising students with problem areas, concepts, and essential materials related to social justice (in both its conventional and critical-theory-based interpretations) should still be part of the academic English curriculum. The key stipulation here is that only a more indirect, sensitive, even furtive, approach can result in more lasting ethical and intellectual transformations than any form of overt 'social action-teaching'. Allowing time and space for reflection and critical engagement with such issues involves a more measured teaching approach, mindful of potential drawbacks. It might include explorations of various historical and cultural settings, demands, expectations, and values, and taking them into consideration through reflective writing and open discussions. Students need to be taught how to recognise and acknowledge multiple positions on a topic, while also learning to have *their* views challenged by *different* views and modify them without feeling threatened and becoming defensive and/or hostile.

In other words, it is only through internalising and contextualising the principle of social justice that social change can be ushered. In the words of the already cited UN report: 'The application of social justice requires a geographical, sociological, political and cultural framework within which relations between individuals and groups can be understood, assessed, and characterised as just or unjust' (UN 2006: 12).

It can be seen that the unique setting of Education City, combined with fluid and often problematic conceptualisations of social justice and women's issues, warrant a nuanced and discerning discussion, focused on parsing the most effective and engaging ways of interpreting and making use of social justice in EAP. A discussion of this kind is badly needed so that instead of what some might see as bombastic, hollow, Western-centric 'woke' rhetoric assuming righteousness and censuring opposing views, social justice can become a universal goal achievable locally through conscious, multilateral conversations facilitating fairness not through injunction but through language education that enlightens minds and sets people free.

References

Atkinson, D. (1999), 'TESOL and Culture', *TESOL Quarterly* 33(4): 625–54.

Atkinson E. (2002), 'The Responsible Anarchist: Postmodernism and Social Change', *British Journal of Sociology of Education*, 23(1): 73–87. Available online: https://doi.org/10.1080/01425690120102863 (accessed 29 September 2022).

De Wit, H. (2013), 'Reconsidering the Concept of Internationalization', *International Higher Education*, (70): 6–7.

Edge, J. (2003), 'Imperial Troopers and Servants of the Lord: a Vision of TESOL for the 21st Century', *TESOL Quarterly* 37(4): 701–9.

Edge, J., ed. (2006), *(Re-)Locating TESOL in an Age of Empire*, Basingstoke: Palgrave.

Felder, D. and Vuollo, M. (August 2008), *Qatari Women in the Workforce* (PDF). RAND-Qatar Policy Institute. Retrieved from: https://www.rand.org/content/dam/rand/pubs/working_papers/2008/RAND_WR612.pdf (accessed 29 September 2022)

Findlow, S. (2007), 'Women, Higher Education, and Social Transformation in the Arab Gulf', *Aspects of Education in the Middle East and North Africa*, Symposium Books, January 2007, 57–76. PDF.

Findlow, S. (2008), 'Islam, Modernity and Education in the Arab States', *Intercultural Education* 19(4): 337–52.

Findlow, S. (2013), 'Higher Education and Feminism in the Arab Gulf', *British Journal of Sociology of Education* 34(1): 112–31.

Firor Scott, A. (2002), 'Epilogue', in J. H. Baker (ed.), *Votes for Women: The Struggle for Suffrage Revisited*, Oxford: Oxford University Press.

Folarin Iman, I. (2022), '"Woke" is More than an Insult, it's a Threat to Our Freedom', *The Telegraph*, 13 May 2022. Retrieved from: https://www.telegraph.co.uk/news/2022/05/13/woke-insult-threat-freedom/

Golkowska, K. (2017), 'Qatari Women Navigating Gendered Space', *Social Sciences*, 6(123): 1–10

Golkowska, K. (2018), 'Developing Symbolic Competence on a North-American Branch Campus in Qatar', in M. Rajakumar (ed.). *Western Higher Education in Global Contexts*, 97-111, London: Lexington Books.

Golley, N. Al-Hassan. (2004), 'Is Feminism Relevant to Arab Women?', *Third World Quarterly* 25(3): 521–36.

Grady, C. (2018), 'The Waves of Feminism, and Why People Keep Fighting Over Them, Explained', *Vox*, 20 July 2018. Retrieved from: https://www.vox.com/2018/3/20/16955588/feminism-waves-explained-first second-third-fourth

Hobson, J. M. (2007), 'Is Critical Theory Always for the White West and for Western Imperialism? . . .', *Review of International Studies*, 33: 91–116.

Lauder, H., Brown, P., Dillabough, J. A. and Halsey, A. H., eds (2006), *Education, Globalization, and Social Change*, Oxford: Oxford University Press.

Leung, K. and Stephan, W. G. (2001), 'Social Justice from a Cultural Perspective', in D. Matsumoto (ed.), *The Handbook of Culture and Psychology*, 375–410, Oxford: Oxford University Press.

Marmolejo, F. (2010), 'Internationalization of Higher Education: the Good, the Bad, and the Unexpected', *The Chronicle of Higher Education*, 22 October 2010. Retrieved from: https://www.chronicle.com/blogs/worldwise/internationalization-of-higher-education-the-good-the-bad-and-the-unexpected (accessed 29 September 2022).

Mirzaei, A. (2019), 'Where "Woke" Came from and Why Marketers Should Think Twice Before Jumping on the Social Activism Bandwagon', *The Conversation*, 13 September 2019. Retrieved from: https://theconversation.com/where-woke-came-from and-why-marketers-should-think-twice-before-jumping-on-the-social-activism bandwagon-122713

MOFA (May 2021), 'Global Praise for Qatar's Role in Improving Status of Women in the World', *Ministry of Foreign Affairs NEWS*. Retrieved from: https://mofa.gov.qa/en/all-mofa-news/details/1442/10/13/global-praise-for-qatar's-role-in-improving-status-of-women-in-the-world

Mohanty, C. T. (2003), *Feminism without Borders: Decolonizing Theory, Practicing Solidarity*, JSTOR Duke University Press. Available online: https://doi.org/10.2307/j.ctv11smp7t (accessed 29 September 2022).

Murray, D. (2020), *The Madness of Crowds,* London: Bloomsbury.

Pessoa, S. and Rajakumar, M. (2011), 'The Impact of English-medium Higher Education: the Case of Qatar', in A. Al Issa and E. L. Dahan (eds), *Global English and Arabic Issues of Language, Culture and Identity*, vol. 31, 153–78, Peter Lang. https://www.peterlang.com/view/9783035301205/9783035301

Rauch, J. (2021), 'The Danger of Politicizing Science', *Persuasion*. Retrieved from: https://www.persuasion.community/p/the-danger-of-politicizing-science (accessed 29 September 2022).

Rostron, M. (2009), 'Liberal Arts Education in Qatar: Intercultural Perspectives', *Intercultural Education* 20(3): 219–29.

Rostron, M. (2014), 'Exploring Identity of Non-native Teachers of English Through Narratives of their Experience', in P. Breen (ed.), *Cases on Teacher Identity, Diversity, and Cognition in Higher Education,* 140–70, Hershey PA: IGI Global.

Rostron, M. (2016), 'A Cultural Other in Transnational Education: Impact of Globalization on Student and Teacher Identities', in L. Seawright and A. Hodges (eds), *Learning Across Borders: Perspectives on International And Transnational Higher Education*, 1st edn, 193–215, Cambridge: Cambridge Scholars Publishing.

Rostron, M. (2018), 'Students' Experiences of Othering: an Ethnographic Case Study of an English Language University Preparatory Programme in Qatar', PhD thesis, The University of Manchester.

Said, E. (1993), *Culture and Imperialism,* New York: Knopf.

Szyliowicz, J. S. (1973), *Education and Modernization in the Middle East*, New York: Cornell University Press.

Telafici, M., Martinez M. and Telafici M. (2014), 'East of West: Rearguing the Value and Goals of Education in the Gulf', *The Journal of General Education* 63(2–3): 184–97.

The Borgen Project 2021. Available at: https://borgenproject.org/womens-rights-in-qatar/ (accessed 29 September 2022).

UN (= United Nations) (2006) *The International Forum for Social Development: Social Justice in an Open World. The Role of the United Nations. Department of Economic and Social Affairs Division for Social Policy and Development*, New York: United Nations, 2006.

Val L. and Wright, N. D. (1993), 'A Critique of Critical Theory: Response to Murray and Ozanne's The Critical Imagination', in L. McAlister and M. L. Rothschild (eds), *Advances in Consumer Research*, vol. 20, 439–43, Provo, UT: Association for Consumer Research.

Ware, S. (2020), 'Leaving All to Younger Hands: Why the History of the Women's Suffragist Movement Matters', *Brookings,* May 2020. Retrieved from: https://www.brookings.edu/essay/leaving-all-to-younger-hands-why-the-history of-the-womens-suffrage-movement-matters/ (accessed 29 September 202).

Ware, S. (2019), *Why They Marched: Untold Stories of the Women Who Fought for the Right to Vote*, Harvard, US: Belknap Press.

Women and the Community (2022), 'About Qatar', available at: https://www.ashghal.gov.qa/en/AboutQatar/Pages/Women.aspx#:~:text=Politically%2C%20women%20in%20Qatar%20achieved,an%20investment%20company%20for%20ladies (accessed 29 September 2022).

Woodworth, A. (2014), 'Exporting Acting Curricula from the Midwest to the Mideast: Seriously?', *The Journal of General Education*, 63(2–3): 138–51.

12

The Journey of *Develop EAP*: From a Single Step to a More Sustainable and Shared Practice

Averil Bolster

Starting out as a novice English language teacher in 1995 in my first English Language Teaching (ELT) job in Ankara, Turkey, all my colleagues were newly qualified too, clutching our certificates from courses of varying weeks in length to prove it. With long hours, little pay and constant referral to the twin pillars of Murphy's (1994) 'bible', *English Grammar in Use* and Swan's (1995) *Practical English Usage*, it was either sink or swim. Together, we managed to keep our heads above water. From this initial forging of collegial bonds, I realised the importance of sharing ideas and materials with fellow teachers, as we were all in it together.

Little did I know at the time how this innate belief in collegiality and sharing was in line with the concept of a Community of Practice (COP), which Breen (2018: 15) points out is a fundamental aspect of English for Academic Purposes (EAP), when he states that Community of Practice literature is 'particularly salient to the EAP context, which has historically encouraged collegiality'. This was the case when working in EAP in Asia and seeing some of the exciting work coming out of conferences hosted by institutions in mainland China, Hong Kong and Singapore, where there was a lot of discussion about establishing and formalising an EAP COP. The centrality of collegiality in EAP is also reflected in Breen's (2018: 15) identification of BALEAP, the British-based EAP organisation, as a 'collegial organisation'.

Fast-forward more than twenty-five years from my initial ELT job, after acquiring lengthier and more recognised qualifications, and a wide range of teaching, examining and management experience, and that appreciation of support and camaraderie of colleagues has never left me. While that appreciation of shared knowledge and materials is something that shaped my personal philosophy of practice, it is also one of the four pillars of medical ethics: justice (the others being beneficence, non-maleficence and autonomy). Within this pillar, the equal distribution of resources is a cornerstone. In social justice, resource distribution is also a key factor to consider, and the field of education is no stranger to the inequalities of resources. There is an increasing discussion about open access research, making research available for everyone, navigating the tension between quality assurance and accessibility. This is a growing trend at the Finnish university where I work, the University of Turku, and several UK universities featured in this publication, such as UCL and the University of Westminster. What is discussed less is the potential of open access EAP teaching materials.

In June 2017, course materials that I had designed together with Peter Levrai (who I met during that initial formative year in Turkey) won a British Council ELTons Innovation Award. The ELTons have been dubbed 'the Oscars of ELT' and celebrated their twentieth year in 2022. According to the British Council, the ELTons 'celebrate the most original courses, publications, projects, apps and platforms, and more, which are finding new ways to help English language learners and teachers around the world achieve their goals' (British Council 2022: para. 1). Our course materials won in the category of Innovation in Learner Resources. This chapter discusses my experience of releasing those materials under a Creative Commons licence, making them openly available to all.

The course, 'Develop EAP: A Sustainable Academic Skills Course', consists of a downloadable booklet, an accompanying Virtual Learning Environment (VLE) open-source Moodle and editable PowerPoint slides for lessons. It aimed to develop students' academic skills through exploration of topics from the United Nations' Sustainable Development Goals (The UN's SDGs). The SDGs are seventeen global goals that were agreed by world leaders in 2015 to tackle the greatest issues facing humankind. According to the United Nations (2022: para. 1), the SDGs provide a plan 'for peace and prosperity for people and the planet, now and into the future'. The SDGs have wide ranging implications, and The British Council supported the development of teaching materials related to the SDGS in 2017 by publishing a free book of teaching resources. In this book, I contributed a chapter with my fellow author, Peter Levrai, titled, 'Using the Sustainable Development Goals in the EAP Classroom' (Bolster and Levrai 2017a).

Develop EAP (for short) evolved from materials I codeveloped in 2016 for an English for general academic purposes course (EGAP) when I was working at the only English-medium public university in Macau. I was responsible for redeveloping a mandatory EAP course that students from all faculties took, meaning an annual cohort of over 1,000 students. Using the SDGs as a core to the course came while pondering what topics or themes might be not only flexible and engaging but also have some actual meaning and relevance to the students from diverse backgrounds with different interests.

Having completed an MA in ELT and Materials Development, I was heavily influenced by Tomlinson's (2007: 162) concept of 'humanising the coursebook', adapting published materials and developing one's own localised and personalised materials for learners. While the SDGs are global, they are also actionable on a local scale and hence, very much 'glocal' (based on the term, glocalization, credited to the sociologist Roland Robertson in the early 1990s (Featherstone 2020)). This means they would also lend themselves to the localisation and personalisation I was looking for.

There certainly seemed to be a relevance between the SDGs and the local context I was working in. Macau's economy is dominated by the gambling industry. In 2013, the year I began working there, the gaming industry's contribution to GDP peaked at 63.1 per cent (Sheng and Gu 2018: 75). Many, if not most, of the students at my university would go on to careers that would be in some way connected to the region's biggest (and most dazzling) industry. While contributing hugely to Macau's revenue and providing employment, the vast construction and running of the numerous energy consuming casinos there, are not what one would call environmentally friendly, and the model did not seem sustainable.

Ensuring environmental sustainability had been one of the Millennium Development Goals (MDGs) that I had remembered from a course in my previous job at a British university branch campus in China, in which the MDGs were a topic for a written assignment. The MDGs were the measurable goals the nations of the UN agreed upon in 2000, with the achievement target date of 2015. Having found the MDGs inspiring, I wondered what had happened now that it was 2016 and their deadline had been reached. Upon checking the UN website, I was delighted to find that the eight MDGs had been followed by the more extensive seventeen SDGs. These new goals also differed from the previous ones in that the MDGs tended to focus on developing countries whereas the SDGs are more global. The SDGs seemed to fit with the ethos I was hoping to incorporate into the EGAP course, as the SDGF (2022: para. 3) states, 'The focus is now on building a sustainable world where environmental sustainability, social inclusion, and economic development are equally valued'.

Having the SDGs as a central theme of *Develop EAP* at a time when it was not common, was one of the reasons for winning the ELTons innovation award, but other innovations in the course included QR codes and the curation of open access materials from various university websites and the semi-academic media site *The Conversation*, interspersed with our original materials. *The Conversation* (theconversation.com) is a collaborative project which allows for the reading and republishing free of charge under Creative Commons of articles from academics who write in a more journalistic style. They make complex issues more digestible, providing valuable inputs and resources for all educators, and can be of particular use to EAP practitioners. As we had no funding, making use of freely accessible resources was essential, including royalty free images from Pixabay and hosting the VLE on Moodle Cloud.

Once we had written *Develop EAP*, the question became what to do with it. With a structure that is different from typical coursebooks, my co-author Peter and I knew that *Develop EAP* would not fit with traditional publishers. Rather than chapters of similar length and predictable activities, *Develop EAP* moved through the process of generating academic work, looking at research and reading strategies before moving into writing orientated activities, from brainstorming, through drafting to editing and final proofreading. Our book, *Academic Presenting and Presentations*, which had been a finalist in the 2016 ELTons awards for Innovation in Learner Resources, found a home in a niche publishing house and while seeing the course in print was great, it did limit the potential for where it could be used as teachers would have to both know about it and purchase it.

To pay forward our use of open access resources in the course, and to avoid prohibitive costs for users and gatekeeping access to materials that traditional publishers may pose for teachers in some contexts, we prioritised free and swift access to *Develop EAP* and accompanying materials. This way, practitioners from all backgrounds, including those with limited (or no) budgets could have them at the click of a button. They could then adapt the materials to their specific contexts, including the editable PowerPoint slides, which could be used as a starting point for lessons. Personalisation and (g)localisation are again encouraged since 'all teaching is local' (Mann 2005: 112). This was in line with my beliefs about teaching and learning which developed from that first ELT job, when sharing with fellow teachers was so vital, and consolidated by my MA studies after which I saw myself as a materials developer.

Developing teaching and learning materials is such an important part of a teacher's work, but it is time-consuming and its value is often overlooked by institutions. One organisation which I found to be a champion for encouraging teachers and researchers in the area of materials development, is the aptly named Materials Development Association (MATSDA: https://www.matsda.org/). Founded by Brian Tomlinson in 1993, MATSDA holds annual conferences and publishes its own journal, *Folio*. In a 2018 article in *Folio*, I wrote about what it is like to write materials (including *Develop EAP*) with a collaborator with my regular co-author (Bolster and Levrai 2018). Twenty years after the founding of MATSDA, another materials development organisation was created: the Materials Writing Special Interest Group (MaWSIG: https://mawsig.iatefl.org/). This SIG is part of IATEFL (the International Association of Teachers of English as a Foreign Language) and also holds events and shares resources on its webpage.

In order to share the *Develop EAP* booklet and its accompanying course materials, we built a website with the free website host Weebly (Bolster and Levrai 2017b) under a Creative Commons non-commercial license. To get the word out and raise awareness of *Develop EAP* in professional circles, we sent a message via some professional network mailing lists and channels, such as BALEAP, EATAW (European Association for the Teaching of Academic Writing) and CercleS (European Confederation of Language Centres in Higher Education). In 2019, the course was reviewed in the *English Australia Journal* (Falkinder 2019). It was positively received and later that year we expanded the materials to build on some constructive observations that had been made, namely about critical thinking, listening skills and note-taking. This 2019 update was based on my and Peter's intrinsic motivation to maintain as high a standard as possible for the materials we had created. Although it is not part of our current work or PhD studies, we still keep the *Develop EAP* site updated by adding links to other useful SDG-related sites and curating academic English language and skills resources, which fellow practitioners might appreciate.

Since it was first made available online in March 2018 to December 2022, more than 930 practitioners from 560 tertiary level institutions spanning eighty-five countries have downloaded the course directly, and it is also known to have been taken on as a central resource in locations as disparate as the UK, Japan and Turkey. Something that is particularly pleasing is that without any kind of advertising, *Develop EAP* has reached EAP practitioners in locations as diffuse as Mauritania, Kiribati and Peru. In addition to the Falkinder (2019) review, feedback on the course has come informally through direct contact from teachers who have downloaded and used *Develop EAP*. It is a small fraction of overall downloads, but those teachers who have reached out have been very positive, and appreciate high quality free materials being made available. Several teachers who wrote to me or my co-author are not EAP practitioners but found that the academic skills and SDGs theme fit their communications and policy studies courses well. Most recently, we gave permission for *Develop EAP* to be used on the UK-based RefugEAP project, an 'online programme of free non-formal

English for Academic Purposes (EAP) classes and independent learning resources, specifically for refugee-background students' (RefugEAP 2022: para. 3). The use of *Develop EAP* in such varied contexts highlights what we had hoped for: that good academic skills materials based on relevant topics could be used in non-EAP and/or first language English classes too.

Although 2017 was not that long ago, much has changed since then (apart from the obvious impacts of the Covid-19 pandemic), including a greater awareness of social justice issues in EAP and ELT as well as the incorporation of the SDGs into many higher education curricula and mission statements (Hessen 2020). The SDGs are even included in the Times Higher Education (THE) university impact ranking lists, with a 23 per cent increase in participating universities in 2002 compared with the previous year (Expanded Impact Rankings Reflect 2022). Whether or not institutions are genuine about playing their part in solving the world's most pressing problems by the target year of 2030 remains to be seen. What is encouraging, however, is that whatever the motivation, the SDGs and issues of sustainability have a higher profile and are attracting more attention.

Creating the *Develop EAP* course was a lot of work, and that work has more value and more impact if it is shared and available to all. Sharing materials with teachers, and by extension their students, in areas which may have fewer resources is especially important for social justice. We could have sought a traditional publishing or commercialised self-publishing route for the course, but I am proud *Develop EAP* is available to any teacher, anywhere. I hope that in our own small way, through the Creative Commons release of *Develop EAP*, some EAP teachers might be empowered to empower their students to address the multifaceted challenges in achieving a more equitable, sustainable world.

References

Bolster, A. and Levrai, P. (2017a), 'Using the Sustainable Development Goals in the EAP Classroom', in A. Maley and N. Peachey (eds), *Integrating Global Issues in the Creative English Language Classroom: With Reference to the United Nations Sustainable Development Goals*, 195–203, London: British Council. Available online: http://www.teachingenglish.org.uk/sites/teacheng/files/PUB_29200_Creativity_UN_SDG_v4S_WEB.pdf (accessed 15 October 2022).

Bolster, A. and Levrai, P. (2017b), 'Develop EAP: a Sustainable Academic English Skills Course', available at: https://developeap.weebly.com/ (accessed 30 December 2022).

Bolster, A. and Levrai, P. (2017c), 'Building Sustainability into an EAP Course [Webinar]', *TeachingEnglish*, https://www.teachingenglish.org.uk/article/building-sustainability-eap-course (accessed 15 October 2022).

Bolster, A. and Levrai, P. (2018), 'Writing Together: Storming to Success', *Folio: Journal of the Materials Development Association*, 18(2): 20–4. Available online: https://www.matsda.org/Folio_sample_2.pdf (accessed 16 October 2022).

Breen, P. (2018), *Developing Educators for the Digital Age: A Framework for Capturing Teacher Knowledge in Action*, London: Westminster University Press.

British Council (2022), 'ELTons Innovation Awards', *TeachingEnglish*, October 2022, https://www.teachingenglish.org.uk/news-events/eltons-innovations-awards (accessed 16 October 2022).

'Expanded Impact Rankings Reflect Rising Interest in SDGs' (2022), *University World News*, 30 April 2022, https://www.universityworldnews.com/post.php?story=20220430080957202 (accessed 16 October 2022).

Falkinder, N. (2019), 'Develop EAP: a Sustainable Academic Skills Course Review', *English Australia Journal,* 35(1): 98–100. Available online: https://eajournal.partica.online/digital/eaj351_web/flipbook/1/ (accessed 15 October 2022).

Featherstone, M. (2020), 'Whither Globalization? An Interview with Roland Robertson', *Theory, Culture and Society*, 37(7–8): 169–85. Available online: https://journals.sagepub.com/doi/full/10.1177/0263276420959429 (accessed 20 October 2022).

Hessen, D. O. (2022), 'Universities as Catalysts of Transition to Sustainability', *University World News*, 20 April 2022, https://www.universityworldnews.com/post.php?story=20220413105333128 (accessed 20 October 2022).

Levrai, P. and Bolster, A. (2015), *Academic Presenting and Presentations: Student's Book*, Norderstedt: Linguabooks.

Mann, S. (2005), 'The Language Teacher's Development', *Language Teaching*, 38(3): 103–18.

Murphy, R. (1994), *English Grammar in Use: a Self-study Reference and Practice Book for Intermediate Students of English-with Answers*, 2nd edn, Cambridge: Cambridge University Press.

RefugEAP (2022), *University of Leicester*, https://le.ac.uk/cite/sanctuary-seekers-unit/initiatives/refugeap (accessed 17 October 2022).

Sheng, M. and Gu, C. (2018), 'Economic Growth and Development in Macau (1999–2016): the Role of the Booming Gaming Industry', *Cities*, 75: 72–80.

SDGF (2022), 'From MDGs to SDGs', *Sustainable Development Goals Fund*, https://www.sdgfund.org/mdgs-sdgs (accessed 20 October 2022).

Swan, M. (1995), *Practical English Usage,* 2nd edn, Oxford: Oxford University Press.

Tomlinson, B. ([2003]2007), 'Humanising the Coursebook', in B. Tomlinson (ed.), *Developing Materials for Language Teaching*, 162–73, London: Continuum.

United Nations (2022), 'Sustainable Development Goals', *United Nations: Department of Economic and Social Affairs*, https://sdgs.un.org/goals (accessed 20 October 2022).

13

English for Research Purposes and Linguistic Diversity: Researcher Reflexivity and Social Justice

Magdalena De Stefani, Richard Fay and Zhuomin Huang

Introduction

English has become a global lingua franca for both academic purposes (EAP) and research purposes (ERP). This status merits problematisation: on the one hand, English seems to offer a shared linguistic vehicle for knowledge development, dissemination and exchange, but on the other it also carries with it the dangers of linguistically-driven epistemological and methodological centralisation at the expense of knowledge-work in other languages. With language diversity, epistemological diversity, and social justice to the fore of our thinking (e.g. Andrews and Fay 2020; Andrews, Fay and White 2018; Andrews et al. forthcoming; Fay et al. 2021, forthcoming), in this chapter we begin to tease out some of the possible implications for us as researchers and, as relevant for the field of EAP, for those that train researchers linguistically as well as methodologically.

Even where English is the main conduit for research activity, many researchers possess deep and varied linguistic resources, and they may be working in contexts characterised by linguistic diversity, and/or collaborating in teams possessing rich linguistic resources with participants and/or data demonstrating similar linguistic range and depth. If researchers are to maximise the value of the lingua franca functions of English for research purposes, whilst at the same time guarding against the risks of epistemic injustice (Fricker 2007), epistemicide (de Sousa Santos 2015), and knowledge colonisation, they need to be attentive to, and we would argue, reflexive regarding, the linguistic aspects of their research practices. In this chapter, we briefly consider some of the features and debates regarding ERP contexts, and then outline our position on researcher reflexivity.

As a research team, we are spread across two hemispheres, and we bring to our joint work diverse linguistic resources, professional identities and experiences, and methodological interests and expertise. As underpinned by these team characteristics, we reflect on the importance of individual and collaborative reflexivity, first in a project we are jointly developing, and then in two other contrasting and illustrative research studies involving some of our authorial team. We conclude with some discussion of the lessons that might be drawn from these cases for EAP students and teachers regarding the conduct of English-foregrounded research in a socially-just manner.

English for research purposes

We favour the term English for Research Purposes (ERP) – rather than the prominent term English for Research Publication Purposes (ERPP) (e.g. Flowerdew 2013) – because we are concerned with all aspects of research arising from the linguistic diversity evident in the research and researched contexts, in the linguistic repertoires of the researchers and participants, and in the diversity of languages used in the relevant literatures. It is not just a matter of publishing in English (with all the implications that the dominant role of English for research publication has for scholars with differing relationships with this language, e.g. Curry and Lillis 2013a, 2013b, 2017, 2019; Lillis and Curry 2010, 2016), it is also a matter of all aspects of research mediated through primarily English-medium communications and understandings. This extensive role of English in ERP contexts is one reason why those teaching English for Academic Purposes (EAP) have a broader remit than that of primarily supporting their students' development of English-for-publication writing skills including the academic writing activities that pave the way for this (e.g. assessed assignments, dissertations, theses).

ERP contexts can be understood as the languaging of research primarily through English. The concept of 'languaging' foregrounds how people both shape and make sense of their worlds through language (Phipps and Gonzalez 2004: 167). Thus, Samy Alim, Rickford, and Ball (2016) consider the role of language in the languaging of race and how this shapes and constructs race. For our researcher purposes, we might ask 'What are the implications of research being languaged in globally dominant languages and in less globally-dominant languages?'. The hegemonic status that English (as a key lingua franca of research) has acquired can lead to a privileging of certain (often English-medium) voices in international scholarship (Curry and Lillis 2013, 2017) despite monolingual-English academic environments not being the academic norm around the world (Robinson-Pant and Wolf 2016). That being so, researchers and those that educate them (including supervisors, mentors, EAP tutors) may benefit from developing a translingual mindset (Andrews and Fay 2020; Andrews, Fay and White 2018) and being more attentive to 'the linguistic features of the context of the research ... the language preferences and habits of the participants in that research; and the way in which the linguistic is understood in the disciplinary research tradition in which the research has been designed' (Andrews and Fay 2020: 190–1). These ideas resonate with calls for translingual practice (Canagarajah 2013), and the educational embrace of plurilingualism (Choi and Ollerhead 2018) especially in largely Anglophone higher education contexts (Preece and Marshall 2020). Inherent in these calls is the problematisation of languages as separate, bounded, labelled entities and the recognition of the fluidity with which the diverse linguistic resources individuals possess may be operationalised.

Underpinning these moves to recognise and value the available linguistic resources lies a concern for what is lost epistemologically when knowledge-work is channelled through a few dominant languages such as English. For example, early childhood specialist Moss (2020) asks what is lost when one language becomes the lingua franca for the exchange of ideas across cultural contexts. For him, 'the dominance of English has been matched by the dominance of a way of thinking about early childhood education: positivistic, instrumental, reductionist and technical, averse to context, diversity and complexity' (ibid.: 433). This theme of linguistic colonisation of epistemology and the loss that this represents for our collective wisdom (Fay et al. forthcoming) is discussed not just in educational debates, but also much more widely, for example in global mental health research and practice (White, Fay, Phipps, Giurgi-Oncu and Chiumento 2022).

Our own research experiences take place in the contested, complicated space where lingua franca utility meets hegemonic language consequences, such as epistemic injustice, colonisation of the curriculum, loss of epistemological, methodological, and linguistic diversity, and so on. We are attempting to navigate this problematic space through a foregrounded reflexivity in our work.

Researcher reflexivity

Reflexivity is an active, ongoing process of critical reflection that occurs during every research stage (Guillemin and Gillam 2004: 274), characterised by 'detachment, internal dialogue, and constant (and intensive) scrutiny of "what I know" and "how I know it"' (Hertz 1997: vii). According to Mason (1996: 6), it implies that researchers 'should constantly take stock of their actions and their role in the research process and subject these to the same critical scrutiny as the rest of their data'. For Mauthner and Doucet (2003: 418), researchers tend to over-simplify the issue of reflexivity by assuming that the voices of research participants will speak for themselves. Instead, they should acknowledge the fact that these voices are being presented through their own choices.

A reflexive positioning requires accounting for ethical issues throughout the research process, and the continuous assessment of conscious and unconscious decisions and their potential impact (Holmes, Reynolds and Ganassin 2022). Researchers need to examine the language-related choices they make and how these may impact on issues related to social justice, such as language dominance, unequal language positioning or potential shifts in the researcher-participant power balance. Yet, reflexivity is not only an aid in the quest for social justice, it is also a tool for researchers to explore their role in greater depth, and thus reach conclusions which might otherwise not be so readily accessible. A reflexive mindset is therefore an aid to the collaborative construction of knowledge, 'creating enriching and empowering research relationships' (Mao, Mian Akram, Chovanec and Underwood 2016: 1). For this, it is important for researchers to situate themselves in relation to participants, not only socially and emotionally, as suggested by Mauthner and Doucet (2003: 419), but also linguistically.

Attia and Edge (2017: 35) argue for a developmental approach to research methodology, in which reflexivity is a key element, offering 'increased hope for researchers to exceed the limitations of (albeit arguably useful) pre-determined hegemonic models by synthesising new possibilities in interaction'. In the three cases we present below, we illustrate some of the complexities of linguistic diversity in different settings and how these become opportunities for researcher reflexivity.

Three cases

Performing arts teachers in Uruguay

This ongoing study explores issues of 'professional personhood' among performing artists turned teachers in the context of a university college in Montevideo, the capital city of Uruguay. Professional personhood is understood as 'the web of roles and relationships that are acquired and enacted in professional arenas' (Dombeck 1997: 11). The concept of personhood involves a systemic and inward-looking understanding which is based on 'first-person meaning-makings' (Huang 2021: 84), rather than on externally defined characteristics. It was within this conceptual framework that two Uruguayan Spanish-speaking artists agreed to participate in the study and do so under their own names (rather than being anonymised or given pseudonyms in the dissemination of the study). Mariana and Maria José, a dancer and a singer respectively, are lecturers at the *Instituto Universitario de Artes Escénicas* in Uruguay (IUDAE), where one of the researchers, Magdalena, is head of the research department. The institution promotes a participatory, collaborative model of research, where lecturers and students take an active part in the construction of the institutional research narrative. As was the case with these two lecturers, IUDAE favours the idea of conducting research *with* participants, so that knowledge generation occurs throughout the educational community and not just, in this case, through the research team.

Adopting a narrative research perspective, this study uses an arts-based research method, with the aim of capturing meanings that extend beyond language (Hickey-Moody 2020). We used 'blind-portrait' (Huang 2022), an arts-based method which involves asking each participant to draw a portrait of their professional self with their eyes closed. This portrait may be abstract, concrete, or metaphorical, and participants are then engaged in a discussion with researchers as to what is represented in their portraits. Both stages of the blind portrait interview were conducted online, in English, as recorded using Zoom. Afterwards, we constructed a narrative of the explorations, attempting to capture the process in which participants and researchers created a shared understanding of these teachers' professional personhood. The second data generation stage involved a follow-up interview in Spanish with each participant, in which Magdalena, the Spanish-speaking researcher, shared with them the analysis of the data gathered in the first stage. During this second interview, the participant's impressions of the analysis and the narrative were discussed. This was, on the one hand, a data analysis validation procedure, and, on the other, a move to foster participants' active involvement in the research process. At the time of writing this chapter, this second stage has been completed with María José and Mariana's contribution still to follow.

The study was conducted by our multinational and multicultural research team which is also multilingual – with first language speakers of Chinese (Zhuomin), English (Richard) and Spanish (Magdalena), as well as a shared use of English as a lingua franca. Even though participants were native-speakers of Spanish with different degrees of English proficiency, English was used for most of the data generation and analysis, as well as the research narrative. From a social justice perspective, we addressed this choice reflexively, foregrounding the implicit effects of using English as the lingua franca in a Spanish-speaking setting. From our perspective as researchers in a linguistically-diverse research team, we continue to reflect on the impact of language-related decisions in this study, addressing issues of ethics, trustworthiness, and power.

This reflexive approach is informing our decision-making as the study evolves. Thus, as we continue to navigate the second data generation stage, we are reflecting on the same issues when we use arts-based methods to generate further data, this time with Spanish-foregrounded rather than English. How might this bring to the fore different perspectives from the performing arts teachers? What might be the implications for the researchers given that Spanish is not a team lingua franca? These questions were also present in our second case where the researchers involved have begun to develop reflexive strategies to address them.

Ladino speakers in Bulgaria

This study (Davcheva and Fay 2012; Fay and Davcheva 2014[2016]) explored the narrativised understandings of middle-aged and elderly Sephardic Jews in Bulgaria regarding the language which participants tend to call *Judesmo* but which is often referred to as *Ladino*. This is a Romance language with roots in Old Spanish which travelled with the Sephardic Jews (*Sephardim*) who were expelled in 1492 from the Iberian Peninsula. Although now an endangered language, for many centuries *Ladino* played an important cultural and communicational dimension for Sephardic Jewish communities. During the Holocaust, many *Ladino*-speaking communities were largely destroyed. Those in Bulgaria were an exception, but even this community dwindled after the Second World War. The study was motivated by the desire to collect the stories of some of the remaining *Sephardim* in Bulgaria before it was too late.

The researchers (Leah and Richard) shared some characteristics broadly relevant for this study, including: professional backgrounds (both being language teachers, intercultural communication educators); personal interests (both being interested in cultural, including musical and linguistic, aspects of different communities in the Balkans); and research experience (individual and collaborative experience of narrative-based methods). They also both have some linguistic competence in Spanish. But there were also significant differences between them (see Table 13.1).

Table 13.1 Insider and outsider perspectives in the research

	Leah	Richard
Culture	A *cultural insider* in the worlds of Bulgarian-*Sephardim* including some familiarity with *Ladino*	A *cultural outsider* (i.e. non-Jewish, non-Bulgarian in background, and only relatively recent awareness of the existence of *Ladino*)
Bulgarian Context	A *contextual insider* in her home country (Bulgaria)	A *contextual outsider* (infrequent short-term sojourner) in Bulgaria
Languages	A *linguistic insider* in the Bulgarian-Sephardic worlds and in Bulgarian-medium and (in many ways) English-medium scholarship	A *linguistic outsider* in the Bulgarian-Sephardic worlds and in Bulgarian-medium scholarship; a *linguistic insider* in English-medium scholarship
Research Sites	A *fieldwork insider* with 'front-of-house' roles in interactions with the storytellers and a *university-outsider* for desk-based research activities	A *fieldwork outsider* with no roles in the field for desk-based research activities and a *university-insider* with ease of access for 'back-stage' desk-based research activities
Research Methodology	Developing *research insider* vis-à-vis understandings of narrative research and methodological issues such as reflexivity	More experienced *research insider* vis-à-vis understandings of narrative research and methodological issues such as reflexivity

The study used participant narratives (generated largely in Bulgarian but then re-storied and translated into English) to explore their understandings of *Ladino*. This fieldwork stage of the research was undertaken almost exclusively by Leah. The resulting corpus of re-storied narratives in both Bulgarian and English was completely available to Leah for analysis whereas Richard could only work with the English version. He was, therefore, once removed from the re-storied data and two steps removed from the original storytellings (for which Leah was the audience). These asymmetries also played a part when the research was presented and published variously in Bulgarian, English, Spanish and German. These researcher asymmetries – regarding the research and researched contexts, the languages used in the research, the processes of data generation, management, and analysis and dissemination writing – were a source of design complexity in the study in which English functioned as the main lingua franca for the researchers.

To transparently manage the subjectivities involved in the study, Leah and Richard developed the technique of 'researcher narratives' whereby they told each other – through largely English-medium written texts – stories about their relationships with both the linguistic focus of the study (i.e. *Ladino*) and the methodological aspects of it (i.e. narrative-based research undertaken multilingually). The objective was to develop a shared sense of what they brought individually and collectively to the research, and thereby to individually and jointly reflect on how their diverse researcher perspectives and experiences might shape the study. This process of story-exchange can be seen as a technique through which reciprocal or collaborative reflexivity might be pursued.

念 (niàn) and mindfulness

In a conceptual 'think-piece' Huang and colleagues (Huang 2020, 2023; Huang, Fay and White 2017) problematise the ways in which researchers and practitioners from different disciplinary and practitioner domains, and with differing linguistic and cultural backgrounds, have engaged with the concept (and associated practices) of 念 (*niàn*) in Chinese, or 'mindfulness' in English. This concept has migrated over time and space, being taken from its original context within Buddhist philosophy, in Asia, and brought into largely Western psycho-therapeutic and educational healthcare domains. The authors' concerns resonate with others; for example, Asher (2017) argues that the use of thinking in a new context needs to be sensitive regarding, and to avoid the risks of, the simplistic use of sources of knowledge from another source context.

For such conceptual migrations to be fully respectful and ethical, Huang, Fay and White 2017) argue that researchers and practitioners need to be attentive to: a) the origins of the concepts being used; b) the migrational history (and its geographical, contextual, disciplinary, temporal and other dimensions); and c) the current vitalities of the concept – that is, the ways in which it is currently being understood and used should be similarly noted. When ways of thinking are taken into new contexts and then return to their original contexts, as in the case of 念 (*niàn*) / mindfulness, the authenticity and/or appropriacy of the new meanings may be contested. In light of this possibility, the authors (Huang Fay and White 2017: 53) call for an 'intercultural ethic' inviting scholars and practitioners to 'recognise the debt incurred to those using the idea before them and to accept the imperative this creates for them to be informed, respectful and transparent in their usage of the ideas in question.'

Their own work seeks to exemplify the ethic in practice. With due diligence, they trace the historical, geographical and philosophical origins of the concept, and, even though the shared language of the researchers was English – and the study thus forms part of the ERP canon – the team explicitly drew upon its collective linguistic resources to engage with literatures in languages other than English. The creation of research teams with diverse linguistic resources available to them is one step towards challenging an unthinking reliance upon English-medium thinking. It is a step which also requires the research team to remain reflexive regarding the ways in which the available (and unavailable) linguistic resources might shape the research.

Discussion / recommendations

Our central argument is that the potential negative effects of the hegemony of English in linguistically-diverse research settings might be counterbalanced with explicit, reflexive researcher positioning. This linguistic reflexivity needs to be an ongoing part of the research process, rather than a by-product which is assessed at the end. Such ongoing reflexivity regarding linguistic matters in the research process can be seen in the discussion (Stelma, Fay and Zhou 2013) regarding the opportunities provided by Zhou's Chinese and English linguistic resources in her doctoral study involving Chinese participants, data and literature whilst being resourced in a UK-based university, and supervised and examined through English. Similar linguistic pulls and pushes are evident in the three cases discussed above.

In the first of the three case studies, the fact that the participants and one of the researchers were contextually native and shared their cultural orientation, not only enhanced trustworthiness in terms of data representation but also shifted the traditional power imbalance between researchers and participants. There was no information that was inaccessible to participants due to language, and we had the flexibility of using different languages and research strategies to co-construct meaning, i.e. 'flexible multilingualism' (Ganassin and Holmes 2013: 349) as part of the research design. Therefore, what is described as monopoly of power in the process of meaning construction (Shklarov 2007: 535) was counterbalanced in the joint construction of the narrative.

In the second case, the researchers' reflexive stance is evident in their decision-making regarding languages and their own linguistic resources and those of their participants and audiences during dissemination. There was a significant degree of asymmetry in these resources, but the researchers were keen to avoid the impetus towards English as the lingua franca with the risk of eclipsing the other linguistic resources in play as well as the worldviews articulated through them. The management of linguistic resources was innovatively accompanied by the process of drafting and exchanging researcher narratives, a technique building on the power of the narrative construction of meaning (Bruner 1991). Here, reflexivity is operating both individually and reciprocally or collaboratively. The process of each researcher narrating their understandings of both *Ladino* and research methodology not only brought these meanings to the fore, but also made them available to the other researcher as a reference point when developing shared interpretations of the participant narratives generated in the study. This second case study is also interesting because of its multiple lingua franca possibilities: all those involved had some competency in a version of Spanish. How might the research process manage such options, especially if one or more of the shared languages involved is less dominant, or if there is a significant hegemonic gradient evident between the languages concerned?

In the third case, the researchers were concerned about what is transformed when terms and concerts are taken from one context (in this case, a Chinese-medium, ancient philosophical and spiritual practice) and used for another (largely English-medium, relatively recent, psycho-therapeutic and educational practices). What are the linguistic, epistemological, methodological and other responsibilities of those involved in this transformation? To support such scholars, Huang, Fay and White (2017) propose an intercultural ethic that respects historical developments and preserves the conceptual and epistemic integrity of the concepts researched. Such a stance requires that each researcher brings a reflexive perspective to the translinguistic and trans-epistemological processes involved. As they trace the development of the concepts and practices they want to use, what are they bringing to the epistemological table and what are they taking away from it? In the development and enactment of an intercultural ethic, the diversity of linguistic resources available through multilingual teams provides new opportunities to exercise team reflexivity.

Concluding comments

In this chapter, we have begun to tease out some of the possible researcher implications for ERP contexts of a reality that is richly diverse but also inequitable linguistically and epistemologically. There are many implications for researchers. For us, these include the valuing of, and need for, linguistic reflexivity, and the recognition also of research teams where the individual and collective linguistic resources are intentionally valued and utilised in challenging the limitations of an

Anglocentric research process and an over-reliance on the lingua franca research function of English at the expense of knowledge-work in other languages. But there are implications not only for researchers but also for the field of EAP and all those that train researchers linguistically as well as methodologically. Not only do researchers need to balance the pull towards English as a research lingua franca and the push against the limitations of a mostly English knowledge landscape, so, too, EAP practitioners need to balance the need to prepare their students for studies (and future academic, researcher and other roles) undertaken largely in English with the need to provide them with an intercultural ethic regarding their knowledge-work. This needs to occur alongside a habit of linguistic reflexivity regarding the linguistic opportunities and challenges of their study and research activities, and the challenging of enduring myths in some contexts, such as the premium placed upon solo-authored, English-medium work. We have experienced first-hand the value of being a research team in which linguistic, cultural, epistemological, and methodological diversity is both present and embraced, while continuing to foreground the role of researcher reflexivity.

References

Andrews, J. and Fay, R. (2020), 'Valuing a Translingual Mindset in Researcher Education in Anglophone Higher Education Settings: Supervision Perspectives', *Language, Culture and Curriculum*, 33(2): 188–202. Available online: https://doi.org/10.1080/07908318.2019.1677701 (accessed 8 August 2023).

Andrews, J., Fay, R., Huang, Z. M. and White, R. (forthcoming), 'From Translanguaging to Transknowledging: Exploring New Epistemological and Linguistic Approaches in Higher Education', in J. Huisman, and M. Tight (eds), *Theory and Method in Higher Education*, vol. 9, Bingley, UK: Emerald.

Andrews, J., Fay, R., and White, R. (2018), 'From Linguistic Preparation to Developing a Translingual Orientation – Possible Implications of Plurilingualism for Researcher Education', in J. Choi and S. Ollerhead (eds), *Plurilingualism in Learning and Teaching: Complexities across Contexts*, 220–33, London: Routledge.

Asher, K. (2017), 'Spivak and Rivera Cusicanqui on the Dilemmas of Representation in Postcolonial and Decolonial Feminisms', *Feminist Studies*, 43(3): 512–24. Available online: https://doi.org/10.15767/feministstudies.43.3.0512 (accessed 8 August 2023).

Attia, M., and Edge, J. (2017), 'Be(com)ing a Reflexive Researcher: a Developmental Approach to Research Methodology', *Open Review of Educational Research*, 4(1): 33–45. Available online: https://doi.org/10.1080/23265507.2017.1300068 (accessed 8 August 2023).

Bruner, J. (1991), 'The Narrative Construction of Reality', *Critical Inquiry*, 18(1): 1–21. Available online: https://www.jstor.org/stable/1343711 (accessed 8 August 2023).

Canagarajah, S. (2013), *Global Englishes and Cosmopolitan Relations*, London: Routledge.

Choi, J. and Ollerhead, S. eds (2018), *Plurilingualism in Learning and Teaching: Complexities Across Contexts*, London: Routledge.

Curry, M. J., and Lillis, T. (2013a), 'Introduction to the Thematic Issue: Participating in Academic Publishing – Consequences of Linguistic Policies and Practices', *Language Policy* 12: 209–13. Available online: https://doi.org/10.1007/s10993-013-9286-7 (accessed 8 August 2023).

Curry, M. J., and Lillis, T. (2013b), *A Scholar's Guide to Getting Published in English: Critical Choices and Practical Strategies*, Clevedon: Multilingual Matters.

Curry, M. J., and Lillis, T. eds (2017), *Global Academic Publishing: Policies, Perspectives and Pedagogies*, Clevedon: Multilingual Matters.

Curry, M. J., and Lillis, T. (2019), 'Unpacking the Lore on Multilingual Scholars Publishing in English: A Discussion Paper', *Publications* 2019, 7(27): 1–14 Available online: https://doi.org/10.3390/publications7020027 (accessed 8 August 2023).

Davcheva, L., and Fay, R. (2012), 'An Examination of the Research and Researcher Aspects of Multilingually Researching one Language (Ladino) Through Fieldwork in Another (Bulgarian) and Analysis and Presentation in a Third (English)', Paper Presented at the First AHRC Researching Multilingually Seminar: Durham University, 28th – 29th March 2012.

de Sousa Santos, B. (2015), *Epistemologies of the South: Justice against Epistemicide*, London: Routledge.

Dombeck, M. T. (1997), 'Professional Personhood: Training, Territoriality and Tolerance', *Journal of Interprofessional Care*, 11(1): 9–21. Available online: https://doi.org/10.3109/13561829709040239 (accessed 8 August 2023).

Fay, R., Andrews, J., Huang, Z. M. and White, R. (2021), 'Bringing the Critical into Doctoral Supervisory Praxis: What Can we Learn from Debates on Epistemic (In)Justice and the Languaging of Research?', *Journal of Praxis in Higher Education* 3(2): 104–27. Available online: https://doi.org/10.47989/kpdc109 (accessed 8 August 2023).

Fay, R. and Andrews, J., Huang, Z. M. and White, R. (forthcoming), 'Linguistic Diversity in Research with and by International Students: Considerations for Research Design and Practice', in J. Mittelmeier, S. Lomer, and K. Unkule (eds), *Research with International Students: Critical Conceptual and Methodological Considerations*, London: Routledge.

Fay, R., and Davcheva, L. (2014[2016]), 'Zones of Interculturality and Linguistic Identity: Tales of Ladino by Sephardic Jews in Bulgaria', *Language and Intercultural Communication*, 14(1): 24–40. Available online: https://doi.org/10.1080/14708477.2013.866122 (accessed 8 August 2023). Subsequently republished as Fay, R., and Davcheva, L. (2016), 'Zones of Interculturality and Linguistic Identity: Tales of

Ladino by Sephardic Jews in Bulgaria', in P. Holmes, M. Dooly, and J. P. O'Regan (eds), *Intercultural Dialogue: Questions of Research, Theory and Practice*, 24–40, Abingdon: Routledge.

Flowerdew, J. (2013), 'Some Thoughts on English for Research Publication Purposes (ERPP) and Related Issues', *Language Teaching*, 2013: 1–13. Available online: https://doi.org/10.1017/S0261444812000523 (accessed 8 August 2023).

Fricker, M. (2007), *Epistemic Injustice: Power and the Ethics of Knowing*, Oxford: Oxford University Press.

Ganassin, S., and Holmes, P. (2013), 'Multilingual Research Practices in Community Research: the Case of Migrant/Refugee Women in North East England', *International Journal of Applied Linguistics*, 23(3): 342–56. Available online: https://doi.org/10.1111/ijal.12043 (accessed 8 August 2023).

Guillemin, M., and Gillam, L. (2004), 'Ethics, Reflexivity, and "Ethically Important Moments" in Research', *Qualitative Inquiry*, 10(2): 261–80. Available online: https://doi.org/10.1177/1077800403262336 (accessed 8 August 2023).

Hertz, R. ed. (1997), *Reflexivity and Voice*, London: Sage.

Hickey-Moody, C. (2020), 'New Materialism, Ethnography and Socially Engaged Practice: Space-Time Folds and the Agency of Matter', *Qualitative Inquiry*, 26(7): 724–32. Available online: https://doi.org/10.1177/1077800418810728 (accessed 8 August 2023).

Holmes, P., Reynolds, J., and Ganassin, S. (2022), 'Introduction: the Imperative for the Politics of 'Researching Multilingually', in P. Holmes, J. Reynolds, and S. Ganassin (eds), *The Politics of Researching Multilingually*, 1–27, Bristol: Multilingual Matters.

Huang, Z. M. (2020), 'Learning from the 'Right' Ground of Mindfulness: Some Insights for the 'Good' Interculturalist', *Language and Intercultural Communication*, 20(1): 50–61. Available online: https://doi.org/10.1080/14708477.2019.1672711 (accessed 8 August 2023).

Huang, Z. M. (2021), 'Intercultural Personhood: a Non-Essentialist Conception of Individuals for Intercultural Research', *Language and Intercultural Communication*, 22(2): 176–90. Available online: https://doi.org/10.1080/14708477.2020.1833898 (accessed 8 August 2023).

Huang, Z. M. (2022), 'The Use of Blind-Portrait: an Opportunity to De-Essentialise Intercultural, Educational Research', *Language and Intercultural Communication*, 21(1): 83–101. Available online: https://doi.org/10.1080/14708477.2022.2041653 (accessed 8 August 2023).

Huang, Z. M. (2023), 'Intercultural Mindfulness: Artistic Meaning-Making about Students' Intercultural Experience at a UK University', *Language and Intercultural Communication*, 23(1): 36–52. Available online: https://doi.org/10.1080/14708477.2022.2162064 (accessed 8 August 2023).

Huang, Z. M., Fay, R. and White, R. (2017), 'Mindfulness and the Ethics of Intercultural Knowledge-Work', *Language and Intercultural Communication*, 17(1): 45–57. Available online: 10.1080/14708477.2017.1261672 (accessed 8 August 2023).

Lillis, T., and Curry, M. J. (2010), *Academic Writing in a Global Context: the Politics and Practices of Publishing in English*, London: Routledge.

Lillis, T., and Curry, M. J. (2016), 'Professional Academic Writing by Multilingual Scholars: Interactions with Literacy Brokers in the Production of English-medium Texts', *Written Communication*, 23(1): 3–35. Available online: https://doi.org/10.1177/0741088305283754 (accessed 8 August 2023).

Mason, J. (1996). *Qualitative Researching*, London: Sage.

Mao, L., Mian Akram, A., Chovanec, D. and Underwood, M. L. (2016), 'Embracing the Spiral: Researcher Reflexivity in Diverse Critical Methodologies', *International Journal of Qualitative Methods*, 15(1): 1–8. Available online: https://doi.org/1609406916681005 (accessed 8 August 2023).

Mauthner, N. S., and Doucet, A. (2003), 'Reflexive Accounts and Accounts of Reflexivity in Qualitative Data Analysis', *Sociology*, 37(3): 413–31. Available online: https://doi.org/10.1177/00380385030373002 (accessed 8 August 2023).

Moss, P. (2010), 'English as a Problem Language', *Contemporary Issues in Early Childhood*, 11(4): 432–4. Available online: https://journals.sagepub.com/doi/pdf/10.2304/ciec.2010.11.4.432 (accessed 8 August 2023).

Phipps, A, and Gonzalez, M. (2004), *Modern Languages: Learning and Teaching in an Intercultural Field*, London: Sage.

Preece, S., and Marshall, S. (2020), 'Plurilingualism, Teaching and Learning, and Anglophone Higher Education: an Introduction', *Language, Culture and Curriculum*, 33(2): 117–25. Available online: https://doi.org/10.1080/07908318.2020.1723931 (accessed 8 August 2023).

Robinson-Pant, A., and Wolf, A. (2016), *Researching Across Languages and Cultures: a Guide to Doing Research Interculturally*, London: Routledge.

Samy Alim, H., Rickford, J. R. and Ball, A. F. (2016), *Raciolinguistics: How Language Shapes our Ideas about Race*, Oxford: Oxford University Press.

Shklarov, S. (2007), 'Double Vision Uncertainty: the Bilingual Researcher and the Ethics of Cross-Language Research', *Qualitative Health Research*, 17(4): 529–38. Available online: https://doi.org/10.1177/1049732306298263 (accessed 8 August 2023).

Stelma, J., Fay, R., and Zhou, X. (2013), 'Developing Intentionality and Researching Multilingually: an Ecological and Methodological Perspective', *International Journal of Applied Linguistics*, 23(3): 300–15. Available online: https://doi.org/10.1111/ijal.12040 (accessed 8 August 2023).

White R. G., Fay R., Phipps A., Giurgi-Oncu C. and Chiumento A. (2022), 'Multi-language Communication about Wellbeing and Distress: Epistemic and Ethical Considerations', *Transcultural Psychiatry*, 59(4): 413–24. Available online: https://doi.org/10.1177/13634615221082795 (accessed 8 August 2023).

14

Los de la UABJO: Resisting Linguistic Imperialism in Southern Mexico through the Indigenisation of Language Pedagogy

Alexander Black and Mónica Sánchez-Hernández, with contributions from Mario E. López-Gopar and illustrations from Katia González

Introduction

We write this text as authors with desks in the Global North and hearts rooted in the Global South. We write collaboratively, occasionally expressing our truth through the dialogue of duoethnography. We write in the hope of inspiring and amplifying Global Majority voices. For this reason, we look to multimodality for an opportunity to render our writing more accessible; we use images to set the stage for the various voices within our text. We aim to provoke reflection in our readers, and perhaps to inspire the 'subaltern' to speak (Spivak 2015), to take the microphone, to feel a sense of legitimacy, and to consider their own voice as relevant. We embrace translanguaging as a means of creating space within the narrow paradigm of Academic English.

Our title alludes to a classic novel of the Mexican Revolution, *Los de Abajo* (*The Underdogs*), whose narrative charts and critiques revolutionary praxis through the character of a student-academic joining the war (Azuela 2008). Our hope is to hint at the sense of radical change underway within and without the academy in this region in regard to language, knowledge and power. Our aim is to explore these themes and how they might suggest new directions for practice in the field of EAP.

This chapter is divided into three sections. First, we introduce the context of the region and of the English for Academic Purposes (EAP) at local universities. Second, we situate ourselves as researchers and our interviewee: Dr Mario López-Gopar. Our third and final segment interlaces an edited interview with a commentary on three broad themes related to EAP and social justice, those of: multimodality, education technology and decolonising pedagogies.

Oaxaca: the valley of *guajes* and *lenguajes*

Oaxaca finds its name in the nahuátl word *huaxyácac* or 'land of the *guajes*', and in many ways the *guaje* tree offers an apt analogy for the region. For indigenous communities, this endemic species facilitates an easy symbiosis with their natural environment: its vines prevent erosion and soil degradation; its nutritious and plentiful seeds can be consumed; its robust fruit is used to make water bottle gourds,

Figure 14.1 *Los de la UABJO* graphic depiction one.

Figure 14.2 *Los de la UABJO* graphic depiction two.

decorative bowls and even musical instruments. Yet, in Spanish, the word *guaje* means 'foolish' or 'worthless', a hint, perhaps, at modern perceptions of the people, language, and knowledge systems it represents. In this section, we shall offer a brief background of Oaxaca as a demographic, educational and linguistic context.

Oaxaca is a region of great contrasts: of profound poverty and of unimaginable wealth. At ninety-four square kilometres (INEGI 2022), it is roughly two-thirds the size of England with a geography spanning snow-capped mountains and tropical beaches. Infrastructure and transportation are poor, with a journey by car between the coast and the county seat of Oaxaca de Juárez taking roughly seven hours. Indeed, Oaxaca has historically been one of the poorest states in Mexico, with its daily minimum wage of $88.36 in 2018 (STPS 2018): roughly £3.53, only recently significantly modified (STPS 2023). Oaxaca's economy is largely agricultural and boasts a strong legacy as the likely site of domestication of crops including corn, beans, chilli peppers and cocoa (Casas et al. 2007; Flannery 2021).

Oaxaca is the indigenous bastion of Mexico (Sánchez-Hernández 2022). The region is known for its social and cultural diversity with a great linguistic diversity. The territory hosts eleven indigenous languages (INALI 2008), with 31.2 per cent of the population still conversing in one or more of these languages (INEGI 2021: 48). As a point of comparison, only 1.4 per cent of inhabitants speak an indigenous language in the Mexican capital of Mexico City (INEGI 2021). Indigeneity is not only present in the language, but also in the *usos y costumbres* political system of self-governance, which allows Oaxacan *pueblos* to determine their own policies on key issues such as land ownership and the enforcement of justice (UN 2007). This partial autonomy has faced broad developmentalist critiques (García-Jiménez 2016); we argue, however, that while self-organising communities often fall short on many measures, they have successfully prevented extractivist agendas from appropriating the rich resources of this region. To quote another of the region's most emblematic spokespersons, Emiliano Zapata, 'The land belongs to those who work it.'

Not all resources are equally distributed across the region, however, and educational achievement in Oaxaca is one notable example. The average Oaxacan adult left school at the age of twelve (INEGI 2021: 67) and 11.8 per cent of Oaxacans are deemed illiterate (INEGI 2021: 62). Under-resourced public schools are impacted by regular and protracted strikes, a situation which has worsened considerably since the 2013 Educational Reform, whose proposals included compulsory English language teaching at all levels of education (López-Gopar 2016a). Like Spanish, proficiency in English is perceived as possessing an aspirational, 'whitening' quality, which will offer improved economic opportunities (López-Gopar and Sughrua 2014). The neoliberal logic underlying these beliefs is uncritically reproduced in academia, a field where English exerts a uniquely hegemonic grip.

Public universities are key to social mobility in the region, yet places are limited. Despite efforts to widen participation in Higher Education (HE), less than a third of applicants to the UABJO won a place this year, leading to protests and hunger strikes (Rodríguez 2022). This institution, founded in 1827, is not the only university in the area, however. It was later followed by the addition of the SUNEO network, whose ten universities were established in the early 1990s (Seara Vásquez 2022). A further eighteen *Universidades del Bienestar Benito Juárez* have also recently been announced (UBBJ 2023). While recent reforms have introduced universal studentships for all public university students (Pells 2018), competition for places remains fierce.

English proficiency has historically held a gate-keeping function in determining university access, funding, and successful graduation, both at undergraduate and postgraduate level. A stark illustration of this is that in some disciplines, up to 80 per cent of Oaxacan students are unable to graduate from their main course of study simply because they failed their English exam (López-Gopar 2021: 681). Given these conditions, student motivation is typically extrinsic, with teaching oriented toward exam skills specific to the ubiquitous TOEFL ITP Test: namely receptive skills and knowledge of grammar and vocabulary (Hernández 2021). Productive skills are consequently afforded little attention, with one study even suggesting a decline in this area of student proficiency following a five-year course of EAP study at one Oaxacan university (Jelen and Hetrick 2009). Criticality has also often proved notably lacking in both the learning and teaching process, instilling a number of invasive language ideologies (Clemente et al. 2006). The most insidious of these ideologies is perhaps the essentialist 'native-speaker' fallacy (Phillipson 1992), which both prevents Oaxacans from perceiving themselves as legitimate speakers of English (Sayer 2012) and brands speakers of indigenous languages as *bene tonts* or 'retards' in a context where such languages are still widely perceived as dialects rather than complete languages (López-Gopar 2009). This dehumanising dimension of coloniality has of course found some of its most ardent and articulate critics in Latin America (Freire 1971; Quijano 2007; Mignolo 2012), yet these ideologies prevail.

Decolonisation is a topic of discussion which is far less present today in periphery contexts than the academic centre. That is not to say that it does not permeate every aspect of contemporary life in Oaxaca. Long before the arrival of Europeans, the region once hosted prosperous, complex, and unusually egalitarian societies (Nicholas and Feinman 2022) with several major cities, such as Monte Albán (*c.* 500 BCE–900 CE). The scale of the subsequent demographic collapse of indigenous Mexicans following the arrival of the Spanish, however, remains without historical precedent. The population collapsed from an estimated 21 million to just three million within the space of twenty years (Acuña-Soto et al. 2002). The languages, cultures, and onto-epistemologies of these peoples were often intentionally destroyed and replaced with Western systems. Yet, despite the unrelenting spiritual conquest, indigenous epistemes prevailed, occasionally embedding themselves so inextricably within the colonial culture as to become defining features of it, as is perhaps the case with the celebration known as *Día de muertos*.

Race is likewise conspicuous in its absence from discussion in Mexico. Racial categories themselves have evolved considerably since the initial arrival of the

Spanish, though the structural inequalities they represent seem to have changed little. Since the end of the Mexican Revolution in 1920, the notion of *mestizaje* has held that all Mexicans are essentially of mixed heritage with both European and indigenous ancestry; this 'post-racial' discourse has now become central to the modern Mexican identity (Moreno-Figueroa and Saldívar-Tanaka 2016). However, this platitude masks a reality of structural racism where 70 per cent of indigenous persons live in poverty, compared with 39 per cent of the general population (CONAPRED 2018). Few Mexicans self-identify as indigenous, which further complicates statistical analysis and affirmative action initiatives. As a consequence, the Mexican authorities have opted to use proficiency in an indigenous language as the primary indicator of this ethnic category: a further indication, perhaps, of the invasive reach of the native-speaker ideology.

Another minority group can yet claim a more marginalised place in the racial hierarchy of the Mexican state: the *afrodescendientes*. Around 200,000 enslaved Africans were brought to New Spain as part of the colonial project, and many of those escaping slavery went on to establish *palenques* or 'free communities' in the westernmost regions (Valdés 1987). Today, self-identified *afrodescendientes* constitute 5 per cent of the population of Oaxaca (INEGI 2021), though they have only been recognised constitutionally as a racial category within Mexico since 2015 (Moreno-Figueroa and Saldívar-Tanaka 2016).

The land of the *guaje* is indeed a region of great contrasts, but also great contradictions. In some ways it offers us a perfect example of the 'modernity-coloniality' (Mignolo, 2012) paradox within the Americas. In this chapter we shall consider our own positionality and relationality within this context, with a particular interest in our relationship to the learning and teaching of EAP, and the struggle for social justice.

Academic English and us

We situate ourselves alongside those who believe social studies cannot be understood without acknowledging the role we ourselves play as researchers in the field. Therefore, in this section we discuss both our positionalities (hooks 2014) and relationalities (Smith 2021) as authors; we also take the opportunity to introduce our interviewee Dr López-Gopar. We use the third person to situate ourselves both as subjects and objects of geopolitical changes. We agree that our understandings have been imprinted by our lived experiences (or lack thereof), and therefore we include a reflective account as a mere honest exercise of explaining where we are writing from.

Indigeneity, coloniality, and the *prieta*

Mónica has always been a *prieta*; but it is only now that it has stopped hurting. From an early age, she understood that terms like *naca*, *prieta*, or *del cerro* were insults rather than neutral descriptions. She daydreamed of being white, or at least less *prieta*. 'I wish I were tall, I wish I were white' were some of the phrases she wrote in English class at ten years of age.

Contrary to many of her compatriots, however, she had access to English classes from an early age. Her *Má* insisted it would open doors for her; her *Pá* agreed, in spite of the substantial economic burden. It seemed a worthwhile 'investment' for a small but exemplary student. She was schooled in Mexico City: the burgeoning capital her parents had both migrated to alone as children in search of better work opportunities. However, as that sneering saying reminds us, 'You can leave the *pueblo*, but the *pueblo* will never leave you.' Neither her mum nor dad ever left their *pueblo* behind, and neither did her brother nor herself.

Every snatch of holiday meant a return to the *pueblo*, a safe haven for her values, her food, and her relationships. That was a different epistemology which held a profound dissonance with the urban context which surrounded her as a child. As a *morena*, and a *prieta*, she learned to assimilate to a Westernised urban context, muting her indigenous roots and packing up her *huaraches* as soon as she returned to the city.

She was often *el frijolito en el arroz*: the odd black bean in the rice. Learning English – and learning it well – became *her* form of 'whitening'. She was an indigenous Oaxacan Zapotec girl, yet Spanish had already become her mother tongue. Her father was keen to shield her from the stigma he had faced. Instead, his daughter's language acquisition would focus on English, and later, the other modern languages: French, Portuguese – even German and Japanese. Some feminists have argued that to succeed in a patriarchal world requires adopting male behaviours: in her case, as she allowed her thoughts and words to be shaped by these colonial languages, she slowly began to see the doors of opportunity opening to her. Her father's short-lived primary school education was delivered in a language he never understood, and his subsequent childhood was characterised by long hours of manual labour. His daughter, however, would find herself with a seat at the table of global academia.

Such linguistic entrepreneurship (Tupas 2022) is common in contexts where language proficiency acts first and foremost as a marker of social class (López-Gopar and Sughrua 2014). Oaxaca has somehow resisted both the nationalist logic of Spanish and the neoliberal logic of English. Yet, being indigenous in a country where great efforts have been made to establish Spanish as the sole national language (Sierra and Yáñez 1984) has marginalised the lives and epistemologies of many.

'We, the Indigenous, face racialisation and discrimination even when undertaking the simplest of bureaucratic procedures – such as opening a bank account– in our own home countries' sustains Monica, joining the Zapotec actress, Yalitza Aparicio, who observes that 'for many of us, we end up believing the only way to avoid discrimination is to simply become invisible' (*Peace Peace Now Now* 2021).

English teaching and the native speaker

Alex is a white, male, British teacher of EAP in his mid-thirties. Awarded an admittedly unexceptional first degree from a prestigious UK university, he taught at various schools and colleges across Europe while accumulating a string of useful but unimposing postgraduate qualifications. In 2016, he took the almost inevitable decision to seek out more exciting prospects in overseas territories and was delighted – yet somewhat unsurprised – to be offered a position at a public university in a distant corner of the Global South.

Oaxaca was a world away from the grey London suburb he left behind. Yet, to his surprise, the communicative canon of his training and concentrated criticality of his studies seemed absent in this new learning environment. Lecturers mostly endorsed a grammar-translation method in preparation for the bi-monthly reading exams, which instilled a combination of anxiety and apathy amongst students. Alex had some empathy with these students, having himself grown up in the rural backwaters of mid-Wales. *Why learn a foreign language when nobody in your family has ever left the country?* In the psychogeography of many Oaxacans, England belonged to that same distant and inaccessible category as their northern neighbour. *Oh, England... That's near Canada, right?*

Alex was often told he was an excellent teacher, though of quite what, he occasionally wondered. Student motivation remained ever inscrutable, in spite of his most creative attempts to stimulate some curiosity in the Anglosphere. When later promoted to head of department, he railed against the regressive assessment practices and slowly succeeded convincing students, staff, and management that change was needed in this area.

One day, Alex was called in to speak to senior management. They seemed surprisingly open to substituting the outdated examinations for something more modern. *Cambridge, perhaps?* But there was a more immediate problem. It was to do with the new EAP lecturer Alex wanted to hire. He smiled and insisted she was as qualified and experienced for the position as he was, if not more so. He stood corrected: she lacked two key qualities necessary to excel in instructing students in EAP at this university: 'nativeness' and 'whiteness'.

Race, legitimacy and the decoloniser

Mario is a Oaxacan, *afrodescendiente*, and a leading academic in the field of decolonial approaches to language teaching. He has a humble demeanour and likes to make jokes. His family first moved to the city so he and his siblings might one day receive an education at the UABJO. Mario would study hard to perfect his English, but his motivation had little to do with university. Mario had always been impressed by the example of his older brother who would return from the US with extravagant gifts. This led to his own decision to make the dangerous journey to cross the border, where he found work in construction (López-Gopar 2016a).

Mario would later return to Oaxaca and study for a degree in languages at the UABJO, only to return north to work, this time, as a primary school teacher. His new colleagues seemed relieved: many of the children at his school had Mexican heritage and he seemed uniquely positioned to help them integrate into the broader community. Yet Mario himself struggled to achieve his own sense of legitimacy as a speaker of English. Many years later, having completed his PhD in Second Language Acquisition under the supervision of Jim Cummins at the University of Toronto, this sense of legitimacy would continue to elude him. He would catch himself boasting to students at the UABJO of his many years spent in the United States.

Mario's first book sought to address this issue using decolonising approaches to language teaching (López-Gopar 2016a); his second documented the lives of ten indigenous students and obstacles they faced in HE (López-Gopar 2016b). Subsequent publications include collaborations with prominent academics, colleagues and his own students. A commitment to social justice remains a constant in Mario's work. In 2020, as keynote speaker at the British Council's annual conference in Mexico on ELT, he did not miss the opportunity to publicly observe that he was in fact the conference's first ever Mexican keynote speaker.

(Un)writing the future: an interview with Dr Mario López-Gopar

Decolonizing is about 'undoing' and 'redoing' (Smith 2021), and, perhaps, recycling. The subtitle for this section – '(Un)writing the future' – is a recycling of the name of a recent governmental programme *'Jóvenes escribiendo el futuro'* (Young people writing the future) that offers bursaries to all Mexican students in public HE. Here, however, we problematise conventional notions of academic literacy, as well as the genres often centered as a primary form of knowledge transfer. We also contest the notion of 'future' as a singular linear point of arrival. Instead, we argue that 'horizons' are more representative of the broad terrain ahead of us (Segato 2018).

As a prelude to our interview with Dr López-Gopar in the summer of 2022, we chose to 'exorcise the demons' of this field in a collage we named 'The Seven Deadly Sins of English for Academic Purposes' which *undoes* the original work of nineteenth-century Mexican artist Guadalupe Posadas, and *repurposes* it to critically assess the role of EAP in HE within our context (Figure 14.3). Through

Figure 14.3 *Los de la UABJO* collage for stimulating conversation.

this collage, we hoped to initiate a conversation on three distinct aspects of social justice in EAP and ELT contexts: multiliteracies, digital technologies and decolonisation.

Mario examines our collage for a moment. 'It is an accurate illustration of the kinds of demons we face', he comments, further elaborating:

> The truth is that this could be an endless list of demons, including social class, gender, sexual orientation... We might also want to consider the question of nationality or citizenship. The positioning of one of our students here in Mexico would be quite distinct to how they are positioned as an undocumented immigrant in the United States. We might also think of the additional challenges faced by a mother with caring responsibilities. There are an endless number of factors to take into account, but sure – these are certainly seven of the sins of EAP, though they are not the only ones.

Indigenous multiliteracies: texts, textiles, and tweets

The first topic we discuss in our interview is multiliteracies. In 1996, the multiliteracies pedagogy (Cazden et al. 1996) anticipated a significant expansion in literacy practices which would necessitate a 'new norm of lifelong learning' (ibid.: 18). New genres would include alphabetic texts, but also visual, audio, digital, and gestural texts. Mario argues this is nothing new to indigenous communities for whom textiles may be as valid a medium of knowledge transfer as texts: 'though it's difficult to convince a student that an image can also function as a text', he adds.

Indigenous multiliteracies contain complex logograms, ideograms and pictograms which can be found in the pre-Hispanic codices, and which are now woven into the fabric of the everyday. Mario argues that indigenous students should not be forced to express themselves using an alienating alphabetic literacy, nor should they necessarily be expected to do so through textiles or codices. Instead, as educators, we must create space in our classrooms for indigenous people to feel heard and to undertake their own multimodal texts (López-Gopar 2007).

We agree that Western academia is complacent. 'There is a great arrogance in assuming that knowledge can only be shared in one specific form, when in fact there are so very many', remarks Mario. He elaborates:

> As a professor, I am obliged to publish in specific journals in order to keep my job and this may lead me to focus exclusively on this area, even though at times my articles may only be read by my own colleagues. Unfortunately, we continue to think of knowledge as being primarily disseminated through articles which

are very graphocentric, when in fact, a tweet or even a cartoon can prove far more powerful, despite being accorded so little value by the academy.

While technology appears to continually accelerate both the speed and reach of communication, we reflect on the place of academia amongst screens and social media. A global majority exists for whom connectivity and access to technology is not a given. Within the field of EAP, how can we offer a platform to students and academics existing in situations of digital poverty?

Pasando el micrófono: educational technologies in contexts of digital poverty

Technology is inescapably entangled with the educational experience in the digital age (Breen 2018), yet educators must account for variable access to these technologies. To illustrate this, Mario cites the example of the Enciclomedia project (López-Gopar et al. 2009), where an American university developed innovative software to teach English in Oaxacan schools. The local response to this project can be best summarised by the headline of a local newspaper at the time: 'Harvard Discovers that Enciclomedia Works Better in Schools which have Electricity' (Aviles and Vargas 2006, cited in Gopar, Méndez and Medina 2009).

Educational technologies have been used as a means to seek out new markets in Mexico, but there is of course a place for educational technologies as part of a humanising pedagogy for languages and literacy. A key consideration is the dialogical quality of its use:

> The possibilities offered to us by digital technologies extend far beyond the reach of neoliberalism. Perhaps the most obvious illustration of this is in the manner that narratives, such as those of the Zapatista peasant's movement, have reached a public that would have been unthinkable prior to the advent of the Internet. This is the great power offered to us by digital technologies. These media have a far greater reach than we do and their impact touches on an entirely different public, a general public where these questions of ideology can truly play out. We may talk of modernity, decoloniality, and other movements: it is the general public who are their true mouthpiece.

Accessible, mobile technologies offer a voice to young people in contexts of poverty. EAP practitioners have a responsibility to engage with mobile devices to help nurture subaltern voices by 'passing the microphone' (Sánchez-Hernández 2022) and by multiplying those microphones.

New media offer ordinary people an opportunity to amplify their voices. A young man can create and share a video, it goes viral, and it is then able to achieve a huge impact. Engaging with new technologies is not just about taking computers out to remote villages and giving them software to learn; it is about empowering them to get their message out and tell their own stories.

By ensuring each other's stories are heard, we can erase the elitist paradigm of the academic ivory tower. This is a first step toward a 'decolonising' praxis in our field.

Decolonising EAP

Much has been written critiquing English and other imperial languages as perpetuators of coloniality and 'soft power' (Phillipson 1992; Pennycook 2002). This poses the question of how we can reconcile ourselves with this reality as EAP practitioners. Educators in Oaxaca and beyond continue to refuse to teach English on an anti-imperialist basis. We agree that to deprive our students of the language, nevertheless, is irresponsible.

> I may perceive the global reach of English as a form of linguistic imperialism, but the language will nevertheless continue to hold great currency. Rather, we have to approach our academic study of English as a challenge and an opportunity.

One of the many obstacles is the way English proficiency is often framed. We discuss some of the underlying assumptions about English in local media and how they arise:

> By conflating English with a sense of modernity, we pity the student with limited English. *Poor him! Perhaps one day he will have enough money to pay for a decent school where he can learn to speak English properly.* We are often sold this idea that poor Mexicans need to be taught English so they can somehow stop being poor. This aspirationalist, neoliberal approach is obviously misguided. Nevertheless, there are legitimate, specific purposes for learning English in the interests of promoting, for example, intercultural cohesion and transnational business. These are the ones we should certainly focus on.

This line of argument underpins the critical approach to language teaching which has long been articulated by members of the UABJO (Clemente et al. 2006).

> We need to take our focus away from consumption and from receptive skills; we need to encourage a productive approach, to tell stories, to put forward our own narrative. We should not be teaching our students to read magazines and consume goods; neither should we encourage them to simply consume theories and ideologies.

Pedagogy is not exempt from such considerations with practice and materials developed in the Global North widely implemented across the Global South. A notable exception to this rule might be Task-Based Language Teaching (TBLT), an approach developed by Prabhu (1987) in Bangalore, India, which has come to inform ELT practice around the world. TBLT should not, however, necessarily be considered a decolonising approach.

> The real question is what kind of 'task' we are talking about: are we learning to place or take orders at a restaurant? Is the task a modernist or a colonialist one? Or does it involve communicating a different kind of narrative? What are we training our students to do?

A decolonising pedagogy is not necessarily one that emanates from the Global South, but one whose everyday praxis challenges the colonised mindset in the context within which it is applied.

> For me, the question is how to find some activity which is *relevant, practical* and *empowering* to my students. I structure my courses using 'Critical Thematic Units'. How are languages important to our lives? What social issues do we face? How can we nourish ourselves sustainably? One example of a useful task for a child might be to appreciate the value present in his mother's cooking, for example: the recipes, the chemistry, the economics, the nutritional content, all of these elements. This is how to exert a genuinely decolonising impact.

Critical pedagogies are of course a useful tool in informing decolonial praxis. EAP should be about learning to 'talk back' (Anzaldúa 2021) and to 'think back' (hooks 1989). A tolerance of transgression is necessary where the speaker is seeking linguistic and epistemic justice.

> Our students should be learning English to communicate their own theories through critically minded texts. If we are going to learn colonial languages, it should be to communicate something to the world; if we are to learn theories grounded in modernism, it should be to create our own theories.

For indigenous students and their communities in Oaxaca, the most important aspect of decolonisation may be a recognition of their epistemologies, their rights and their relationship with the land. This can be illustrated in the diverse ontolo-epistemologies coexisting within the region, including one provided by one of Mario's students.

> [My student's] community go and ask permission from the river to go fishing. For him, it is not a question of appropriating the land so much as respecting and connecting with it. This is an important point of reflection where we sometimes have to acknowledge our own ignorance. There are innumerable ways in which we are able to commune with nature.

The gradual extinction of non-Western knowledge systems is no accident, and we are under no illusions that our institutions have played a role in their disappearance.

> A major reason for this is that our schools and universities have spent the past 500 years denying the importance of our relationality with those around us, with ourselves, with our emotions, with our environment. Our knowledge systems have been historically denied any legitimacy. It is important to end our complicity in this delusion.

Conclusion

Is it possible to decolonise EAP? If so, it necessarily requires acts and not just words. EAP can certainly serve decolonisation, if it is humble enough to listen and to pass the microphone. In this chapter, we invite EAP practitioners to re-think how their work could be used as a practical tool to give voice to others, so that others may defend their values, their epistemologies, their lands. We invite you to consider how you might nurture dialogue, share your tools, make a megaphone of every student's microphone.

Global South writing and thought must be placed at the centre of our syllabi. The bread and butter of the EAP practitioner cannot continue to consist of demanding papers at the gates of the academy or policing the perimeters of academic writing. A decolonising EAP practice will instead be situated on the picket lines of a neoliberal university for whom 'internationalisation' increasingly seems a subterfuge for new forms of domination. We must act as allies and self-effacing editors to the brave new voices emerging from the periphery. We must maintain a constant critical curiosity toward the technologies which are transforming knowledge production. We must recognise that any other approach is a quiet complicity in the ongoing project of empire and the accelerating process of linguistic and epistemic genocide.

We are aware that indigenous examples are imperfect. As authors, we are also wary of romanticizing indigeneity. Indigenous voices can speak for themselves, and EAP has a responsibility for making space for them at the table of academia.

Oaxaca, the land of the *guaje,* offers us an example of resistance. Here we find one example among many of indigenous and enslaved peoples refusing to be exiled from their own land, to have their voices silenced, to allow their worldviews to be extinguished. At an historical moment where it is Western science, rather than Mesoamerican calendars, warning of imminent environmental collapse, we should consider centring the knowledge systems of Indigenous communities who have long prioritised coexistence over conquest.

References

Acuña-Soto, R., Stahle, D. W., Cleaveland, M. K. and Therrell, M. D. (2002), 'Megadrought and Megadeath in 16th Century Mexico', *Emerging Infectious Diseases*, 8 (4): 360–2. Available online: https://www.doi.org/10.3201/eid0804.010175 (accessed 26 September 2023).

Aviles, K. and Vargas, R. E. (2006), 'Descubre Harvard que enciclomedia funciona mejor en escuelas con luz', *La Jornada*, 7 November. Available online: https://www.jornada.com.mx/2006/11/07/index.php?section=sociedad&article=046n1soc (accessed 9 August 2023).

Azuela, M. (2008). *The Underdogs: a Novel of the Mexican Revolution*, London: Penguin Group.

Breen, P. (2018), *Developing Educators for the Digital Age: A Framework for Capturing Knowledge in Action*, London: University of Westminster Press.

Casas, A., Otero-Arnaiz, A., Perez-Negron, E. and Valiente-Banuet, A. (2007), 'In Situ Management and Domestication of Plants in Mesoamerica', *Annals of Botany*, 100 (5): 1101–15. Available online: https://www.doi.org/10.1093/aob/mcm126 (accessed 9 August 2023).

Cazden, C., Cope, B., Fairclough, N., Gee, J., Kalantzis, M., Kress, G., Luke, A., Luke, C., Michaels, S. and Nakata, M. (1996), 'A Pedagogy of Multiliteracies: Designing Social Futures', *Harvard Educational Review*, 66 (1): 60–92.

Clemente, A., Crawford, T., García, L., Higgins, M., Kissinger, D., Lengeling, M., López-Gopar, M., Narvaez, O., Sayer, P. and Sughrua, W. (2006), 'A Call for a Critical Perspective on English Teaching in Mexico'. *Mextesol Journal*, 30 (2), pp. 13–18.

CONAPRED. (2018), *La pobreza en la población indígena de México, 2008 – 2018*, Mexico City: Comisión Nacional para la Prevención de la Discriminación.

Flannery, K. V. (2021), *Guilá Naquitz: Archaic Foraging and Early Agriculture in Oaxaca, Mexico*, New York: Routledge.

Freire, P. (1971), *Pedagogy of the Oppressed*, New York: Herder and Herder.

García-Jiménez, R. (2016), 'La violencia de género en Oaxaca, una explicación desde la victimología', *Revista Contribuciones a las Ciencias Sociales*, (octubre-diciembre 2016). Available at: http://www.eumed.net/rev/cccss/2016/04/victimizacion.html (accessed 3 May 2022).

Hernández, I. F. (2021), 'The TOEFL as Exit Criteria in English as a Foreign Language (EFL) Programs in Mexico: a Discourse Historical Analysis (DHA) Approach', *Open Journal for Educational Research*, 5(1): 105–18.

hooks, bell (1989), *Talking Back, Thinking Feminist, Thinking Black*, Cambridge: South End Press.

hooks, bell (2014), *Teaching to Transgress*, New York: Routledge.

INALI. (2008), *Catálogo de las Lenguas Indígenas Nacionales: Variantes Lingüísticas de México con sus autodenominaciones y referencias geoestadísticas*, Mexico City: Diario Oficial de la Federación.

INEGI (2021), *Censo de Población y Vivienda 2020*. Mexico: Instituto Nacional de Estadística y Geografía.

INEGI (2022), *Cuéntame Inegi. Información por entidad*, Mexico: Instituto Nacional de Estadística y Geografía. Available at: https://cuentame.inegi.org.mx/monografias/informacion/oax/territorio.

Jelen, B. F. and Hetrick, R. (2009), *A Case Study in Organizational Dynamics and Foreign Language Acquisition: the Story of UMAR Puerto Angel and the E.L.L.,* Puerto Angel: Universidad del Mar.

López-Gopar, M. (2007), 'Beyond the Alienating Alphabetic Literacy: Multiliteracies in Indigenous Education in Mexico', *Diaspora, Indigenous, and Minority Education*, 1(3): 159–74. Available online: https://www.doi.org/10.1080/15595690701394758 (accessed 9 August 2023).

López-Gopar, M. (2009), *'What Makes Children Different is what Makes Them Better': Teaching Mexican Children English to Foster Multilingual, Multiliteracies, and Intercultural Practices*, Toronto: University of Toronto.

López-Gopar, M. (2016a), *Decolonizing Primary English Language Teaching*, Bristol: Multilingual Matters. Available online: https://www.multilingual-matters.com/page/detail/Decolonizing-Primary-English-Language-Teaching/?k=9781783095766 (accessed 9 August 2023).

López-Gopar, M. (2016b), *Historias de vida de estudiantes universitarios de origen indígena*, Oaxaca: Universidad Autónoma 'Benito Juárez' de Oaxaca.

López-Gopar, M. (2021). 'Citizenship in Language Testing: a Call for Respectful Collaborations', *Language Testing*, 38(4): 649–53. Available online: https://www.doi.org/10.1177/02655322211022061 (accessed 9 August 2023).

López-Gopar, M., Núñez-Méndez, O., Montes-Medina, L. and Cantera-Martínez, M. M. (2009), 'Inglés Enciclomedia: a Ground-Breaking Program for Young Mexican Children?', *Mextesol Journal*, 33(1): 67–85.

López-Gopar, M. and Sughrua, W. (2014), 'Social Class in English Language Education in Oaxaca, Mexico', *Journal of Language, Identity and Education*, 13(2): 104–10.

Mignolo, W. (2012), *Local Histories/global Designs: Coloniality, Subaltern Knowledges, and Border Thinking*, New Jersey: Princeton University Press.

Moreno-Figueroa, M. G. and Saldívar-Tanaka, E. (2016), '"We Are Not Racists, We Are Mexicans": Privilege, Nationalism and Post-Race Ideology in Mexico', *Critical Sociology*, 42(4–5): 515–33. Available online: https://www.doi.org/10.1177/0896920515591296 (accessed 9 August 2023).

Nicholas, L. M. and Feinman, G. M. (2022), 'The Foundation of Monte Albán, Intensification, and Growth: Coactive Processes and Joint Production', *Frontiers in Political Science*, 4: 1–19. Available online: https://www.doi.org/10.3389/fpos.2022.805047 (accessed 9 August 2023).

Peace Peace Now Now (2021), [TV series] Star+. Trailer available at: https://www.youtube.com/watch?v=WVVESU7Yf4Y (accessed 26 September 2023).

Pells, R. (2018), 'Plan for 100 New Universities in Mexico "Totally Impractical"', *Times Higher Education*, 7 August. Available at: https://www.timeshighereducation.com/news/plan-100-new-universities-mexico-totally-impractical (accessed 9 August 2023).

Pennycook, A. (2002), *English and the Discourses of Colonialism*, London: Routledge.

Phillipson, R. (1992), *Linguistic Imperialism*, Oxford: Oxford University Press.

Pineda, I. (2019), *Chupa ladxidua'- Dos es mi corazón. Irma Pineda para niños*, Juchitán de Zaragoza: Alas y Raíces.

Prabhu, N. S. (1987), *Second Language Pedagogy*, Oxford: Oxford University Press.

Quijano, A. (2007), 'Coloniality and Modernity/Rationality', *Cultural Studies*, 21:(2–3): 168–78.

Rodríguez, Ó. (2022), 'Aspirantes rechazados a la UABJO se declaran en huelga de hambre', *Grupo Milenio*, 2 August. Available at: https://www.milenio.com/estados/aspirantes-rechazados-uabjo-declaran-huelga-hambre (accessed 9 February 2023).

Sánchez-Hernández, M. (2022), 'Indigenous Masculinities in the Dock: Intimate Partner Violence, Serious Offences and Manhood in Oaxaca, Mexico', MA diss., University of Bristol.

Sayer, P. (2012), *Ambiguities and Tensions in English Language Teaching: Portraits of EFL Teachers as Legitimate Speakers*, 1st edn, New York: Routledge.

Seara Vázquez, M. (2022), Hechos. Oaxaca: UMAR. Available at: https://www.suneo.mx/libros/2022-Hechos-Web.pdf (accessed 9 August 2023).

Segato, R. L. (2018), 'Fundamentalismo, masculinidad y crueldad.' [Lecture] Mexico City, Mexico. Available at: https://ibero.mx/prensa/antropologa-rita-segato-reflexiona-sobre-violencia-crimen-y-religion (accessed 9 August 2023).

Sierra, J. and Yáñez, A. (1984), *Obras completas del Maestro Justo Sierra: la educación nacional*, Mexico City: Universidad Nacional Autonoma de México.

Smith, L. T. (2021), *Decolonizing Methodologies: Research and Indigenous Peoples*, 3rd edn, London: Zed Books.

Spivak, G. C. (1988), 'Can the subaltern speak?' in *Marxism and the Interpretation of Culture, eds. Cary Nelson and Lawrence Grossberg*, 271–313, Basingstoke: Macmillan.

STPS (2018), *Salarios mínimos vigentes a partir del 01 de enero de 2018*, Mexico City: Gobierno de México.

STPS (2023), *Salarios mínimos vigentes a partir del 01 de enero de 2023*. 001/2023, Mexico City: Gobierno de México.

Tupas, R. (2022), 'The Coloniality of Linguistic Entrepreneurship', *UNITAS: International Online Journal of Advanced Research, Literature and Society*, 95(2): 170–88.

UBBJ (2023), 'Universidades para el Bienestar "Benito Juárez García"', *Gobierno de México,* https://ubbj.gob.mx/carrera (accessed 5 February 2023).

UN (2007), 'United Nations Declaration on the Rights of Indigenous Peoples', *Department of Economic and Social Affairs*, https://www.un.org/development/desa/indigenouspeoples/declaration-on-the-rights-of-indigenous-peoples.html (accessed 9 August 2023).

Valdés, D. N. (1987), 'The Decline of Slavery in Mexico', *The Americas*, 44(2): 167–94. Available online: https://www.doi.org/10.2307/1007289 (accessed 9 August 2023).

CONCLUSION

Concluding Reflections Upon Social Justice in EAP and ELT Contexts

Paul Breen

In the introductory reflection of this book, I suggested that there is a need for the activity system of ELT and EAP to incorporate aspects of social justice into our work in a way that does not dilute our primary activity. Such an approach was also taken by the authors in Chapter One who presented a framework for incorporating social justice into the design of learning materials, wherein the final outcome was deemed to be awareness of topics which discuss and promote social justice.

Expanding upon this, and a conceptual framework shaped by the work of Yrjö Engeström in the various publications cited in this book, I have now tried to develop a broader Activity System for EAP as a whole. However, in keeping with the values espoused throughout this book, the idea of presenting this framework is not to be seen as a closing of the conversation. Rather, it is intended as a stimulus for further development wherein categorisations have been left loose and up for discussion. I have no desire to say that this is a definitive model for what we do. Maybe a better way of describing it would be as a model or framework of possibilities. If anyone wants to situate their approach to social justice in a conceptual form, then this is one suggestion, whilst remembering that not everyone sees this as a pressing need. However, for some of us, the incorporation of social justice makes complete sense as a result of how it synergises our personal, political and professional interests.

The outline of this proposed model is presented below and provisionally named in such a way that it can be adapted according to context. Thus, although I prefer the term 'social justice in English Language Teaching (SJ-ELT) model of activity', the design can alternatively be labelled as 'social justice in English for Academic Purposes (SJ-EAP) model of activity.' This has been developed in conjunction with the aforementioned work of Robert Farag, Katherine Mansfield,

AN ADAPTED FRAMEWORK FOR PUTTING SOCIAL JUSTICE INTO PRACTICE

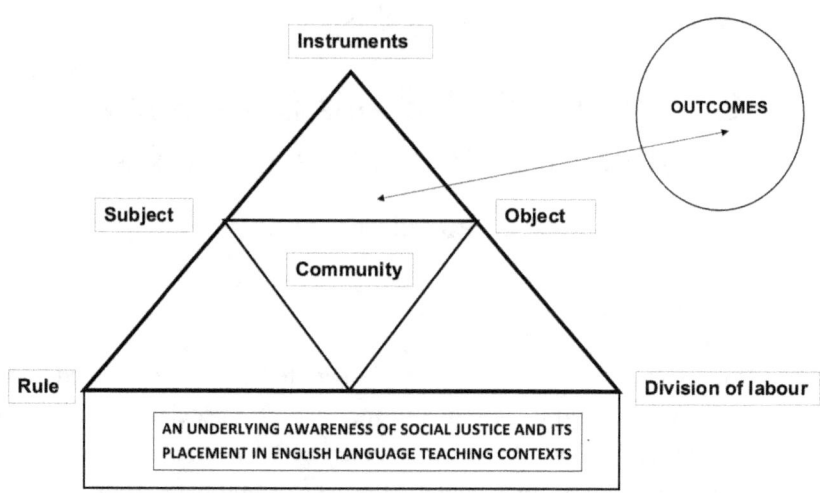

Figure 15.1 The SJ-ELT or SJ-EAP model of activity: a framework for integrating a social justice epistemology into the activity of English for Academic Purposes and English Language Teaching. Adapted from Engeström (2001) by Breen, Farag, Mansfield, McDowell, Page and Pereira (2023).

Hilary McDowell, Svetlana Page and Ignez Pereira (2023). However, where that mainly differs is in the nature of the expected outcome and the positioning of social justice.

In the SJ-ELT or SJ-EAP model, social justice takes the form of a foundation stone for the pillars upon which all other activity is built. Therefore, it is a value set not interfering with our pedagogy, but acting in the same way as our knowledge base impacts what we do in our classrooms or associated activities, such as many of those seen in this book. Those could include assessment practices as discussed in Jan McArthur's Chapter 4, the design of materials in Chapters 1 and 12 or curriculum design as in Chapter 2. The role of social justice then is to be a fuel for activity rather than a focus for activity, shaping our pedagogic approaches rather than shaping the content that we teach. In this way, there is no fear of social justice delimiting the language focus or falling into the pitfall of prioritising aspirations over practicable outcomes, as voiced in some of the literature that criticises such approaches.

In this model (see Figure 15.1), the emphasis is very much upon outcomes that are both a product of activity and feed back into a more cyclical process of generating developments. Community too has been symbolically placed in a more central position than in Engeström's earlier models because of the particular nature of EAP and English Language Teaching, wherein it is more of a shared and inter-relational habitat. The definitions of the core tenets are also provided below, but again it should be stressed that these are intended as a stimulus for discussion and not the finished article. It has also been left with skeletal details sketched in because the work that we do is context specific, and although I have argued that we are all part of the same field, the nature of our activity crosses the very broad spectrum seen in this publication. This sense of leaving the model as flexible as possible also fits in with Roth's (2004) argument about the historical dynamism of the Activity Theory model, which in itself, as he also argues, is highly suited to application in a social justice context because of how it has been shaped by the wider political context of where and how it originated. Furthermore, the idea of allowing contextual influences to shape and re-shape the parameters of theoretical paradigms, is something that has become an increasing feature of educational activity. One such model which incorporated a greater element of context into its depiction over time, was that of Technological Pedagogical Content Knowledge (TPACK), for example. Therein, Mishra and Koehler's original (2006) model was subsequently adapted to include an outer ring of contextual influence.

The various labels in our model represent the following:

1. *Subject* refers to English Language practitioners in whatever particular domain they are working, whether EAP, ELT, ESOL or teacher education.
2. *Object* refers to the enactment of a social justice epistemology fuelling the synergy of pedagogy and language that shapes our practice.
3. *Instruments* refer to the combination of curriculum, materials and artefacts through which we mediate our practice, such as those that are technological.
4. *Community* is placed at the heart of what we do and again is context specific. Other parts of the book have presented depictions of community in various frameworks such as the Community of Inquiry Model (Garrison et al. 2000) or Wenger's (1998) Community of Practice Framework. In the context of our framework, *community* might be best defined as our primary workplace. However, because of the ecosystem language teachers inhabit, space must also be allowed for the many overlapping professional communities we belong to. These too significantly shape the outcomes of our activity.

5. *Rules* work on two levels: referring to those that are formal and shape our practice, such as university regulations or assessment requirements; and then those that are informal and shaped more by the values we espouse and the underlying awareness of social justice as a foundation for the model.
6. *Division of labour* refers to the ways in which work is assigned in light of an ethical foundation that all those in our field are asked to adhere to – particularly those in positions of management.
7. *Outcome* refers to the ultimate goal of activity, which again is context dependant but will generally involve a synchronisation of language and pedagogy fuelled by an underlying awareness and enactment of social justice in our practices.

Having outlined these, it is important to note that this is not a framework where everything is expected to run smoothly or uncritically. There are often complete contradictions in aspirations and actualities in the situations we work in. A prime example can be found in Jan McArthur's Chapter 4 where she looks at a university system that is essentially based on distrust. Fundamentally, the rules are designed around what is seen as an institutional or sector-wide need to prevent cheating. That in turn influences the almost ubiquitous usage of Turnitin to police our entire assessment system. As long as we have such a culture in higher education, our activity is not going to be socially just, since it feeds the environment that Nguyet Luu rallies against in Chapter 5. Similarly, if more general English language education remains shaped around commercial or visa compliance purposes, there is less space for justice to breathe. But if there is more work with groups such as refugees, greater outreach to fragile environments and language taught for purposes of intercultural exchange rather than primarily for profit, a sense of justice can prevail.

Right now, in a time of impending climate change and endless wars, there is a need for the countries and the peoples of this world to work together, as we have seen happening in Chapters 9 and 10 particularly. Universities are in pole positions of influence in this regard, and within universities, language educators occupy the same slot. We can help build a world that is less colonial, less capitalist and less militaristic. Attaining that is not easy though. It requires both vision and the willingness to change. There is no point in embracing individual tenets of justice unless the whole system is set up to produce just outcomes. As stated in my opening reflection, there has been too great a commodification of the language of social justice at a superficial level. Outside of education, the English

Premier League's endorsement of BLM is seen by some as an example of that. Menter (2021) contends that even within education there is a danger of 'fashionable and changing nostrums' being sold in the manner of 'snake oil' (ibid.: 41). Often, we see a 'pick and mix' approach (Dart 2022: 164) to who and what is deserving of justice. In the university sector this is true of the divergence in the emphasis in terms of social justice for staff and social justice for students. As John Gray said at the outset, there can be no true justice if all that we are fighting for is a cultural justice without socio-economic justice.

To conclude then, this fight for social justice across multiple dimensions is one that must go on. Hopefully, in some small way this book has contributed to addressing some of the challenges and showcased the benefit in what we do. There is enough good practice happening in our field to hopefully sustain it for the future. The climate of the ecosystem that we inhabit may be changing but time and again we have proven ourselves to be an adaptable species in the world of ELT and EAP. This is because, as stated at the beginning, there is a humanity at the heart of our pedagogic practices. That is why in the Activity System we have created, the structure is based around an equilibrium of language, pedagogy and people, drawing upon Activity Theory in the dynamic sense of Engeström's original intention (1987), as argued by Roth (2004). However, this book is not about the creation of an Activity System alone. It is about stories and instances of practice that incorporate aspects of social justice into our work, to enhance and not replace a focus on language. Through these stories it is hoped that everyone will come away from reading this work with a sense of positivity. So much good is happening in our field and we need to share it with the wider world.

In this publication we have tried to synergise the different strands of ELT into a united front rather than mirroring the class-systems of academia. This is why we have incorporated as wide a range of voices as possible, bringing in a mix of experience and those new to publishing. By doing so, we hope that we can use this book as a call to action for others to join in our efforts of shaping a new and sustainable framework for the future, which will thrive and survive even in the changing climate of our times. Through all such changes, language education remains our core activity and as seen in so many instances of practice herein, it can be a major force for good.

This book has brought us as readers, writers and editors to places that stretch across continents, methodologies, ethnographies and contexts. Whether Mexico, Vietnam, Qatar, Syria, Bloomsbury, Bulgaria or all the rest, there is some vital element in what we contribute to the periodic table of educational knowledge. The stories that the authors have shared show just how resource-rich an environment we live and work in. That is largely because of the people, the practitioners at the heart of the ecosystems we inhabit; people with a genuine passion for teaching and learning, and for making the world a better and more equitable place as a result of such activity. It has been a joy to participate in the editing of this work, from first word to last.

References

Breen, P., Farag, R., Mansfield, K., McDowell, H., Page, S. and Pereira, I. (2023), 'The SJ-ELT/SJ-EAP Model of Activity', in P. Breen and M. Le-Roux, *Social Justice in EAP and ELT Contexts*, p. 230, UK: Bloomsbury.

Dart, J. (2022), 'From Ferguson to Gaza. Sport, Political Sensibility, and the Israel/Palestine Conflict in the Age of Black Lives Matter', *European Journal for Sport and Society*, 19(2): 151–69.

Engeström, Y. (1987), *Learning by Expanding*, Helsinki: Prienta-Konsultit Oy.

Engeström, Y. (2001), 'Expansive Learning at Work: Toward an Activity Theoretical Reconceptualization', *Journal of Education and Work*, 14(1): 133–56.

Garrison, D. R., Anderson, T. and Archer, W. (2000), 'Critical Inquiry in a Text-Based Environment: Computer Conferencing in Higher Education', *The Internet and Higher Education*, 2: 87–105.

Menter, I. (2021), 'Snake Oil or Hard Struggle? Research to Address the Reality of Social Injustice in Education', in Ross, A. (ed). *Educational Research for Social Justice: Evidence and Practice from the UK*, 29–44, Cham: Springer International Publishing.

Mishra, P. and Koehler, M. (2006), 'Technological Pedagogical Content Knowledge: a Framework for Teacher Knowledge', *The Teachers College Record*, 108(6): 1017–54.

Roth, W.M. (2004). 'Activity Theory and Education: an Introduction', *Mind, Culture, and Activity*, 11:1: 1–8. Available at: https://www.doi.org/10.1207/s15327884mca1101_1 (accessed 1 March 2023).

Wenger, E. (1998), *Communities of Practice: Learning, Meaning, and Identity*, Cambridge: Cambridge University Press.

Index

activism 64–6, 109–10, 183
Activity Theory/Activity Systems 2–4, 7, 12, 18, 23–6, 32–4, 231–6
Afghanistan 12, 137–40, 142, 144, 145, 149
assessment 8, 13, 18, 20, 46–7, 49, 73–87, 95–6, 109, 119, 167, 219, 232, 234

BALEAP 4, 7, 58–9, 66, 68, 99, 189, 193
Benesch, Sarah 8, 19, 46, 49–50, 57–8, 61, 63–4
Black Lives Matter (BLM) 4, 28, 43, 179, 235
blackout poetry 6, 103–4
brave spaces 4, 10–11
British Council 20, 139, 141, 143, 146, 190

cancel culture 118
China 159, 189, 191
Chinese (language) 201, 204–5
Chinese (students) 7, 64, 67, 94
Council for At-Risk Academics (Cara) 4, 11, 157–75
Community of Enquiry model 21–3, 233
communities of practice 25, 41, 68, 142, 189, 233
compassion 1, 4, 9, 10, 107, 111, 113, 121–31
connected curriculum 47
Critical EAP (CEAP) 8, 49–50, 57–68
cultural justice/injustice xix, xx, xxi, 46, 235
curriculum 20, 26–8, 57–8, 63, 92, 109–10, 180, 233
curriculum for change 39–51

decolonisation xix, xx, 40, 61, 67, 199, 211, 219, 223–5
Develop EAP: A Sustainable Academic English Skills Course 4, 20, 189–94
Digital Teaching and Learning Ecosystem (DTLE) 20–1

EAP for Social Justice (EAP4SJ) SIG 4, 99–100, 104, 107, 109
Engeström, Yrjö 2, 19, 23–6, 231–2
English for Research Purposes 166, 198–9
ethics of care 111–12

feedback 29, 34, 47, 81, 129, 144, 149, 163, 171, 174, 193

gender xix, xxi, 28, 40, 49, 61, 107, 112, 138, 177–84, 221
glocalisation 3, 7, 10–11, 191

honesty 78, 82–3
Honneth, Axel 46, 74, 76–7, 83–4.
Hyland, Ken 5, 8, 17, 41, 58, 92, 159, 166, 167

IELTS 78, 96, 137

Journal of English for Academic Purposes (JEAP) 58

LGBTQ xix, xx, 4, 7, 108, 112
lingua franca/English as a lingua franca 11, 85, 197–9, 201–3, 205–7
linguistic diversity 7, 11, 96, 197–207, 214

Marxist ideology 2, 42, 178
Mexico 6, 12, 211–26, 235
militarism 234
mindfulness and 念 (*niàn*) 204–5

native-speakerism 65, 108, 215–18

online learning 20, 122, 144–6, 148

Palestine 143–4
plagiarism 79–81
plurilingualism 94, 199
postcolonialism 160, 179

precarity 1, 3, 6, 32, 63, 65, 67, 76, 107, 158
pre-sessional courses 7, 17–18, 20, 28, 30, 59, 65, 76, 81, 85

Qatar 11, 12, 181–4, 235
queer identity 108–9
Queer Theory 179

racial justice xix, 4, 40, 49, 119, 178, 198, 215–16
reflexivity 11, 197–207
RefugEAP 4, 193–4
refugee(s) 4, 13, 137, 141, 143, 147, 149, 194, 234
resilience (language as) 143–4

social change and education 42–3
socioeconomic justice/injustice xix, xx, xxi, 86, 235

Sri Lanka 10, 12, 123
sustainable development/sustainable development goals (SDGs) 4, 11, 18, 20, 40, 42–8, 50, 190
Syria 4, 11, 12, 137–9, 142–5, 156, 158–71, 235

teacher education 233
technology 3, 43, 146, 211–12
translanguaging xx, 6, 9, 66, 91–6, 211
trust 9, 78, 79–81, 102, 106
trustworthiness 78, 202, 205

University College London (UCL) 5, 190

Vygotsky 2, 23–5

Westminster (University of) 7, 11, 17–18, 190
white gaze 9, 91–6

www.ingramcontent.com/pod-product-compliance
Lightning Source LLC
Chambersburg PA
CBHW071820300426
44116CB00009B/1382